DISASTER
IN CHILE

Communist Party headquarters in Santiago.

DISASTER IN CHILE

ALLENDE'S STRATEGY AND WHY IT FAILED

Edited with an introduction by Les Evans

PATHFINDER PRESS, NEW YORK

First Edition, 1974

CONTENTS

V. THE APPROACHING SHOWDOWN

VI. THE DOWNFALL OF POPULAR FRONTISM

APPENDIX

NOTES ON CONTRIBUTORS

JEAN-PIERRE BEAUVAIS is editor in chief of *Quatrième Internationale*, the French-language journal of the International Executive Committee of the Fourth International, the world Trotskyist organization.

HUGO BLANCO has spent the last decade in prison and exile for his role as a leader in the peasant movement in his native Peru. He lived in Chile during the months prior to the coup and was an eyewitness to the military takeover in September 1973. He is the author of *Land or Death: The Peasant Struggle in Peru*.

PETER CAMEJO, a leading member of the Socialist Workers Party in the United States, has traveled extensively in Cuba, Chile, and other countries of Latin America.

LES EVANS is editor of the *International Socialist Review*, a monthly Marxist magazine, and former managing editor of *Intercontinental Press*. He is coauthor of *Watergate and the Myth of American Democracy*.

GERRY FOLEY, a staff writer for *Intercontinental Press*, has written extensively on events in Ireland, including firsthand reports from Derry and Belfast.

JOSEPH HANSEN is the editor of *Intercontinental Press*. He served as secretary to Leon Trotsky during the Russian revolutionist's final exile in Mexico, and is a longtime member of the National Committee of the Socialist Workers Party.

DICK ROBERTS has lectured widely on Marxist economics. He is a staff writer for the socialist newsweekly *The Militant* and is completing a book on the economics of U.S. imperialism.

DAVID THORSTAD is a former staff writer and translator for *Intercontinental Press*.

INTRODUCTION

The right-wing military coup that toppled the government of Salvador Allende Gossens on September 11, 1973, ushered in a wide-ranging repression against the working class. It was a tragic setback for the Chilean revolution, for the peoples of Latin America, and for the world working class as a whole. Why did it happen? Who was responsible? How could it have been prevented? Is it possible to guard against such a defeat in other Latin American countries? These are life and death questions that will be central to the debate over strategy and tactics in the Latin American revolutionary left for years to come.

This collection of articles, taken mainly from the international Trotskyist newsmagazine *Intercontinental Press*, constitutes an invaluable record of the three years of the Unidad Popular — Allende's Popular Unity coalition — from its electoral victory in September 1970 to its overthrow in the U.S.-sponsored coup. More than that, they provide a political axis for judging the worth of the popular front strategy of a "peaceful road to socialism" in alliance with the "progressive" bourgeoisie propounded by Allende's coalition partners. Except for minor abridgements to eliminate repetition, and editing for consistency of style, the articles in this book are republished here as they originally appeared, without the benefit of hindsight. It has been said that one of the greatest merits of the Marxist method is its ability to predict. Judged by that criterion these articles stand up remarkably well. Except for the Trotskyists, every other tendency on the left misunderstood — willfully or otherwise — in face of mounting evidence — the inherent and self-imposed limitations of the Allende government. Thus *Political Affairs*, the theoretical journal of the Communist Party, USA, editorialized on the UP victory in its December 1970 issue:

"This was no ordinary electoral victory, no mere victory of a Socialist over the other candidates. Rather, in the words

9

of the Basic Program of the six-party coalition which backed Allende, it represents a 'transfer of power from the old ruling groups to the workers, to the peasantry and to the progressive sections of the middle class of the city and country.'"

But this picture was entirely false. Allende's popular front coalition contained the bourgeois Radical Party which had not and never would agree to a real "transfer of power from the old ruling groups to the workers." Moreover, Allende had failed to win a majority in the September 1970 election. To secure the votes of the major bourgeois parties — the Christian Democrats and the Nationalists — in a runoff election in Congress in October he publicly pledged to leave the military and the police intact, not to reduce the size of the army, and not to appoint any officers who had not graduated from the bourgeois military academies. He also agreed to outlaw any independent workers' militias. How, then, was the "transfer of power" to be carried out? Peter Camejo, in an article that first appeared in the August 6, 1971, issue of the New York socialist weekly *The Militant*, included in this collection, put his finger on the essential flaw in Allende's reformist strategy and graphically predicted the outcome. He wrote:

"The politics of the Allende regime are by nature forced into a balancing act between the oppressed and oppressor classes. While his regime began with the enthusiastic support of the masses and the grudging support of the ruling class, it is bound to end, after a period of vacillation, by satisfying neither the rulers nor the ruled. . . .

". . . Undoubtedly the masses will press for more meaningful social reforms; the bourgeoisie will await the moment to stifle and then, literally through murders and imprisonment, behead the workers' movement.

"While the bourgeois armed forces remain intact, organized, disciplined, and centralized, the workers and peasants have no organization, no arms, and no leadership. They have only numbers and a willingness to sacrifice.

"For the present experience to end in a better way than the previous one [the popular front governments in Chile from 1938 to 1952], a leadership willing to struggle against the opportunist and corrupt Communist and Socialist parties is necessary. If such a leadership does not develop, the results might be even worse than in the 1940s."

Of course, the main criminal in the Chilean coup was American imperialism, which armed, trained, and inspired the reactionary forces of General Pinochet. The left around the world is duty bound to seek by all means at its disposal to alleviate the present sufferings of the Chilean working class at the hands of the new military masters of the country. But at the same time, no one who aspires to the leadership of the revolutionary movement should have the right to claim surprise that the pro-American armed forces of Chile used their arms against Allende's reforms and against the working class. We know what to expect from the executioner. But what can be said of a strategy for revolution that leads the masses barehanded to the place of execution?

We still do not know the full extent of the repression in Chile following Allende's overthrow. The junta has sought to cover its bloody deeds with a shroud of secrecy. All leftist parties have been outlawed. Marxist books have been burned — as if ideas could be put to the torch like the witches of old. There are no reliable figures on the number of assassinations or on the number of political prisoners held by the regime. The November 6, 1973, *New York Times* attempted an assessment — almost certainly very conservative:

"At least 2,000 people died throughout the country, most of them victims of unreported executions carried out after the initial heavy armed resistance to the military had ceased. . . .

"A . . . tour made in the last three days indicates that in the Santiago area at least, summary executions have become relatively rare. On the other hand, officially announced executions of people reportedly tried by closed military tribunals or caught attacking security forces are continuing throughout the country. . . .

"There is still no indication of how many people initially listed as prisoners have in fact been killed. Although the junta has repeatedly set deadlines for clearing the National Stadium of prisoners, 1,036 were still held there this morning."

The coup was met with determined resistance by the Chilean workers. But without leadership, without a mass revolutionary party that had the will to fight, this heroic resistance was doomed to defeat. What was lacking in Chile was not guns. Many thousands of the workers were armed. Just as essential, as every successful revolution has shown, was the necessity and the real possibility of splitting the army. This could not be done by placating the right-wing officer corps and inviting the generals into the government, as Allende did. Only through an organized, nationwide show of force by the workers could the ranks of the armed forces be broken from their officers and brought over to the side of the revolution. The sporadic and disorganized fight put up by the vanguard factory and neighborhood committees was not sufficient to accomplish this.

Yet such a showdown with the army was implicit from the moment the Unidad Popular came to power. Its electoral victory was made possible by a deep radicalization of the workers that terrified the ruling class. When the Unidad Popular adapted to the radical mood by instituting significant reforms the question was immediately posed of how it would defend these advances when the powerful institutions of the bourgeois state mobilized against them.

Unquestionably the Unidad Popular carried out many progressive measures that earned it the distrust and hatred of the Chilean bourgeoisie and its imperialist backers in Washington. These included the recognition of Cuba, the nationalization of a major portion of the foreign imperialist investment in Chile, a sweeping land reform, substantial increases in workers' wages, and the granting of political asylum to left-wing exiles from all over Latin America. The majority of the country's workers, as well as many of the poorest peasants, looked on the Unidad Popular as their representative and were prepared to defend it against the impending reactionary assault. The leaders of the Unidad Popular proved incapable of utilizing this support in their own defense because of their unquestioning commitment to the bourgeois governmental structure they had inherited along with the presidency. Nixon and his Chilean agents, of course, were bound by no such scruples.

Allende's strategy was not new. It was first propounded by Stalin in 1935 under the name of the "popular front." Stalin claimed that the ultimate goal of socialism could be promoted by a political alliance with bourgeois liberalism — on the basis of the liberals' program. The real aim of the popular front was never a socialist revolution, but rather the inclusion of Communist Parties in bourgeois governments which could then become allies of the Soviet Union. This electoralist, class-collaborationist strategy had been tried and had led to disastrous defeats long before the UP electoral victory of 1970. In 1936 in Spain the Communist and Socialist parties participated in a liberal capitalist government. They, like Allende, sought to convince the army that their reforms would be held within the framework of bourgeois legality. And there also the army was unpersuaded. It revolted under Franco to crush the Popular Front government in a prolonged civil war.

Allende quite truthfully insisted on many occasions that his

government was not a socialist regime, although he claimed
to favor socialism for Chile at some unstated future time.
Concretely his government limited itself to an attempt to improve the standard of living of the working masses through
concessions that would not challenge the private ownership
of property or the existing institutions of bourgeois rule. The
most radical of Allende's reforms was the expropriation of an
important segment of foreign-owned business, particularly the
U. S.-dominated copper companies.

Allende and the Chilean Stalinists hoped to win acceptance
for their program from the "progressive" wing of the Chilean
bourgeoisie, organized in the Christian Democratic Party. If
the Christian Democrats could be persuaded to restrain their
criticisms of the UP government to hostile articles in the press,
the more openly right-wing National Party could be neutralized
and prevented from taking extralegal actions. The bait for
the Christian Democrats was the anti-imperialist nationalizations, which could be expected to strengthen Chilean capitalism
by removing a powerful imperialist rival from the scene.

Allende's popular front strategy was fatally false on two
counts. First, there is no truly nationalist bourgeoisie in the
colonial world. Whatever ephemeral economic benefit the businessmen of the Christian Democracy might have gained from
the take-over of U.S. holdings, they would at the same time
lose the protection of their benefactors in Washington in a
period of deepening working-class radicalization. The bourgeoisie is not easily fooled when its fundamental class interests
are at stake. After all, it was this same "nationalist" party of
the Chilean bourgeoisie, and not the right-wing National Party,
that had received the backing of Washington in the 1964 and
the 1970 elections.

Allende's second fatal misconception was that the bourgeoisie
would remain bound by the rules of bourgeois democracy
when these conflicted with its class interests. Allende acted from
beginning to end on the premise that if he never overstepped
the bounds of constitutional legality the bourgeois opposition
would never have a credible excuse for trying to topple his
regime. On the contrary, the effect of this stance was to disarm
the working class and prepare its defeat.

The Chilean bourgeoisie took its time in overthrowing Allende.
It followed a strategy of wearing down and discrediting the
regime before moving to direct confrontation. It waited quietly
through the first euphoric year when reform followed reform
and the self-confidence of the masses was on the rise. But be-

hind the facade of progress was the stark fact that every one of Allende's reforms had to win the votes of the Christian Democrats in Congress, and Allende's popular front government had no plans for what to do if Congress lined up against it.

By the end of 1971 bourgeois sabotage of the economy had begun to stalemate Allende's reforms. Inflation hit record highs, combined with a growing shortage of essential goods. The real offensive opened with the "bosses' strike" of October 1972, which closed factories and halted truck transport. When Allende, instead of mobilizing the workers to take over the factories and move the trucks, brought the army into his cabinet, he sealed the fate of his government. The futile and self-defeating effort to neutralize or win over the army high command bore its fruit in the September 11 coup.

What was missing in Chile was a mass revolutionary party with a perspective of struggling against the military for power, not collaborating with the generals and urging the workers to trust the local agents of imperialism. Neither the Communist nor Socialist parties, which dominated the Unidad Popular, was such an organization. Tragically, none of the organizations that stood to the left of the CP and SP were capable of displacing the popular front reformists from the head of the mass movement. The largest organized force to the left of the CP was the Movement of the Revolutionary Left (MIR). The MIR began as a Castroist current, enamored of the elitist schema of guerrilla warfare carried out by a vanguard group without direct involvement by the masses. Years of precious time were lost while the reformists deepened their influence over the radicalizing workers.

It was only with Allende's election in 1970 that the MIR turned to mass work. But even then, despite many correct and cogent criticisms of the capitulationist policies of the Unidad Popular, it posed as a critical supporter of the popular front coalition and not as a revolutionary alternative to it. The MIR's switch from ultraleftism to opportunism never produced a concrete program of transitional demands that could have won the masses away from the reformists in the course of the unfolding struggle. Moreover, the MIR retained certain of its ultraleft conceptions, which proved fatal when the showdown came. It expressed distrust in the military, while at the same time voicing some dangerous and unfounded illusions in the revolutionary potential of a sector of the officer corps. It advocated arming the workers, but in practice it looked to the atomized slum dwellers rather than to the organized working class in the factories. The steps it took to militarily prepare its followers for the coming confrontation were vitiated by its previous guerrillaist conceptions: it set up small clandestine armed groups subordinate to its party organization rather than seeking to build mass workers' militias that could have had a fighting chance against the coup.

The clandestine commando squads fought heroically against the military putsch, but they were not and could not have been a substitute for the self-acting armed organizations of the masses. This failure to understand the real dynamics of a *mass* armed struggle robbed the MIR's fighting units of any capacity to seriously affect the outcome when the bourgeoisie struck.

The Chilean Trotskyists sought to build the independent organizations of the workers in the factories and to prepare them to engage in battle against the military. This was a correct perspective. Unfortunately they did not have the membership or resources to implement this program on a large enough scale to turn the tide against the reformists of the CP and SP or to outflank the vacillating MIR.

But the defeat in Chile was not inevitable. With a correct program and a determined leadership with genuine roots among the masses—that is, with a mass Leninist party—there is every reason to believe that a socialist victory was possible. The purpose of this book is to draw the lessons of the Chilean disaster so that it will not be repeated.

LES EVANS
December 1, 1973

I

THE VICTORY OF THE
UNIDAD POPULAR

The End of Frei's
"Revolution in Liberty"

By Les Evans

Chileans went to the polls September 4 to deliver a smashing defeat to the ruling Christian Democratic Party and an unexpected victory to Socialist presidential candidate Salvador Allende.

Final results gave Allende 1,075,616 votes (36.3 percent). He narrowly defeated former president Jorge Alessandri, candidate of the right-wing National Party, who received 1,036,278 votes (34.9 percent). The Christian Democrat, Radomiro Tomic, handpicked heir to President Eduardo Frei, and until recently Chilean ambassador to Washington, ran a poor third, finishing with only 824,849 votes (27.8 percent).

Because Allende received only a plurality of the popular vote, the election is to be decided by Congress at a session October 24. In the past Congress has automatically selected the candidate with the larger vote, but it is not required to do so by law.

Some 30,000 supporters of the multiparty coalition backing Allende took to the streets to celebrate their victory. The army deployed tanks and troops around government buildings, but withdrew them when it became clear that Allende was the winner. In a victory speech to the giant crowd Allende declared: "I will not be just one more president. I will be the first president of the first authentically democratic, popular, national and revolutionary government in the history of Chile."

During his campaign the Socialist Party senator promised to

From the September 14, 1970, *Intercontinental Press*

restore diplomatic and trade relations with Cuba and to carry out extensive nationalizations, particularly of foreign-owned businesses.

The election marked a sharp polarization in Chilean politics. Eduardo Frei's "Revolution in Liberty" that swept him to power in 1964 appeared finished. Even the future existence of his Christian Democrats seemed in doubt. In 1964 the right-wing parties had formed an electoral bloc behind Frei's candidacy to prevent Allende from winning office. (Allende has been the perennial candidate of the Socialist Party since 1952, his 1970 victory representing his fourth try.) The Christian Democrats won 42.3 percent of the vote in 1964. In the legislative elections of 1967 this dropped to 35.6 percent and dropped still further in 1969 to 31.1 percent.

Alessandri's Nationalists broke with Frei to the right over the government's token agrarian reform and minimal social welfare measures. There has been a growth on the left as well, further isolating the Christian Democratic center and reducing the room for maneuver of bourgeois reformism.

Frei's reputation as a protégé of Washington proved to be a liability for his candidate. Tomic's record as a Washington ambassador only further strengthened his image as the U.S. State Department's choice. The Nixon administration did not hesitate to meddle directly in the campaign. (The American government has long given open support to politicians of its choice in Chile. Malcolm Browne reported in the March 9, 1969, *New York Times* that Washington "had heavily subsidized Mr. Frei's campaign" in the previous presidential election in 1964.)

The U.S. Information Agency organized frequent showings of a propaganda film on Czechoslovakia purporting to "prove" that voting for Communist candidates in 1948 had paved the way for a Russian dictatorship in that country.

Rumors were circulated that the army would stage a coup rather than accept Allende as president. Whether this was intended merely to frighten voters away from Allende or was a serious project, it was clear at least that the mysterious comings and goings of U.S. military personnel made even the Frei government nervous enough to publicly question Washington on its intentions. The September 5 *New York Times* reported: "The United States Navy has applied for Chilean visas for 87 officers, noncommissioned officers and civilian employes over the last eight months, a development that has left the Chilean Government deeply worried. . . .

"At one point the Chileans were told that the visa applicants made up a Navy band — an explanation that they did not believe and that was later withdrawn." Later explanations, including the claim that forty-nine of the men were to take part in naval exercises that had been canceled, and that thirty-eight of the others were to help in the rotation and resupply of a staff of ten at an Antarctic naval station, have not added to Washington's credibility.

Allende has been declared the official winner of the popular vote by the Frei government. But several hurdles lie ahead that will determine whether he will be able to take office and what he will be free to do if he does finally become president.

First he must win a majority in the joint session of Congress October 24. It is here that the bourgeois parties will be free to demand programmatic concessions in return for their votes, and where the composition of the broad coalition that backed Allende will be put to the test.

There are 150 members of the Chamber of Deputies and 50 members of the Senate, meeting together for a total of 200 votes. The Christian Democrats command 78 votes. The Nationalists have another 39. Together they can easily block Allende's election, although this is not expected to happen.

The Allende forces are a multiclass bloc dominated by the Communist Party (28 seats) and the Socialist Party (20 seats). The coalition also includes the bourgeois-liberal Radical Party (33 seats) and three smaller formations (2 seats).*

It should be pointed out that this election does not represent a sharp shift to the left. Even in 1964, at the time of the Christian Democratic landslide, the combined vote of the Communist, Socialist, and Radical parties amounted to 36 percent of the total, only .3 percent less than the 1970 results. What is new is the split among the bourgeois parties over whether or not to pursue Frei's program of capitalist reforms.

The Chilean Socialist Party stands to the left of the Communist Party, and Allende himself is in the left wing of his party. He is an open supporter of the Cuban revolution, and

---

* The parties composing the Unidad Popular, besides the SP, CP, and Radicals, were the Social Democratic Party; MAPU (Movimiento de Acción Popular Unitaria — United People's Action Movement), a left-wing split-off from the Christian Democrats; and API (Acción Popular Independiente — Independent People's Action), a small bourgeois formation in the right wing of the coalition.

was in turn supported during his campaign by Cuban Premier Fidel Castro.

The Communist Party, however, is one of the most slavishly pro-Moscow in the world and adheres to a rigidly reformist and electoral scheme for the "democratic revolution." Its perspective for maintaining a viable majority in Congress is to preserve the alliance with the Radical Party at all costs and to win an important sector of the Christian Democrats.

Luis Corvalán, the CP's general secretary, spelled out this perspective in an interview with the Cuban news service Prensa Latina, distributed earlier this year: "As Unidad Popular [Popular Unity, the bloc of Allende supporters] becomes an even more powerful force, the only one able to block the right and win, it can be predicted that the popular sector that still backs the Christian Democrats will leave them to join the left. The pro-government and reactionary sector of the CDP would join the traditional right-wing forces. All of this is more than likely."

Allende views himself as in the tradition of the Popular Front government of 1938. In an interview with Sonia Sepulveda of Prensa Latina earlier this year he gave his views of that experience:

"The Chilean parliament has been a going concern for over 120 years, a fact which distinguishes this country to a considerable degree from the rest of the Latin American nations. For example in 1938 Chile had Latin America's only popular front government; it was composed of non-Marxist parties like the Radicals as well as Marxist organizations. At that time the Radical Party was the majority grouping. Thus the president was a Radical, but the government was composed of Radicals, Socialists and members of the Democratic Party plus the parliamentary support of the Communist Party.

"At that time it was said that the situation would not be tolerated. However, the popular front government took decisive steps towards the economic and social development of the country: the incorporation of the middle class, the presence of the organized workers in the CTCH [Chilean Workers Federation, predecessor of the present CUT (Central Unica de Trabajadores — United Federation of Workers)] and the Production Development Corporation, which meant oil, steel, electricity for Chile.

"Our tradition, our history, what we did before allow us to say that Chile represents a social vanguard in Latin America, and that after trying out old formulas of traditional capitalism and Christian Democratic reformism, the way to socialism is now open by way of Unidad Popular."

Undoubtedly Allende's program is more radical, on paper, than the program of the Popular Front of 1938. But it remains to be seen what his bourgeois allies, present and prospective, will allow him to put into practice.

Student Declaration on the September 1970 Election

The following statement was drawn up by a committee of socialist students and professors at the University of Concepción after the Allende victory. It was read September 9, 1970, before an assembly of the Concepción Student Federation. Intercontinental Press printed this translation October 5, 1970.

1. We begin this document by clearly stating that we recognize the political-electoral triumph of the popular forces and already consider Salvador Allende the president of Chile.

Chile has entered a prerevolutionary stage, marked by a change in the relationship of class forces. With the victory of Salvador Allende, the workers have won an important political-electoral triumph. The process of radicalization, expressed in the support of the workers for Salvador Allende, must also be understood to include an important sector of workers, small-town people, and above all, peasants who voted for Tomic. These people did not vote for the Christian Democratic candidate because of his centrist and bourgeois reformist essence but because of his leftist appearance and his demagogic and populist program.

This political-electoral victory does not mean social revolution. Ownership of the means of production is still in the hands of the capitalists; the bourgeois state apparatus and its bulwark, the army, remain intact; and basically workers' and peasants' power has not been established. Social revolution means a qualitative leap from bourgeois democracy to workers' democracy.

2. A *prerevolutionary process* has begun, which opens up three probable alternatives: (a) this process may be crushed in embryo by a proimperialist military coup; (b) it might be canalized toward a center-left course, with a reformist government being maintained, although it would be under the con-

tinual threat of a proimperialist coup d'état if it were consistent with its program; and (c) it can lead into a socialist revolution, into a workers' and peasants' government, if the workers are capable of creating organs of power in the process of struggle and social confrontation.

Between now and November 4 [when the new president is inaugurated], the proimperialist bourgeoisie will probably attempt a coup d'état. If it is unable to do so, it will try to use the joint session of Congress [which will formally choose the new president] and perhaps try to get a second presidential election in order to gain a pretext for a "relatively constitutional" solution. To this end Alessandri's conservatives will provoke apparently tumultuous political acts which could produce a division in the Christian Democratic Party. One sector would then vote for Alessandri in the joint session of Congress. He would resign and the president of the Senate would have to call a new election. The U.S. State Department has not yet recognized the legitimate victory of Salvador Allende.

3. In a seeming paradox, the Christian Democrats, the losers in the election, have become the key party in the postelectoral deals. The importance of this party lies not alone in the fact that it has the decisive votes in the joint session but in that it controls an important sector of the armed forces, which is a card it uses in all its negotiations. A section of the Christian Democrats is acting as a lure for the Unidad Popular, promising the *Allendistas* jesuitically that if they remain quiet they will gain its votes in the joint session and a pledge that the army will not stage a coup. There must be no attempt to mobilize the workers, these Christian Democrats argue, because that would provoke an instinctive reaction by the military. Parallel to this, the ultraright wing of the Christian Democrats, in collusion with the *Alessandristas*, is speculating on a coup or the variant of new elections.

4. The real threat of a coup d'état or new elections means that we must make it our primary political task to prepare right now, without losing a minute, to meet the plans of the right. We must not let our attention be distracted by evocations of the "democratic" tradition of the bourgeois state. We must call for a militant mobilization of the workers, peasants, slum dwellers, and students, without worrying about how this may affect the nerves of the military. The proimperialist bourgeoisie will execute its plans without bothering about whether or not the people's movement has offered a certificate of good conduct. Only a militant mobilization of the popular masses can halt the reactionaries' plot.

If the bourgeoisie fails to put its plans into effect between now and November 4, we will have lost nothing and we will have gained much in preparing the ranks of the workers for the possibility that they will attempt a coup d'état after Allende takes office.

5. The principal task for this period is to organize *Committees Against the Reactionaries and for Socialism.* These committees must develop on the foundation of the Unidad Popular committees, where the politicized masses are. They must not practice any sectarian exclusiveness but join with all those who are for the defense of the people's victory. They cannot be the same as the Unidad Popular committees, which are electoral in nature, but must be able to carry out tasks in accordance with the new political conjuncture. There is no question of forming parallel or divisive committees.

6. The revolutionary left must consider building these committees as anti-imperialist united front work involving a tactical alliance with the Unidad Popular. But we must keep it clear that we are maintaining our strategy of armed struggle, which is the only way to oust the bourgeoisie and establish a workers' and peasants' government.

7. In order to carry forward the tasks outlined above, we consider it urgent to form a revolutionary front which must not only undertake common actions but *a rapid regroupment of the revolutionary left*, above all, those groups whose tactical and strategic positions are the closest.

The greatest dangers facing the revolutionary left in this situation are the following: (1) falling into conciliationist and capitulationist opportunism, which could lead gradually to liquidationism; (2) falling into sectarianism toward the *Allendista* movement, which could lead to suicidal isolation.

Regrouping in a tactical united front with Unidad Popular will enable the revolutionary left to integrate itself in the real process of mass struggle and to give impetus, with determination and revolutionary imagination, to the struggle against the bourgeois and imperialist plot.

We are not trying to deceive any *Allendista compañero* with this policy of a united front. We will be principled and unsectarian in working together with the Unidad Popular *compañeros* in the struggle against the bourgeois and imperialist plot. But at the same time, we make it absolutely clear that we will not retreat an inch from our strategy of armed struggle.

Unite to form committees against the reactionary plot.

Nixon Weighs the Alternatives

By Les Evans

The Nixon administration has said little in public about the September 4 electoral victory in Chile of Salvador Allende. Privately, however, Washington has made it known that it is extremely worried at the possible consequences if Allende should win the presidency in the October 24 runoff vote in the Chilean Congress.

Unnamed White House spokesmen have raised the specter that an Allende regime would mean a communist take-over in Chile, which would be followed in quick succession by similar developments in Argentina, Bolivia, and Peru. These predictions were made at a "background" news briefing in Chicago September 16.

Under White House rules, officials cannot be identified by the press. But it was at a similar briefing in Chicago the next day that an "official" threatened U.S. military intervention in Jordan if Hussein were to lose to the Palestinian commandos. The anonymous spokesman in the latter case, it was soon disclosed, was no one less than Nixon himself.

Charles Vanhecke commented in the September 27-28 Paris *Le Monde* that "In Washington the talk is that Chile has become his [Nixon's] main preoccupation, after the Middle East and Vietnam."

The *New York Times,* a rather selective champion of "free elections," even went so far as to advise the Chilean armed forces on how to find a good pretext for a coup d'état if Allende ultimately won the presidency. In a September 19 editorial the *Times* said: "If Dr. Allende in office tried to withdraw from his commitment—by purging the judiciary, politicizing the schools or canceling elections—Chile's armed forces then would have a legitimate excuse for intervening in defense of the Constitution."

Although Allende's Popular Unity coalition has no intention of instituting a communist regime, it is certainly true that Wall Street would be the biggest loser from any large-scale nationalization of foreign-owned property in Chile.

According to U.S. Commerce Department data, the value

of American corporate holdings in Chile at the end of 1968 (the latest figures available) was $964 million. More than half of this figure ($586 million) represented investments in mining and smelting. Chile is the second largest copper producer in the world, with a capacity to turn out 850,000 tons a year.

There are 110 U.S. companies or agencies of American interests operating in Chile. The largest U.S. investors are the Kennecott and Anaconda copper companies, but firms in other sectors of industry have also been turning a handsome profit. Boise Cascade runs electric utilities which had a gross income of $87 million in 1968. International Telephone and Telegraph (ITT) owns a 60 percent interest in Chile's main telephone company, on which it had a gross income of $60 million in 1968. In the same year Coca Cola, Standard Oil of New Jersey, and General Motors had sales respectively in Chile of $20 million, $46.9 million, and $36 million.

The rate of profit is high. The September 21 *New York Times* reported: "In 1967, the earning ratio on capital invested in mining enterprises was 27.3 per cent. In 1968 it was 26 per cent. . . . The 1968 return on all United States investments in Chile was 17.4 per cent."

President Eduardo Frei Montalva's Christian Democrats have been demanding programmatic concessions from Allende as the price of their votes in Congress October 24. Allende on September 30 refused their demand for constitutional amendments guaranteeing free elections and freedom of the press. He also refused to relinquish his right if elected to name commanders of the armed forces.

Nevertheless, Allende's multiclass coalition has shifted sharply to the right since the September 4 voting. In an interview quoted in the September 26 *Washington Post* Allende declared: "The future government of Chile will not be a Socialist government. It is unscientific to maintain the contrary. I have said repeatedly — and it could not be otherwise — that my government will be multi-party." He assured his critics that the bulk of industry would remain in private hands: "The area of private property will be numerically the biggest."

The September 9 London *Times* reported: "Dr. Allende has told friends that he will rest contented if by his presidency he breaks the power of a few very rich and influential families and the new immigrant rich."

But the rich have no intention of surrendering even a portion of their privileges to Allende's halfhearted reforms. Immediately after the elections a run on the banks began. Joseph Novitsky reported from Santiago in the September 25 *New York Times:* "The Chilean economy went from expansion to recession almost overnight, according to the outgoing government." The Central Bank had to supply Santiago banks with 688 million escudos (22 escudos equal one U.S. dollar) in the first two weeks of September to cover unexpected withdrawals. This was three times the average for a full month.

Money, and its owners, are flowing out of the country in a steady stream. Most of the wealthy Chileans are heading for Argentina — although for some this is just a stopover on the way to the United States. Malcolm W. Browne reported from Buenos Aires in the September 17 *New York Times:* "An invasion of refugees, panic-stricken by the prospect of a Marxist President in Chile . . . has packed hotel rooms here and jolted the Argentine economy." Browne said that "there are thought to be tens of thousands of migrant families" now in Argentina.

"The Chileans have sought to convert as much money as possible into dollars," he added, "much of which has been sent either to banks or to relatives in the United States."

The military regime in Buenos Aires is plainly worried at the prospect of a "leftist" government in Chile, coming on top of the rising radicalization it faces at home. Argentina's lackluster strongman, General Marcelo Levingston, appears to be casting around for a civilian successor who could act as a buffer between the military and the aroused masses.

Marcel Niedergang reported in the September 27-28 *Le Monde* that a whole string of former presidents have visited Levingston recently, at his request. But the most likely candidate, in Niedergang's opinion, was unable to come in person, because he is in exile in Madrid: former President Juan Perón. "The possibility of General Perón returning to Buenos Aires before the end of the year is again the chief topic of commentary and speculation in political circles in the Argentine capital," Niedergang wrote.

Recent months have seen an increase in acts of individual terrorism, sabotage, and attacks on government offices. "Upset by this menacing and uncontrollable rise of violence," Niedergang said, "some Argentine leaders may be tempted to authorize General Perón's 'return to the country' in the hope of disarming the most turbulent elements of revolutionary Peronism.

"Another argument to encourage the Argentinian leaders to take a new look at the 'Perón dossier' is the victory in Chile September 4 of the Socialist Salvador Allende, the standard bearer of the Popular Unity coalition, who is regarded in Buenos Aires as a Trojan Horse of Communism in Latin America. . . .

"Of the two 'evils,' Peronism and Communism, the Argentine officers would still unquestionably prefer the former. Even a temporary accord with the Peronists might seem capable to them of putting off the eventuality that, rightly or wrongly, they dread the most — the rise of a popular movement demanding the establishment of a socialist regime in Buenos Aires, either by force or by the ballot."

Chile's Congress Approves Allende
By Les Evans

"There's no reason at all to be uneasy. We have never claimed that we would form a socialist government November 4. Allende himself has said: Popular Unity is composed of six different groups including the Radicals who have largely dominated Chilean political life for the last thirty years."
— Pablo Neruda, the best-known member of the Chilean Communist Party, in the October 23 *Le Monde*

Salvador Allende passed his last legal obstacle to inauguration as Chile's president when the long-awaited special session of Congress October 24 voted 153 to 35 to abide by the September 4 election results and ratify his victory. The vote was a mere formality inasmuch as the Christian Democrats had pledged to support Allende. Even Jorge Alessandri, candidate of the right-wing National Party and the only other contender, withdrew in Allende's favor on the eve of the congressional runoff.

The assassination of army commander in chief René Schneider Chereau, apparently by right-wing terrorists, did not affect the outcome of the vote. Schneider was gunned down in his automobile October 22 by a well-organized group of assailants. He died three days later. The lame-duck regime of Eduardo Frei proclaimed a state of emergency — amounting to martial law — threatening to shoot civilians caught on the streets between midnight and 6:00 a.m. Press censorship was imposed.

From *Intercontinental Press*, November 2, 1970

Although virtually all of the 150 suspects who were arrested were identified as supporters of extreme right-wing organizations, the left-wing press bore the brunt of the censorship. General Camilo Valenzuela, the military commander of Santiago, warned three leftist newspapers October 23 to cease publishing articles speculating on the origin of the terrorist attack.

One of the papers involved, the Communist Party's *El Siglo*, charged that the U.S. Central Intelligence Agency was responsible for the crime. Columnist Eduardo Labarca wrote in *El Siglo*: "There is no doubt that the group of right-wing extremist commandos that attacked General Schneider belongs to a network of terrorist cells operating in the country under the guidance and control of the North American CIA." Allende's Socialist Party took the same stand. In an October 25 statement to the press, Senator Aniceto Rodríguez, general secretary of the Socialist Party, said: "All these people have been trained by the CIA."

Outgoing President Frei invited representatives of Allende's popular front coalition to help administer the state of emergency. José Tohá, a colleague of Allende, was appointed acting undersecretary of the interior, a post closely associated with the functioning of the police.

The chief suspect in the murder of General Schneider is Roberto Viaux, a retired general who led an abortive military revolt in Santiago in October 1969. The revolt was put down when General Schneider was appointed commander-in-chief of the army. Schneider's assassination was evidently intended to provoke the army into a coup that would prevent Allende from assuming office. Thus far the army has refrained from doing so. Allende was received with full honors at the military academy in Santiago where the slain general lay in state.

The press in the United States has consistently depicted Allende as a fire-breathing Marxist, set on expropriating Chilean capitalists, lock, stock, and barrel. The fears of the privileged sectors in Chile itself are even more extreme. Marcel Niedergang, writing from Santiago in the October 22 issue of *Le Monde*, reported a few of the extravagant rumors that have been circulating in monied circles since the September 4 elections: "They're going to move the workers and the homeless into our houses," "They're going to requisition all the private cars," "They're going to freeze all the bank accounts," "They'll stop us from going abroad." There have been demonstrations in front of the presidential palace with people brandishing signs demanding: "Eduardo Frei, Save Us From Communism."

If Allende were in fact the revolutionary he is represented to be, the army's ambivalence would be difficult to fathom. There is, however, a great disparity between rumor and reality.

Communist Party Senator Volodia Teitelboim told Marcel Niedergang (October 23 *Le Monde*) not to expect any "spectacular upsets" in the first months of the Allende government. "We certainly have no intention of provoking useless confrontations with the United States," Teitelboim said. "We will carefully study all the problems as they come up. We have experts in our ranks — economists, financiers — and we strongly hope that the Christian Democratic technicians who have had the experience of power will give us a helping hand. . . . We hope to lay the basis for something that could later make possible the development of a socialist regime."

Allende himself said to Niedergang: "The American press immediately labeled me a Marxist. The barb is plain, as is the poison. Of course the Socialists adhere to Marxism. They are not the only ones. We are not going to set up a Marxist government. That is senseless. We will have a government in which the six formations of the Popular Unity are represented — the Communists, Socialists, Radicals, MAPU, Social Democrats, and Independent People's Action. That is the truth."

II

POPULAR FRONTISM IN OFFICE:
THE FIRST YEAR

Allende's Chile:
Is It Going Socialist?

By Peter Camejo

The following essay was published as a pamphlet in December 1971; the first part was based on an article that originally appeared in The Militant, *August 6, 1971.*

Was the September 1970 victory of Salvador Allende's Popular Unity coalition in the Chilean elections a victory for socialism? Did it at least set into motion an evolution toward socialism? Does the Popular Unity government represent the interests of the workers and peasants of Chile?

Many radicals in the United States would answer these questions with an unhesitating yes. Foremost among them is the Communist Party, whose mouthpiece, the *Daily World*, has given enthusiastic coverage to events in Chile. "Class struggle sharpens as Chile moves to socialism," reads a *Daily World* headline on May 11, 1971, for example.

This sentiment is shared by many others, and not all of them on the left. From some accounts in the major daily press, one might wonder if a socialist revolution had not already taken place in Chile.

What are the facts?

Since his election, Allende has implemented a number of reforms, some of them significant. Probably the most important was the general pay increase, averaging approximately 35 percent. Some very poorly paid workers received even more.

Soon after his election, Allende announced and sent to Congress his plans for nationalization of the copper mines and a few other corporations. By February 1971, the Senate had endorsed his project with only moderate alterations, and the mines are expected to be completely nationalized by 1972.

The land reform initiated by the previous government prior to Allende's election has been speeded up.

The income of families with children has been supplemented with free milk for each child.

A special riot police unit of 2,000 was disbanded and its men sent into other units of the Chilean national police, which is called the Carabinero Corps.*

Political prisoners were set free. Most of these were young revolutionaries who had engaged in expropriation of banks and other armed actions; in return for their freedom, they called for a moratorium on such actions.

The reforms the Allende government has implemented are a direct product of mass pressure generated by the struggles of the workers and peasants of Chile. The reforms brought him increased popularity, which was reflected in the municipal elections last April in which the Popular Unity coalition received more votes than all of its opponents combined.

Can these and other proposed reforms be taken as a sign that Chile is moving toward socialism? To answer this question, we should look at how Allende became president of Chile, what the Popular Unity is, exactly what his reforms are, and how they are being implemented.

"The program of the Popular Unity is not a Communist program," declared Allende in the October 4, 1970, *New York Times*, "nor is it a Socialist program, nor a Radical program, nor the program of the MAPU, or the API. It is the convergence of opinion." In other words, it is a program that is acceptable to all the parties involved.

The Popular Unity coalition is a familiar combination of bourgeois and working-class political parties. The MAPU is a left split-off from the Christian Democratic Party with some support among the peasantry. The API has its historical roots in the movement of ex-dictator Carlos Ibáñez del Campo in the 1950s.

But foremost among the bourgeois parties participating in the Popular Unity coalition is the Radical Party. Back in 1964, Allende ran for president because of what he called "betrayal" of the people by the Radical Party. He declared that the people have "no possibility whatever with the Radicals." Before the

---

*At the time this article was written the UP government had announced it was disbanding the Grupo Móvil, but this was actually never carried out.

year was out, however, he had made an impassioned plea for the Radical Party to join his coalition. It refused.

Yet as time went by, the Radical Party came to realize that a radicalization was occurring that was more intense than a similar one in the mid-thirties, and was considerably broadening the electoral base of the Socialist and Communist parties, as well. An indication of this process was that by March 1969, the Socialist Party had 14.4 percent of the vote and the Communist Party, 15.7 percent. Thus, if the 12.9 percent of the Radical Party were added, the combined total would indicate that the chances in 1970 were excellent for an electoral victory for a popular front coalition among these groups. Such a popular front combination would be similar to the one that came to power in 1938.

Unlike 1938, however, this time there was a new problem: the radicalization was so deep that powerful left-wing pressure within the Socialist Party could have effectively blocked the formation of a popular front. The nomination of SP leader Salvador Allende as the coalition candidate was necessary to placate the left wing and to assure the SP's participation.

And so the Radical Party "betrayers" of yesterday, who only six years earlier had been in a political alliance with the extreme right wing, joined in the formation of a popular front coalition. They received a warm welcome. "We hope that the new situation will allow [the Radical Party] to win back some of the strength which made them the top Chilean formation for a long time," purred the leading Communist Party senator, Volodia Teitelboim, following the elections.[1]*

An Allende victory in September 1970 was made possible by several factors. Among these were the decline in the influence of the Christian Democratic Party (PDC) in the six years since it won the elections in 1964, and the split in the bourgeois forces reflected by the candidacies of Radomiro Tomic of the PDC and Jorge Alessandri of the National Party. (The traditional Liberal and Conservative parties had united to form the National Party.)

Alessandri concentrated his campaign on the danger of a Communist take-over. He combined nationalist demagogy and a hard line on alleged "disruptions" of the economy by labor and peasant strikes.

Tomic put forward a left-reform program designed to attract radicalizing social layers, especially the peasants. At times,

---

*Footnotes appear at the end of this article (p. 61).

Tomic appeared to be to the left of Allende. It was not always easy to distinguish between them.

Because no candidate received more than 50 percent of the vote, the outcome of the election was referred to a joint session of the House and Senate for a decision on October 24.

The Tomic-led PDC agreed to make Allende president if he, along with the rest of Popular Unity, would accept certain constitutional amendments to strengthen capitalist institutions (referred to by the PDC as "reinforcing democracy"). These amendments would limit the authority of the president while increasing the independence of certain bourgeois institutions from Congress and the executive; they constituted a kind of blackmail.

The constitutional changes provided that no military officers would be appointed who had not attended the academies; no changes in the size of the army, navy, air force, or Carabineros could be made by the president; "private" militias would be unconstitutional; Allende must "guarantee" not to tamper with the press, radio, schools, unions, judiciary, and so forth.

When discussions about these proposals began between the Unidad Popular and the Christian Democrats, the Communist Party reacted with indignation. "We understand, from this dialogue, that there is not and could not be on the part of this party [the Christian Democrats] any question about the prerogative of the next president of the Republic or any conditions imposed on the Unidad Popular or any concessions to the blackmail of 'Alessandrism,'" declared Orlando Millas in his report from the CP's Political Committee to its Central Committee on September 14, 1970.[2]

On September 30, Allende released a seven-page statement in which he indignantly refused to accept the proposal of the Christian Democratic Party.

The PDC's purpose was not to extract a promise from Allende that he would attempt to maintain capitalism; of that they had no fear. "The new Chilean chief of state has at least as many friends in the Christian Democratic ranks as in those of the left," wrote Marcel Niedergang in the Paris daily *Le Monde* October 23. "While some of his daughters, who are also his collaborators, are considered to have 'leftist' sympathies, he himself is not loath to frequent Santiago high society. Throughout his long career he has always strictly respected the rules of the democratic game, and this 'detail' has certainly helped temper the fears of some right and center leaders."

No, the PDC had another purpose in mind: to take advantage of the situation created by the closeness of the election to improve its own position in coming battles between the ruling class and the masses by altering some of the rules of the game. The PDC stuck to its demands in spite of declarations by the CP and Allende that they would not capitulate.

In less than two weeks Allende capitulated. The agreement was signed and Allende's election to the presidency was assured with the support not only of the PDC, but even of Alessandri, who said, "My best wishes for success go to the next president of Chile, whose long and proven democratic convictions, reflected in attitudes of constant respect for the constitution and the laws, are well-known."[3]

The majority of the Chilean ruling class would have preferred Alessandri or Tomic as president. The masses, however, could not be persuaded to go along with the ruling class's first choice, and so an alternative had to be accepted, one that would be able to coopt the electorate's desire for change by granting reforms without exceeding the bounds of capitalist property relations. This alternative was Allende.

Nevertheless, Allende and his government constitute a reformist regime driven considerably to the left by the general radicalization among the masses and the economic instability that plagues Latin America. To be sure, the ruling classes in Chile and the United States do fear that under Allende the masses may become uncontrollable; they are afraid that the masses, believing Allende represents them, may grow more daring in both their demands and their actions. At the same time, however, Allende warns the ruling class that unless it accepts him, the masses will certainly revolt. It is precisely this misguided faith of the masses in Allende that makes him so useful to the ruling class in its efforts to contain the radicalization.

In return for the bourgeoisie's endorsement, Allende set up a cabinet in which the majority (eight out of fifteen) of the members come from the bourgeois parties in the Popular Unity coalition, in spite of the fact that these parties accounted for only a small fraction of the Popular Unity vote. Of the remaining seven cabinet ministers, three are Communists and four are Socialists.

Allende's inaugural speech opened with a call for "work and sacrifice" from the masses.[4] He pledged before Congress to "keep and obey the constitution."[5] Once installed in the presidential palace, he made a speech rendering homage to the armed forces and the national police: "Permit me, on this solemn occasion . . . to voice our people's thanks to the armed forces and to the Carabinero Corps, which abide by the constitution and the rule of law."[6] Although he paid homage to army Commander in Chief René Schneider, assassinated by the right wing, he had not one word for the martyrs among the miners, the landless, the homeless, and the Mapuche Indians, murdered in cold blood by this same police and army.

Of Chile's youth, Allende said: "A rebellious student in the past, I will not criticize their impatience, but it is my duty to ask them to think calmly."[7]

The inauguration ceremonies included a visit to church, where Allende was greeted by Cardinal Raul Silva Henriques as the choir sang hallelujahs. The reactionary Catholic church, which is attempting to adapt to the rhetoric of revolution only to better swindle the masses of Chile, was defended by Allende last October in these words: "Before, for centuries, the Catholic Church defended the interests of the powerful. Today the church, after John XXIII, has become oriented toward making the Gospel of Christ a reality. . . . I have read the declaration of the Bishops of Medellin, and the language they used is the same that we have used since we were born into political life thirty years ago. I believe the church will not be against the Popular Unity government. On the contrary, they are going to be a factor in our favor. . . ."[8]

With the blessings of outgoing President Frei, the army, and the church, Allende took office and promised to lead Chile to socialism by obeying the constitution based on capitalist property relations and upholding the primary defenders of capitalist private property, the army and police.

Thus, in order to remain in power, Allende must constantly demonstrate to the ruling class that he can contain the masses. Most crucial in this respect is keeping the mass organizations disarmed. On the other hand, if he loses his mass support, the ruling class would no longer need to tolerate him. Therefore, Allende must bend sufficiently to mass pressure to maintain his mass support.

The politics of the Allende regime are by nature forced into a balancing act between the oppressed and oppressor classes. While his regime began with the enthusiastic support of the masses and the grudging support of the ruling class, it is bound to end, after a period of vacillation, by satisfying neither the rulers nor the ruled.

How has Allende's law-and-order road to socialism been working out? Let us look at the program of the Popular Unity coalition (*Programa de la Unidad Popular*, Libreria PLA, 1970) and see how it is being applied in reality.

Despite the leftist tone of its introduction and its vague references to socialism, this program in no way challenges the continued existence of capitalism. It challenges neither the armed defenders of capitalism, the army and police, nor the sacred bourgeois right of private property. It aims to improve the infrastructure of Chile's capitalist economy by helping private business while not eliminating foreign investment.

The nationalization of the mines — copper in particular — is an important part of the Popular Unity program, and it will represent a victory for the Chilean masses. Still, nationalization in and of itself does not mean that the working class is in power or that capitalism is being eliminated. (Bolivia nationalized its mines almost twenty years ago, yet capitalism remains in power and the masses are as exploited as ever.)

Fidel Castro told a delegation from Chile in 1966 that the nature of the Chilean revolution could not be judged by whether the copper industry were nationalized, but that "what really defined a revolution was the will to change the social structure for the benefit of the exploited classes . . ." and that "the nature of the revolution had to be judged by all its acts, by all its policies toward each social class."[9]

Allende's plan for nationalization was to buy the mines from the United States. This policy was actually begun under the previous Christian Democratic regime of Eduardo Frei, which had already bought 51 percent of the major mines by the time Allende was voted into office.

The law authorizing nationalization was passed unanimously in July by the predominantly conservative Congress of Chile. This was first of all a reflection of the mass pressure for the nationalization of the copper mines. Second, in order to improve its position within the context of imperialist domination, the national bourgeoisie is willing to take advantage of the present circumstances of the U.S. — its unpopular war in Vietnam and unfavorable trade situation with other imperialist countries. The Chilean national bourgeoisie, however, fearing both the reaction of the masses and imperialist reprisals, has preferred to postpone or at least modify the nationalization. This was reflected in Frei's earlier hesitant "Chileanization" of the mines. A third and important factor precipitating the nationalization of the copper mines was the government bureaucracy's support for the measure. The Chilean government's funds come from taxes on copper exports. And the government bureaucracy seeks to increase its negotiating power within the economy as a whole in order to guarantee its privileged jobs, many of which are nonessential to the Chilean economy.

Allende's earlier promise to pay about $500 million for the remaining 49 percent of the mines, still formally in American hands, was a huge concession to U.S. imperialism. After all, it was only a year earlier that the Peruvian military dictatorship, much further to the right than the Allende government, had nationalized an important U.S. oil corporation without compensation.

From an original investment of $3.5 million, American corporations have built up their holdings in Chile to the value of close to $1 billion — all of it at the expense of Chile's working people. In addition, the imperialists have drained billions of dollars from Chile since the 1930s. Thus, Chile has already paid for the total U.S. investment many times over. [10]

The way this works is that the American companies first mine the copper in Chile and then sell it to themselves at artificially low prices to avoid both paying taxes and paying Chilean workers a decent wage. In 1966, for instance, the price of copper was set at 36 cents per pound, while the price on the world market was 60 cents per pound. [11]

These facts are common knowledge in Chile. Even the president of Allende's own party was forced to declare against paying for the copper mines. The law approved by the entire Congress permitted a reevaluation based upon the opening of the companies' books. On September 29, 1971, Allende announced that his study had indicated that the U.S. corporations had, in the last sixteen years alone, made $770 million in superprofits, that is, above the 10 percent profit rate considered sufficient. This in effect means that the mines will now be nationalized without additional compensation.

Allende's statement, however, refers only to the 49 percent of the mines still formally in the hands of the North American copper companies. The extent of the profit to the American imperialists from Chile's purchase of the original 51 percent of the mines is still undetermined. It is not ruled out, however, that for decades to come Chile will continue to pay interest on the bonds used to pay for that same 51 percent of the copper mines. Furthermore, the actual money involved could well exceed the cash value of the mines.

On the other hand, Allende may be forced to stop payments on the debt arising from Chile's purchase of the original 51 percent. Two factors push Allende in this direction. First, the Chilean masses want to end the U.S. capitalists' extortion of the wealth created by Chilean labor. And second, Allende may simply run out of money and be compelled to seek at least a temporary suspension of payments.

Allende would prefer, as all reformists do, to satisfy the imperialists and the local ruling class and, in addition, grant reforms to the masses. But already his program of promises to make everyone happy — boss and worker, landlord and tenant, oppressor and oppressed — is falling apart. And, unlike the masses, imperialists are not very understanding when it comes to the personal tragedy of a reformist. Allende, despite his efforts to help imperialism (which, until October 1971, had brought a favorable response in ruling circles), may find himself confronted with ever-growing attacks from the United States.

It is important to note, however, that Allende is not threatening to nationalize the growing U.S. holdings in the industrial sector. The November 4, 1970, *Washington Post*, for example, estimated 1968 U.S. investments in Chile to include $586 million in mining and $377 million in nonmining industries. The 1969 Rockefeller *Report on the Americas* confirms this trend.

In addition, the Popular Unity program guarantees that most businesses in Chile will remain in private hands and be aided by the government. Of the 30,500 businesses in the country, fewer than 1 percent (150) fall into the category for possible purchase, or "nationalization." In banking and other categories the government has given full compensation for any state intervention. Allende has agreed, in addition, to continue payment on the over $2 billion Chilean debt, owed almost entirely to U.S. imperialism. The interest payments on this debt alone drain hundreds of millions of desperately needed dollars from Chile.

Allende is also promising to pay with interest for the land reform. The law under which Allende is operating is the same one passed by the previous, openly proimperialist Frei government.

Because of foot-dragging by both Frei and Allende, peasants throughout the country — including the 250,000 Mapuche Indians in the south — are simply taking over the land. If Allende were to attempt to prevent the take-overs by force, his popularity would plummet and his government might face peasant uprisings or a revolutionary situation. Instead, his government is quick to assure the landowners that they will be paid for their land.

This may not be so easy, however. "The government is financially able only to expropriate about one-eighth of the large farms and estates this year," Rick Nagin wrote in the *Daily*

World in May 1971, following a trip to Chile. Meanwhile, the peasants are supposed to wait around until Allende can find money to pay the rich landowners, because implementing the land reform without paying compensation to the landowners would be "ultraleft": "Unfortunately, certain ultraleft groups have also encouraged illegal land seizures," Nagin complained. (If one went by Nagin's criterion, the Russian Revolution would represent the epitome of ultraleftism.) "Illegal" or not, however, the Chilean peasants are continuing to carry out the land reform on their own.

The "pressure for a faster pace" toward socialism, says the December 6, 1970, *New York Times*, is the "keenest difficulty" Allende faces. It is this pressure which is most dramatically reflected in the occupations of land and unfinished buildings.

In the past, the Communist Party and the Socialist Party associated themselves with similar efforts by the masses to alleviate their oppression. Now that they are part of the bourgeois government, however, they are singing a different tune. CP senator Volodia Teitelboim, for instance, is quoted in the December 3, 1970, *Washington Post* as saying, "We have stopped urging people to go out and take sites for themselves. . . . These invasions must now cease."

On February 13, 1970, Allende announced special legislation to punish land invasion instigators. According to the February 14 *New York Times*, José Tohá, Allende's minister of the interior, warned that "the government of President Señor Allende would act vigorously against any armed group operating in rural areas." These announcements were made following a meeting between Allende and representatives of the National Farm Owners' Organization.

A few days later, all the component groups of the Popular Unity front issued a declaration opposing the land seizures. Tohá was sent to different parts of the country in an effort to talk the peasants out of seizing the land.

In March, Daniel Vergara, undersecretary of the interior, began to warn that force might be used to prevent the land seizures. Juan Rubiliar, the president of the Federación Campesina de la Provincia Llanquihue (Llanquihue Province Peasant Federation) was actually imprisoned, although he was quickly released.[12]   However, the government has recently begun to use force to remove peasants from occupied land.

The Popular Unity program contains a section entitled "National Defense." It not only calls for providing the latest "modern military science" for the armed forces,[13] but it declares: "It is necessary to assure the armed forces the material and technical means and a just and democratic system of remuneration, promotions and retirement that guarantees to officers, noncommissioned officers, and troops economic security during their tour of duty in the ranks and under their conditions of retirement. . . ." [14]

In relation to its population, Chile has the largest armed forces of any South American country. Only the military in Brazil have received more aid from the United States. Between 1960 and 1965 alone, Chile sent 2,064 of its men to the U.S. for military training, a figure surpassed only by Brazil and Peru. [15]

This army and this special police, formed to protect and maintain the privileges of the capitalist ruling class, are not only to remain intact, but workers and peasants who correctly suspect that these forces may soon be used against them again will be forbidden to arm themselves.

"I have absolute confidence in the loyalty" of the armed forces, Allende stated in an interview in the *New York Times*, March 28, 1971. "Our forces are professional forces at the service of the state, of the people. . . ."

"With each day my conviction becomes deeper that the armed forces of Chile are an expression of its people, and therefore are irrevocably and essentially professionals and democratic," Allende said in an interview published in the February 14, 1971, issue of the Buenos Aires daily *Clarín*.

"The Chilean armed forces, which assure the sovereignty, independence and dignity of Chile, are the guarantee of our political process," Allende said at a news conference for representatives of the foreign press, May 25, 1971.

Hand in hand with this confidence in the armed forces goes a fear of the masses being armed. Minister of the Interior Tohá made clear in the same issue of *Clarín* that "the government reaffirms its decision not to accept the existence of armed groups of any kind; the functions relating to order and security are exclusively the armed forces' and Carabineros' jurisdiction."

Luis Corvalán, general secretary of the Communist Party, stated months before the electoral victory of the Popular Unity coalition that the CP opposed proposals to arm the masses as being "equivalent to showing distrust in the army." The army, he explained, "is not invulnerable to the new winds blowing in Latin America and penetrating everywhere." [16]

Yet it does not take much thought or knowledge of history to understand that if the army were on the side of the op-

pressed workers and peasants, there would be no fear of
arming them. These fears are themselves proof that the oppressed do not run Chile. Allende, by refusing to arm the
masses and by supporting the army and police, assures
the capitalist ruling class that as long as he is president, the
workers and peasants will not run Chile. Revolution is not
part of his program.

Allende has declared his intention to maintain relations with
all countries. This represents a victory for the Chilean masses
because it means the establishment of relations with countries
like Cuba and China.

The mere recognition of China and Cuba, however, in no
way changes the capitalist nature of Chile. One of the campaign
promises of the right-wing candidate in last year's elections,
Jorge Alessandri, was that if elected he would recognize Cuba.
And the Frei government had not only considered recognition
of Cuba, but had actually reopened trade with Cuba before
it was voted out of office.

A closer look at Allende's foreign policy will indicate that
rather than being anti-imperialist, it is actually a sophisticated
cover-up for imperialism.

"Our international policy is based, as it was yesterday, on
respect for international commitments freely assumed, self-
determination and non-intervention," Allende is quoted as
saying in the winter 1971 issue of the *New World Review*.
In a feature interview with Prensa Latina, September 5, 1970,
Allende claimed that Chile has never been a puppet of the
United States, and that he only intends to continue a great
tradition of Chilean independence. "We have always stressed
our respect for the self-determination and full sovereignty of
the peoples," he states. "That has also been the policy of the
Christian Democratic government of Sr. Frei, in keeping with
a Chilean tradition. Therefore, relations and ties are above
and beyond regimes, and I think Chile has done well to maintain a position in line with that criterion."

What is the truth behind all this piety?

The "international commitments" Allende referred to include
the $2 billion debt, owed mainly to the United States, "freely
assumed" by Chile's rich, but to be paid by Chile's poor.

Neither the present nor the previous Chilean regimes have
a very good record on the question of self-determination.
Allende knows well that Chile, used as a tool by British imperialism in the nineteenth century, took over through war
the southern parts of Bolivia and Peru that contained the

richest mines. That imperialist-promoted venture left Bolivia landlocked, a handicap it has sought to overcome by requesting an outlet to the sea.

If Allende were a revolutionary, he would support Bolivia's request. But the Chilean bourgeoisie has created a national climate of chauvinism and racism (unlike Chile, Bolivia is predominantly nonwhite) which makes such support unpopular. Allende takes advantage of this to deny Bolivia's just demand.

Allende talks about a policy of opposing imperialist intervention into the affairs of other nations, and the Popular Unity program even contains a sentence calling for "active solidarity" with Vietnam. As president, however, Allende has neither condemned U.S. aggression in Indochina nor done anything to aid the Vietnamese.

Not only does he remain silent in the face of imperialist aggression in Vietnam, but he even tries to play down its interventionist role in Latin America. He was asked in the interview in the *New York Times* March 28, 1971, if he thought the United States would conspire with business interests against Chile. "Obviously I do not think the United States government would lend itself to such efforts . . ." he replied. "I simply cannot imagine that the United States government would make common cause with private enterprise on an issue like this and frame policy accordingly. Unfortunately, history does teach that on occasion in the past this has been the case."

In 1966, Castro insisted that "a government can ask the workers to make sacrifices when a revolution has been made for the workers, when there is a change in the social structure to the benefit of the workers; but no government can tell the workers to make sacrifices for the benefit of the bourgeoisie, for the benefit of the rich. No government can tell the workers not to demand salary increases in order to develop an industry as the private property of the capitalists. . . ."[17]

The Allende government has chosen not to follow this admonition. By the end of February 1971, Allende was already making speeches against absenteeism and "exorbitant" wage demands. In the March 16, 1971, issue of the magazine *Punto Final,* Allende criticized the present wages of copper workers as being too high and he proudly referred to a speech he made to coal workers in which he told them, "You have to work more, produce more, sacrifice more."[18]

By early April, Allende was even calling on workers to work without pay. "Dr. Allende asked for harder work and even called for several hours of voluntary labor each week by the copper workers," reports Juan de Onis in the April 12, 1971, *New York Times*.

The attitude of the Chilean ruling class is to bide its time, looking forward to better days, when it will be in a position to launch an offensive against the working class. The result is that the bourgeoisie is disrupting the economic situation in the country.

Businesses are firing workers or refusing to hire new ones. Unemployment is estimated at around 9 percent of the total work force.[19] (In Santiago alone, 21 percent are unemployed.)[20] Many landowners are refusing to make the necessary expenditures for the next crop, fearing an extension of the land reform. Others are selling even their pregnant cows for slaughter in order to get quick cash. Corporations are slowing production and allowing their stocks to be depleted.

"There are economic problems," Juan de Onis reported in the February 7, 1971, *New York Times*. "Unemployment has risen since October, private investment is at a standstill and the government's public works program has bogged down. Some manufacturing concerns are near bankruptcy because of little business. . . ." In March he reported that Chile was falling behind by about 20 percent in meeting its contracts for copper — a difficulty that was at least partially due to the removal of technical personnel by the imperialist corporations.

With its endless financial obligations to imperialism and the local rich, and in the face of the anarchy of capitalist production and the resistance of the bourgeoisie, the popular front in Chile will find itself compelled to call upon the masses to make further sacrifices to keep the economy above water. The continued hardship on the masses can only lead to disillusionment and demoralization once it becomes clear that their situation remains the same or even becomes more difficult while the millionaires continue to drive luxury cars and find their wealth and privilege untouched.

The capitalist ruling class can, of course, be expected to take advantage of the failures of its own system to campaign against the alleged failures of socialism. This will intertwine with the demagogy of the government and the reformist parties as they call upon the masses to make even greater sacrifices for "socialist" Chile.

The Popular Unity program also provides for a structural change in the parliamentary system. This proposal boils down to replacing the present bicameral system with a unicameral system. Whatever the value of such a reform, Allende has made it clear that this provision does not intend the elimination of the bourgeois parliament. "We shall never make parliament disappear," he said in the April 11, 1970, *New York Times.* "About this there should not be the slightest doubt. It is the essential form of Chilean democracy."

Rather than contenting itself with reform of the bourgeois parliamentary system, the Allende government should have initiated popular forms of dual power in opposition to the bourgeois structure. It could have begun this process with the Popular Unity committees that were organized among the workers, the peasants, and the poor in general during the election campaign last fall. These committees functioned in neighborhoods, factories, and on the land throughout the entire country. Unfortunately, however, following the ratification of the electoral victory on October 24, 1970, the Communist and Socialist parties allowed the Popular Unity committees to be demobilized.

Since Allende took office, the government, as we have already seen, has not had a policy of support to the militant struggles of the peasants and the homeless. Things have not gone well for the revolutionary left either, as one incident last December illustrates particularly well. This was the killing of a revolutionary student and the wounding of another in Concepción by a Communist Party commando. The incident occurred when a group of students belonging to the MIR (Movimiento de Izquierda Revolucionaria — Movement of the Revolutionary Left) attempted to prevent a CP commando group, the Ramona Parra Brigade, from tearing down its posters. It is a telling fact that the CP, which urges the workers not to arm themselves, nevertheless sent an armed commando to tear down revolutionary posters.

Allende immediately intervened to get both the MIR and the CP to put out a joint statement declaring it all a misunderstanding. The CP, in its paper *El Siglo* (which finances itself by publishing "girlie" magazines), condoned the action of the commando.

While the peasants, the homeless, and the MIR were running into difficulties with the government, bourgeois forces were becoming increasingly cooperative. Senator Victor García of the right-wing National Party, for instance, who is a "public-finance expert," has been pitching in to help out the Communist minister of finance, America Zorrilla Rojas.[21] Even the executive director of the right-wing Santiago daily *El Mercurio* declared in January 1971, "the newspaper is willing to support change in Chile's property structure and social relations such Dr. Allende proposes."[22]

But Allende's sources of help are not only in Chile. In October 1970, the *Washington Post* reported that Sir Maurice Parson, chairman of the Bank of London, noted "new signs of hopefulness for private investment, particularly international banking, in Chile."[23]

More significant, however, is the sympathy that has been expressed in Washington, D.C., itself — despite tenseness over the terms of nationalization of U.S. mining interests. As far back as January 29, 1971, the *Washington Post* reported that the United States would give Chile new loans and that the tone of the Nixon administration was changing. "Allende's own political history of playing the game within the system," the *Post* reported, "appears to have convinced the doubters that the Chilean brand of Marxism may not be the menace it was first believed to be. . . . Chile may just find its own road to political and economic development that presents no threat to the hemisphere."[24]

Allende's minister of economy, Pedro Vuskovic Bravo, traveled to Washington, D.C., in February to work things out. Reporting on his discussions in Washington, Vuskovic indicated that the U.S. government, having reviewed the plans of the government of Chile, had received them "with respect, comprehension and promises of help."

Some of that help came June 29 in the form of an announcement by the Nixon administration that it would grant Chile $5 million in credits for purchases of military equipment. Administration officials said that this first such gesture by the Nixon administration was a reflection of Washington's "pragmatic policy" towards the Allende regime.

On July 2, C.L. Sulzberger of the *New York Times* expressed in that paper his admiration for Allende's "virtuoso performance"   and called the Allende regime "a model of the new kind of ballot-box revolution to which Washington cannot object and which rapidly maturing Moscow seems to recognize as helpful in the long run, if only patience is applied."

The popular front represented by the Allende government and the Popular Unity coalition is nothing new. It has been tried before — and with disastrous results.

The concept of a popular front (or people's front) was developed to its current polished form by the Communist Parties during the 1930s. Their claim at that time was that the popular front was a continuation under new conditions of

the original policy of the *united* front advocated by Lenin
and the Communist International in the early 1920s. In reality,
however, it was the exact opposite.

The purpose of a united front is to bring together working-class organizations and other organizations representing
oppressed social layers on the basis of common agreement
on specific issues and above all to engage in united actions
against the ruling class. The united front tactic is an effective
tool for bringing to bear the maximum strength of the oppressed against the ruling class. It is founded on uncompromising independence from and opposition to the ruling class.
Its main purpose is to prevent sectarianism or isolation of
the politically advanced workers from the more conservative
workers who could be won over in struggle.

The popular front is the exact opposite. It seeks to contain
whatever actions the working class undertakes in order to
assure coalition with a section of the ruling class. The most
famous popular fronts were built in France and Spain in the
1930s. Both were miserable and costly failures in terms of
defending the interests of the working class and preventing
the rise of fascism.

In Chile, such a government was formed in 1938, with
Allende as minister of health. That popular front, known as
the Antifascist Popular Front, was so broad its presidential
candidate was endorsed by the Chilean Nazi Party! Popular
front governments continued on and off in Chile until the
1950s.

Others developed in other countries in Latin America, including Cuba, where former dictator Fulgencio Batista came to
power with the support of the Communist Party and even
included some Communists in his government.

Today, similar popular fronts are taking shape in Latin
America. The most important so far is in Uruguay, and is
called the Broad Front (Frente Amplio).

Popular fronts are by their very nature incapable of respond-
ing to the needs of the masses. The solution to the pressing
problems of poverty lies in the abolition of capitalism.

A socialist revolution in Chile would begin, like the Cuban
Revolution, by disarming the army and police and creating
armed units of the working class and peasantry to defend
their interests. Foreign as well as national corporations would
be nationalized without compensation. Democratic control over
Chilean political, economic, and social life would develop
through worker and peasant committees.

A popular front government will be unable to insure that

such anticapitalist transformations take place. The reason is that the essential limitation of a popular front government is that it cannot exceed the bounds of bourgeois legality and respect for private property.

A popular front is characterized by the fact that it *prevents* the working class from struggling for a government of workers and peasants that could abolish capitalism and carry through a socialist transformation of society by going beyond bourgeois property relations. The essence of a popular front is determined not by the relative weight of the various parties involved or the size of the bourgeois component of the coalition, but by the fact that its program insures that the working class is kept corralled *within limits acceptable* to the bourgeoisie, or a section of the bourgeoisie.

In this way, it is possible for a popular front to exist even without any bourgeois parties within it.

In Chile, although the most important bourgeois party, the Christian Democratic Party, does not belong to the Popular Unity coalition, it is in fact functioning as a silent partner. It is the Popular Unity and the Christian Democrats who together constitute the necessary working majority in Congress.

If the Christian Democrats are not a part of the Popular Unity, it is not because the Communist Party has tried to keep them out. CP leader Orlando Millas, referring to these favorites of American imperialism in Latin America in his report to the Central Committee of the Chilean Communist Party, said on September 14, 1970: "The enemy would like to isolate the forces of the left, create splits between the working class, the farmers, the students and the general public and place us in opposition to the Christian Democrats. But they will not succeed. . . ." 25

"Unity at any price" could well sum up the attitude of the Communist Parties to popular fronts. For the price has often been great — even for the Communists themselves. Still, in Chile as elsewhere, they continue to advocate them.

Ceylon is a current example of a popular front government — and one, moreover, in which the Communist Party is participating. Its success at the polls was hailed by the Communist Parties throughout the world as a victory for the masses. Yet, in 1971, the Ceylonese "people's" government is receiving U. S. helicopters and military aid from other imperialist powers in its ferocious campaign to suppress its own people.

Perhaps the best-known "people's" government in recent history was the Sukarno regime in Indonesia. There, as in Chile today, the Communist Party called for a worker-peasant-national bourgeois alliance. The Indonesian CP even went along with the concept that the Sukarno regime represented a peculiar but necessary blend of nationalism, Islam, and socialism. (This has a familiar ring today in the Chilean CP's assertion that "the three great ideological currents will work together: the Marxists, the Christians and the Masonic laity.") 26

Even Communist Parties no longer speak about the "peaceful" road to socialism that was followed by the "people's" government in Indonesia. When the bourgeoisie turned on its working-class and peasant "allies," the massacre that ensued left up to a million worker and peasant militants dead and the third-largest Communist Party in the world (with 3 million members and 20 million in CP-led mass organizations) decimated. None of this would have happened had it not been for the fact that the Communist Party assured the masses that they could trust the armed forces and that to arm themselves would be a provocation.

Similarly, the Guatemalan CP assured the people in 1954 that the army could be trusted and that the masses should not arm themselves. Then, when the CIA-led invasion occurred, the army switched sides, the CP-supported reformist regime fell, and a military dictatorship took over.

Today something very similar is happening in Chile, where the CP campaigns against arming the peasants and workers. Neither its policy nor the arguments used to justify it have changed. Some people never learn.

No ruling class in history has ever relinquished its rule without putting up a fight. The revolutionary forces have had to physically disarm the state apparatus and repressive forces of the ruling class they intended to replace. In light of the lessons of history, to advocate a "peaceful" road to socialism is the same as *not* advocating revolution.

Nevertheless, the Chilean Communist Party (not to mention the American and Soviet parties) deliberately promotes the illusion that a peaceful road to revolution is possible and that one is now being traveled in Chile.

Yet the Chilean capitalist state (its army, its police, its courts, and its governmental bureaucracies) remains intact. To spread illusions that the ruling class can be removed without its resorting to force to prevent such a removal is not only absurd but dangerous. The Chilean bourgeoisie did not create its army and its police in order to allow pieces of paper in a ballot box to abolish its wealth, privilege, and power.

That, however, does not prevent Chile from being held up by the Communist Parties in other countries as a shining example. On April 28, 1971, the *New York Times* reported that the Soviet Communist Party's specialist on developing countries, Rostislav A. Ulyanovsky, called on colonial and semicolonial countries to follow Chile's example.

This has been the approach of the American Communist Party, too. In November 1970, CPUSA General Secretary Gus Hall called the Allende victory "a new revolutionary experience."

An editorial in the December 1970 issue of the CP's theoretical journal *Political Affairs* terms the election of Allende a "transfer of power from the old ruling-class groups to the workers, to the peasantry and to the progressive sections of the middle class of the city and country." It concludes that we should look forward to similar coalitions in the United States as well.

The notion that a ruling class can be defeated by placing enough pieces of paper into a ballot box is a rejection of the Marxist view of the state and bourgeois society. Marxism holds that every state apparatus reflects the interests of the ruling class and that the state apparatus of the ruling class cannot be used to serve the needs of an oppressed class. In Chile and other capitalist societies, this means that the working class must replace that apparatus with one of its own.

Although it is likely, it is not certain that with Allende the Chilean masses will once again be disoriented, demoralized, and demobilized by a popular front government. The objective conditions in Latin America today are very different from what they were during previous popular front governments during the thirties and forties. The "leftism" of the Allende popular front is itself a by-product of the new conditions.

Once again, a left wing is developing within the Socialist Party. This time it is developing under the impact of the Cuban Revolution, which has convinced many young people that a socialist revolution is possible and that armed struggle is necessary to achieve it. In such a context, it cannot be ruled out that a revolutionary alternative could develop from an intensification of the contradictions within the Popular Unity coalition.

Unfortunately, the revolutionary left, particularly the *Fidelista* MIR, is largely confused. The victory of Allende left the MIR and other ultraleft groups disoriented. Since the election, the MIR has tended to give Allende critical support, while at the same time it has found itself forced to reassess some of its positions, especially its lack of work in the mass movement.

The revolutionary left's lack of a political analysis of popular frontism and its critical support of Allende's candidacy in both 1964 and 1970 have tended to diminish the possibility of a revolutionary party developing out of the sharpening class struggle in Chile.

Fidel Castro's support to Allende has only added to the disorientation of the revolutionary left, as have the illusions he has at various times expressed about other bourgeois regimes such as the present military dictatorship in Peru. In a speech last April, Castro expressed "our confidence in the Chilean revolutionary process, in the Popular Unity movement, in the Chilean people and government. . . ."27

In Chile it is only the Trotskyists, both as an independent current and within the ranks of the Socialist Party, who are helping to bring clarity into this confusion. On the eve of the September 1970 election, the Chilean Trotskyists wrote: "If Salvador Allende wins, we will see the formation of a worker-bourgeois coalition government which, under cover of party politics, will block authentic mass participation in the administration of the country and will defend the capitalist structure. . . .

"The arming of the proletariat is the essential condition for further advance of the struggle and for the victory of the revolution. . . .

"The reformist parties refuse to accept the task of arming the people and put all their energy into preventing them from taking up arms. Their refusal to carry out such an urgent task vividly reveals their rejection of revolution.

"The revolutionary vanguard, which has already taken the initiative in this work, will have to raise the level of its activity and extend it, offering the mass movement all its experience and knowledge. By its determination, it will have to carry this process through to its conclusion."28

This, not the popular frontism of the Allende government, points the way for the Chilean masses.

The History of Popular Frontism in Chile

The history of popular frontism in Chile dates back to 1938, with the triumph of a government called the Popular Front. Allende, who became minister of health in 1938, has referred to that government as "unquestionably a great advance." [29] "Chile," he has maintained, "is a country in which Marxists have been in the government. We were in the government in 1938, under Pedro Aguirre Cerda. . . . It was the most progressive government yet . . . [it] took decisive steps towards the economic and social development of the country." [30]

The experience of 1938 was similar to that of today. The Communist Party and the Socialist Party, which were based on the working-class movement, joined with procapitalist parties, the largest of which was the Radical Party, based on the middle class.

The Communist and Socialist parties had grown rapidly in the mid-thirties due to the radicalization of the workers brought on by the world depression. The Radical Party, which until 1937 had been blocking with the two reactionary parties of Chile, the Conservative and Liberal parties, now saw the possibility of winning elections by switching over to a left-center coalition.

The working-class struggles had reached mammoth proportions in 1936 in response to the government's attempt to crush a railroad workers' strike. Each off-year election revealed the workers' radicalization bringing about a shift in the electoral arena.

This set the stage for the formation of a coalition of the Communist Party, the Socialist Party, and the Radical Party. The coalition was formed in spite of the resistance of a few conservative leaders of the Radical Party, including Pedro Aguirre Cerda.

The coalition was known as the Popular Front, a name borrowed from similar formations in Europe at the time. The Popular Front adopted a program upon which all the participants could agree.

To win the support of the masses, the Popular Front labeled its program anti-imperialist, antioligarchic, and antifascist. But it never spelled out what this meant. In reality, the program could not be anticapitalist — otherwise the openly procapitalist parties such as the Radical Party would have withdrawn.

The program was really made up of a list of reforms to be achieved under capitalism. It called for improvement of Chile's economic infrastructure (power supply, transportation facilities, etc.) in order to modernize the economy. It included promises of liberal reforms along the lines of Roosevelt's New Deal legislation in the United States. In general terms it called for an agrarian reform, more planning in the economy, and peace among nations.

A significant section of the Popular Front's program called for "careful maintenance of national defense, granting to the armed forces instruction, equipment, and proper means for their efficient development for the purpose of safeguarding our sovereignty."[31]

Its demagogic cover for an essentially reformist program put the Popular Front in a good position to unite its bourgeois constituency with the peasantry and working class, and to win the elections. However, as the 1938 elections approached, the Popular Front was confronted with a serious problem: a second popular-front-like coalition appeared. This formation, called the Popular Liberation Alliance, was a coalition of individuals and groups including a split-off from the Socialist Party (the Union Socialist Party) and the Chilean Nazi Party. The Popular Liberation Alliance also described its program as anti-imperialist, antioligarchic, and antifascist. Its candidate for the presidency was ex-dictator of Chile Carlos Ibáñez del Campo.

Ibáñez had personally led an artillery massacre of more than 2,000 workers at Iquique in the mid-twenties when he was minister of war.[32] He founded the infamous Carabineros, a special force used against peasants, workers, and radicals. But Ibáñez was also a clever demagogue who favored the modernization of Chilean capitalism. In the mid-twenties he had joined with Arturo Alessandri (president of Chile during the twenties and again from 1932 to 1938) in guiding the drafting of the present-day constitution of Chile.

The presidential candidate of the Conservative and Liberal parties in 1938 was Alessandri's outgoing minister of finance, Gustavo Ross. The Popular Front nominated Pedro Aguirre Cerda, formerly opposed to the coalition, in order to maximize its appeal to the right.

The Communist Party leaders appealed to Ibáñez, urging him to withdraw from the race and join the Popular Front. But he refused. Because Aguirre and Ibáñez were expected to split the left vote, Ross was the expected winner. As it turned out, Ross would have won except for an unexpected incident.

The Nazi Party, knowing that its candidate, Ibáñez, would come in a poor third, attempted a coup. It failed, and Ibáñez was imprisoned along with the Nazi leader, Gonzales von Marées.

Aguirre visited Ibáñez in prison. Soon after, Ibáñez declared for Aguirre, as did Gonzales von Marées. The Popular Front, hailing its new supporters, published pictures of Aguirre and Ibáñez appearing together, and distributed them throughout Chile.

Aguirre received 222,700 votes, and Ross 218,609. Because it had been estimated that Ibáñez would get 20,000 votes, it was clearly his support and the support of the Nazi Party which delivered the winning votes. Aguirre expressed his appreciation by freeing von Marées and offering the Popular Liberation Alliance seats in his cabinet. They refused.

After this down-to-earth election campaign, Aguirre established his government with Allende and other Socialist Party leaders in his cabinet.

The 1938 government was only the first in a series of popular front governments which were to appear in Chile from that time to the 1950s. Because these popular front governments were bourgeois governments, it was a foregone conclusion that they would be exposed sooner or later by their own actions in opposition to the interests of the working class and peasantry.

On various occasions the Communist Party or the Socialist Party would withdraw in protest from the popular front in order to preserve the party's mass base. Nevertheless, throughout this period, both of these parties completely endorsed the strategy of the popular front.

This period was further characterized by continual factional warfare on the left. In 1940, when the Socialist Party of Workers (a split-off from the Socialist Party) quit the popular front, the Communist and Socialist parties joined hands in throwing this group out of the trade unions.

However, most of the factional fighting took place between the two largest parties. The Socialist Party and the Communist Party fought for control of the trade unions and vied with each other for posts in the popular front governments.

With the signing of the Stalin-Hitler pact in 1939, the Chilean Communist Party switched its line, and began to call the United States an imperialist, prowar power. Allende's Socialist Party thereupon tried to throw the Communist Party out of the Popular Front. However, the effort failed because the Radical Party chose to stick it out with the Communist Party. This led to the Socialist Party's withdrawal from the Popular Front in early 1941. Soon after, the Popular Front was formally dissolved. In spite of the Socialist Party's "withdrawal" from the coalition, its ministers remained in the government until the unexpected death of Aguirre in November 1941, which resulted in a call for new elections in 1942.

With the invasion of the Soviet Union by Germany (and consequently the Communist Party's new pro-U. S. line), and the opening of new electoral opportunities, the old popular front groups joined hands behind Juan Antonio Rios, a well-known anticommunist leader in the Radical Party. Both the Communist Party and the Socialist Party supported the government of Rios.

During the war the popular front government kept the masses in check. The Communist Party especially exerted itself to break strikes, in accord with Stalin's international policy of keeping workers under control in the countries allied with the Soviet Union.

But the most destructive period for the unions began after the war. The ruling class maneuvered in the crudest manner between the Communist Party and the Socialist Party, playing upon the divisions in the working class. The end of the war brought a mass wave of independent struggles, reaching a crisis with the killing of six workers during a demonstration in support of a nitrate workers' strike. A general strike was called. The bourgeois government offered the Socialist Party posts in the government if it would call off the general strike. After some negotiating, this same Socialist Party which brought Allende into the government in 1938 and made him general secretary in 1943, accepted and tried to call off the strike.

In consequence, the Socialist Party's trade-union support switched its allegiance to the Communist Party, which in turn accused the Socialist Party of selling out.

The advent of the new elections found the Communist Party on the winning ticket supporting Gabriel González Videla of the Radical Party in September 1946. González Videla did not receive enough votes to win outright, and the decision had to be made by a session of Congress. There the matter was resolved after some back-room deals among the Communist Party, the Radical Party, and the traditional extreme right-wing Liberal Party. The new government was set up with the nine cabinet seats divided equally among them.

With the Socialist Party now out of the government, and the Communist Party in, their roles were reversed. The government backed and helped finance a huge Communist Party-run trade-union conference, even paying the train fares of the delegates. President González Videla spoke to the conference of 15,000, which was deliberately aimed at weakening the Socialist Party unions, whose own trade-union conference drew only a few thousand. Not only was the trade-union movement split, but the Communist Party provoked violence with physical attacks on Socialist Party members.

Usually the bourgeois governments preferred Communist Party-run unions to those run by the Socialist Party. However, once González Videla had gotten what he wanted from the Communist Party, he turned on it and threw it out of the government. This coincided with the cold war and the general anti-communist hysteria in the U. S., which the Chilean bourgeoisie had to imitate if it wished to receive kind treatment in Washington.

In October 1947, a strike of miners took place near Concepción, led by a CP-controlled union. González Videla utilized this as a pretext to outlaw the Communist Party and imprison hundreds of its leaders. (Later, González Videla set up a concentration camp for labor leaders in Pisaqua.)[33] The Socialist Party helped González Videla break the strike; in return, he allowed them back into the bourgeois government.

By 1952, after years of being manipulated, maneuvered, and betrayed by the reformism of the Communist Party and the Socialist Party, the working-class movement was disorganized and demoralized. Let us look at the concrete results of Allende's "great advance" and of the other similar coalition governments.

During the entire period from 1938 to 1952 nothing was done towards land reform. Even large landed estates went untaxed. During the period 1946-1947, the Communist Party had control of both the Ministry of Agriculture and the Ministry of Lands and Colonization under Victor Contreras. But they did nothing to undermine the power of the rich landowners. In 1955, an agricultural census indicated that the old property relations had remained basically unchanged. Fewer than 10 percent of the landowners owned 86 percent of the arable land, while 74.6 percent of the poor peasants owned only 5.3 percent of the land.[34]

Agricultural production rose only 1.6 percent per year, less than the growth rate of the population, thus forcing Chile, with its great agricultural potential, to increase its imports of food. One-sixth of Chile's limited foreign exchange had to be utilized to purchase food.[35] Today this figure is closer to one-fourth.

Illiteracy was 25 percent and hundreds of thousands of children still had no schools.

Eighty-six percent of the people lived in one-room dwellings. So little housing had been built since 1938 (6,000 units from 1939 to 1946) that after all these coalition governments, the situation was worse than before. [36]

Wages fell from 27 percent to 21 percent of the national income during the years 1940-53. [37] This indicates that the Popular Front's call for a "more equitable and just distribution of income" resulted in just the opposite: a less equitable and more unjust income distribution. While the working class gained only a 7 percent wage increase during fourteen years, the middle class gained 46 percent. [38]

Allende himself, according to Stevenson, "conducted extensive investigations of Chile's socio-medical problems and drew up several far reaching public health projects. But none of these ambitious programs ever got far beyond the planning stage. . . ." [39]

The trade-union movement suffered a general disorganization. The dues paid by union membership had declined from a high of 854,000 escudos in the early 1940s to 444,000 by 1954. [40] And these figures alone do not give the complete picture of the confusion, disorganization, and demoralization which plagued the workers' movement.

The only major "victory" of the popular front governments was a rise in corporate profits. During the Aguirre popular front, for instance, profits ran at 14.8 percent as compared to the previous ten years' average of 8.8 percent. [41]

The popular fronts were also a means for individual socialists to make it within capitalist society. During the period between 1933 and 1953, a study showed that 79 percent of elected socialist congressmen used their posts to make their fortunes in the bourgeois world, and had quit the socialist movement by the time they left office. Another study with a larger sample, covering the period up to 1965, revealed approximately the same number of elected socialist officials using their posts to improve their personal living standards. [42]

The Popular Front deflected the 1930s' mass mobilization of workers into the electoral arena, then dissipated its energy under the "people's government" of Aguirre. Instead of reforms, they got a request from Aguirre for a "temporary nation-wide suspension of strikes." [43] Similar electoral illusions and hopes for reforms from above were used throughout this period to paralyze the workers' movement.

John Reese Stevenson, author of *The Chilean Popular Front,* summarized it in this way: "Taking as our standard of judgement its pre-election campaign promises, the Popular Front [of 1938-41] was a failure. . . ." However, Stevenson explains, "the victory of the Popular Front prevented a revolution and taught the masses to resort to the ballot instead of the sword."[44]

James Petras, in his excellent study of Chile, *Politics and Social Forces in Chilean Development,* describes the overall consequences of the popular fronts. "On the one hand the Popular Front made considerable progress in creating an industrial infrastructure, broadening the base of social participation beyond a small elite, and increasing the conscious government involvement in the developmental process.

"On the other hand, these changes tended to enrich the upper and middle class in status, wealth, and power, at the expense of the workers and peasants. Popular Front politics weakened the Left, strengthened the Right, and increased the people's distrust of parliamentary politics. At the end of a decade of working class-middle class coalitions, the Rightist parties were politically, socially, and economically stronger than ever."[45]

The demoralization of the masses, their frustration with parliamentary manipulations, left them susceptible to a demagogue from the right who would promise to clean up the mess with a strong government. Into this situation stepped none other than Ibáñez, the Nazi-backed candidate of 1938. Running as an "antipolitician," and backed by the majority of the Socialist Party, Ibáñez swept the 1952 elections.

It was in the elections of 1952 that Allende began his climb to the presidency. In all the maneuverings of the period 1938-52, the Socialist Party had split at various times. Each time the Socialist Party supported a bourgeois government, a "leftwing" faction would appear, refusing support for the government (usually because the SP was losing its mass support and positions in the unions). The left wing would inevitably split from the SP to solidify its base, only to join another bourgeois government later. Allende's faction, calling itself the Popular Socialist Party, split from the González Videla government in the late 1940s, only to endorse Ibáñez in 1952 and join his cabinet. But Allende bolted from his own organization, joined the SP faction which had supported González Videla, and declared himself a presidential candidate. His goal was to rebuild a "left" popular front in opposition to the rightward drift which had resulted in the González Videla and then the Ibáñez governments.

With the Socialist Party split, its strength depleted, the Communist Party outlawed, and the trade-union movement weakened, an attempt to re-create the old popular front in 1952 did not get very far. Only a few bourgeois groups, mainly the National Democratic Party, agreed to join. The largest socialist group was in the Ibáñez camp, another faction supported the Radical Party candidate, and the Communist Party was suspected of flirting with Ibáñez. The result was that although Allende had the endorsement of the Communist Party, the Socialist Party, and others, his vote totaled less than 6 percent.

After the elections, events began to strengthen the new popular front effort led by Allende. Ibáñez had run a very demagogic campaign, but once in office, his completely reactionary, anti-working-class politics became obvious. Risking the loss of their popular base, the socialists in his government were forced to quit. Eventually they reunited with the Allende-led Socialist Party.

The rate of inflation began climbing incredibly. The cost of living rose 56 percent, 70 percent, 80 percent, 40 percent, and 20 percent, respectively, in the years 1953-57. The working class, faced with a deteriorating economic situation, began to struggle anew, independently of the ruling class.

In 1953, the labor movement underwent a period of reorganization, and the CUT (United Federation of Workers) was formed. Under the leadership of Clotario Blest, the CUT carried out many militant independent struggles. Later, in the early 1960s, the Communist Party and the Socialist Party expelled Clotario Blest from the presidency of the CUT because he was too radical for them.

In 1957, the raising of bus fares touched off mass demonstrations. The Carabineros killed two students. The army was called out when workers began to join the students in protests. The army killed forty to sixty workers, leaving hundreds of others wounded.

Allende's popular front forces, now bearing the name FRAP (Popular Action Front), criticized the government for allowing such a situation to develop, but refrained from the struggle. From the safety of parliament, FRAP quietly dissociated itself from the "violence" of the demonstrators.

In 1958, Allende ran for president again. He was backed

by the growing working-class movement, the now legal Communist Party, the Socialist Party, and some bourgeois parties including some of Ibáñez's former supporters. But the election was won by Jorge Alessandri, the son of Arturo Alessandri who was president in the 1930s. Allende later defeated Alessandri in 1970.

The Radical Party, which in 1938 had blocked with the Communist Party and the Socialist Party in order to get into office, had by now totally reversed itself and was blocking once again with the right. The Radical Party joined with the Conservative and Liberal parties in what was called a "Democratic Front."

The working-class movement continued to grow and struggle. Slowly the peasantry began to move as well. The Communist Party and the Socialist Party, both outside the government, attempted to build a base among the working class and peasantry.

The general radicalization deepened under the impact of the Cuban Revolution in the early sixties.

As the 1964 elections approached, it became clear that the Democratic Front could not win, and it fell apart. The Conservative and Liberal parties threw their support behind the fast-growing Christian Democrats. Their candidate, Eduardo Frei, beat Allende in the 1964 elections because he was able to unite almost all the bourgeois electoral formations behind him.

The Christian Democratic Party offered the Chilean ruling class an exceptional opportunity. Since it had not been discredited by participation in previous governments, its left-demagogic calls for radical reforms appeared credible. Furthermore, its apparatus was not subject to the kind of rank-and-file working-class pressure affecting the Socialist Party and the Communist Party. Thus, the ruling class hoped the Christian Democrats could contain the radicalization of the masses, offering minimal reforms to prevent a social revolution.

The Christian Democrats were also backed financially and politically by Washington. Frei's Chile became the U.S. showcase, its alternative for Latin America.

As could be predicted, the Christian Democratic Party's popularity grew with the expectations created by its promises, and declined with the realization that it would not deliver. As the Christian Democratic Party declined from 1964 to 1970, the workers' and peasants' movements grew in both size and militancy. Instead of placating the masses, the limited Christian Democratic Party reforms only convinced them of the justness of their struggle and of the vulnerability of the ruling class.

The radicalization was especially marked among the peasantry. There were increasing numbers of land occupations by the peasants. Peasant unions grew from a few thousand members in 1964 to over 100,000 by 1969. A strike wave swept Chile after 1967, when the economy took a sharp turn downward. The number of illegal strikes grew rapidly.

The student movement, which had been dominated by the Christian Democratic Party in the mid-sixties, also began swinging to the left. Homeless urban poor began to take over land sites to build homes. The militancy of government and other white-collar workers also grew.

In March 1966, police killed seven miners and injured twenty-five at the well-known El Teniente mine. Carabineros occupied Anaconda's El Salvador and Potrilla mines when the miners came out in support of the El Teniente workers.

The struggles continuing throughout this period reached violent confrontations in which the police or Carabineros murdered workers and students. In 1967, two student members of the MIR were murdered by Carabineros who caught them writing "Che did not die" on a wall.

In November 1967, a twenty-four-hour general strike resulted in the mobilization of all Chile's troops, including the navy and air force. Twenty-two workers were killed and sixty-six injured in the resulting confrontations.

On March 10, 1969, in Puerto Montt, an infamous massacre took place. A thousand homeless poor attempted to use the public land in order to build shacks to live in. The repressive forces were sent in, killing five and wounding thirty-seven. By May and June 1969, the army was running the trains in an attempt to break a railroad workers' strike.

In 1970, students joined clerical workers striking for higher wages to meet the runaway inflation plaguing Chile's economy. Following weeks of confrontations, two students were killed and a state of emergency was declared. The *New York Times* reported June 28, 1970, that "nearly all the leaders of the Chilean Socialist Party have quietly disassociated themselves" from the demonstrations.

Today Allende claims that the Chilean army and the Carabineros can be trusted to defend the interests of the working people. But it is a serious mistake for Allende and the Popular Unity coalition to entrust to the army the defense of the popular front government.

This "mistaken" faith in the army proved disastrous for neighboring Bolivia where, as in Chile, a "progressive" supposedly proworker but in reality procapitalist government assured the masses that they could trust the army. In fact, they had a better argument than Allende, for it was the Bolivian army itself that had placed Torres, leader of the "progressive" government, in power. The "trusted" army turned on the Bolivian workers in August 1971, murdering hundreds and imprisoning untold numbers.

It was under conditions of violent class struggle that the 1970 elections which brought Allende to power took place. His victory was a by-product of popular frontism in Chile and of the new radicalization sweeping the Chilean masses.

And this brief historical background to the development of popular fronts indicates the likely variants for the coming period in Chile: undoubtedly the masses will press for more meaningful social reforms; the bourgeoisie will await the moment to stifle and then, literally through murders and imprisonment, behead the workers' movement.

While the bourgeois armed forces remain intact, organized, disciplined, and centralized, the workers and peasants have no organization, no arms, and no leadership. They have only numbers and a willingness to sacrifice.

For the present experience to end in a better way than the previous one, a leadership willing to struggle against the opportunistic and corrupt Communist and Socialist parties is necessary. If such a leadership does not develop, the results might be even worse than in the 1940s. But precisely because of the depth of the current mass radicalization, a revolutionary vanguard prepared to fight against capitalism could emerge very rapidly. However, such a vanguard cannot develop so long as the working class remains unclear as to the real nature of Allende and popular frontism. Only a leadership pitted against those betrayers of the Chilean people — Allende and the Socialist and Communist parties — can organize the masses to defend their gains and prevent a counterrevolutionary move by the bourgeoisie.

In this sense, because of their misleadership of the mass movement, the present SP- and CP-led government is a major obstacle to the victory of the workers and peasants seeking a social transformation to end capitalism and begin the construction of a socialist society.

In the broader, objective sense, it is the policies of North American imperialism that prevent a solution to Chilean poverty. The capital necessary to industrialize Chile exists in the

United States. But these funds are diverted by the imperialists to the prosecution of the criminal war against the Vietnamese. The U.S. economic system, based on profits for the rich, cannot now raise the standard of living even for the workers in the United States. For Nixon, Kennedy, Rockefeller, McGovern — for the ruling class — the misery of the Chilean people is irrelevant, except insofar as the consequent unrest makes them more difficult to control and exploit. In the last analysis, those responsible for the continued poverty in Chile are the millionaires of the United States. Only their removal from power will ensure a solution to the problems of Chile and all the colonial peoples.

In the immediate future, it is the duty of the American left, regardless of the nature of the Chilean government, to mobilize the American people against any steps taken by the United States against the people of Chile. It is our duty to defend the Chilean people's right to self-determination.

Notes

1. *Le Monde,* October 23, 1970.
2. *Political Affairs,* December 1970, p. 30.
3. *New York Times,* October 20, 1970.
4. Ibid., November 4, 1970.
5. Ibid.
6. *New World Review,* vol. 39, no. 1, p. 31.
7. Ibid., p. 33.
8. *New York Times,* October 4, 1970.
9. *The Militant,* May 2, 1966.
10. Luis Vitale, "Which Road for Chile?" *International Socialist Review,* Summer 1964, p. 67.
11. *New York Times,* January 25, 1971.
12. *La Nacion* (Buenos Aires), March 7, 1971.
13. *Programa de la Unidad Popular* (Santiago: Libreria PLA, 1970), p. 22.
14. Ibid., p. 23.
15. *Monthly Review,* January 1971, pp. 10-11.
16. *Drapeau Rouge* (organ of the Belgian Communist Party), January 1, 1970.
17. *The Militant,* May 2, 1966.
18. *Punto Final,* March 16, 1971, p. 54.
19. *New York Times,* March 12, 1971.
20. Ibid., January 25, 1971.

21. Ibid., February 7, 1971.
22. Ibid., January 31, 1970.
23. Ibid., October 28, 1970.
24. *Clarin* (Buenos Aires), February 25, 1971.
25. *Political Affairs,* December 1970, p. 23.
26. Ibid., p. 30.
27. Speech by Fidel Castro, press release of the Cuban Mission to the United Nations, p. 7.
28. *Intercontinental Press,* October 5, 1970, p. 827.
29. *Punto Final,* March 16, 1971, p. 31.
30. *New York Times,* October 4, 1970.
31. John Reese Stevenson, *The Chilean Popular Front* (Greenwood, 1942), pp. 83-84.
32. James Petras, *The Emergence of Working-Class Politics,* unpublished master's thesis, University of California, 1963, p. 77.
33. Ibid., p. 102.
34. James Petras, *Politics and Social Forces in Chilean Development* (University of California Press, 1970), p. 133.
35. Paul Johnson, "The Plundered Continent," *New Statesman,* September 17, 1960, pp. 381-82.
36. Arturo Aldunate Phillips, *Un pueblo en busca de su destino* (Editorial Nascimento, 1947), p. 107.
37. Frederick B. Pike and Donald Bray, "A Vista of Catastrophe: The Future of U.S.-Chilean Relations," *Review of Politics,* vol. 22, July 1960, pp. 396-98.
38. Petras, *Politics and Social Forces,* p. 133.
39. Stevenson, op. cit., p. 127.
40. Petras, *Politics and Social Forces,* p. 170.
41. Paul Theodore Ellsworth, *Chile: An Economy in Transition* (Macmillan, 1945), p. 178.
42. Petras, *Politics and Social Forces,* p. 161.
43. Stevenson, op. cit., p. 102.
44. Ibid., p. 136.
45. Petras, *Politics and Social Forces,* p. 132.

After the April Municipal Elections

By Jean-Pierre Beauvais

The following article is translated from the April 19, 1971, *issue of* Rouge, *at that time the newspaper of the Ligue Communiste (Communist League), the French section of the Fourth International. (The Communist League has since been banned by the French government.) The footnotes and emphasis appear in the original.*

The recent Chilean municipal elections represented an unquestionable victory for the Unidad Popular government. Receiving 49.75 percent of the votes cast, the coalition headed by Salvador Allende won almost an absolute majority, while in the last presidential election it garnered no more than 36 percent of the vote.

Within the Unidad Popular, these elections marked an important gain in influence for the Socialist Party* and a small but real gain for the Communist Party, while the Radical Party, the third influential component of the coalition, representing the liberal sections of the small and middle bourgeoisie that support the Allende experiment, saw its vote cut in half.

The victory did not surprise anyone in Chile, least of all the Christian Democratic and Nationalist opposition. In the space of six months, the Nationalist Party has lost more than one-fourth of its vote to the Christian Democracy. The Christian Democrats have become the main opposition party and the principal political instrument of the Chilean bourgeoisie, although they in turn have lost a large part of their popular electoral base to the Unidad Popular.

The increased popularity of the Allende government is the direct result of a series of measures benefiting the most disadvantaged sectors of the petty bourgeoisie and the working

---

* The gains of the SP must be qualified, however, by the fact that small formations like MAPU, a grouping of dissident Christian Democrats led by J. Chonchol, the minister of agriculture, were unable to get on the ballot and that their supporters voted mainly for the SP.

class. In January, for example, while the prices of consumer goods were frozen, the lowest category of wages was raised by 50 percent, and the rest by 25 percent to 30 percent. At the same time, family allowances were increased 100 percent, while school supplies were provided free at the end of the vacation period.

These measures came at a time when alarmist rumors about plots and a military coup, circulating more or less everywhere in the country, impelled the broad layers of the population benefiting from the reforms to rally behind the government.

The fact remains, nevertheless, that this victory, however important, in no way changes the basic factors of the Chilean situation.

"Going beyond bourgeois reformism" is a phrase often encountered in the Chilean press and frequently uttered by the main protagonists of the Unidad Popular. It reveals a fact often forgotten, especially in Chile. The reformist measures approved by Allende were already included in the Christian Democratic program in the main, when Frei won the 1964 presidential elections. In this sense the Unidad Popular's slogan, "We Have Done in Four Months What the Christian Democrats Couldn't Do in Six Years," is literally true.

Thus, the agrarian reform projected by the Christian Democrats, which limits landholdings to eighty hectares [one hectare equals 2.47 acres], has begun to be applied "in reality." *
In the same way, the main copper mines are in process of being nationalized, and several banks have been nationalized, as well as a number of other enterprises serving the public.

However spectacular some of these measures may be, the fact remains that they were advocated long ago — if not put into practice — by a bourgeois party. In no case do they represent a change, not even an incipient one, in the class nature of the Chilean state. In no case do they strike at the essential economic base of the Chilean bourgeoisie. As for the imperialist interests in Chile, they have so far been affected only in a marginal way. While the nationalization of the copper mines has a

---

* While the landowners in the barren or uncultivated regions are giving up their land without any difficulty, in exchange for an attractive compensation, in the richer areas, where industrial crops are grown, this is not the case. Here, most often, "they carry out the agrarian reform themselves," dividing their land into eighty-hectare plots and distributing them among the members of their families. This permits them to keep their estates intact!

symbolic value in the eyes of the Chilean people, it must not give rise to any illusions. It has involved the payment of large compensation. Furthermore, *the mining sector accounts for only a small part of the imperialist investments in the Chilean economy.* The essential part of foreign capital is found in the light-industry sector and in the service sectors, which are relatively important in the economy of Chile in comparison with other Latin American countries. And in these sectors, for the moment at least, there is no question of nationalization.

In this framework, the current *wait-and-see attitude* of the Chilean bourgeoisie and the imperialists — after the initial panic over the outcome of the elections — can be easily understood.

As long as their fundamental interests, their economic base, and their main instruments of action — the Christian Democratic Party in the framework of formal bourgeois democracy, and large sections of the army and police — are not touched, why should they take the risk of a confrontation whose dynamic and consequences are unpredictable?

Several factors are important in this connection, above all the immense popular support enjoyed by the Allende government. So far, this support has been expressed in the electoral arena and on rare occasions by limited mobilizations, as on the day Allende was inaugurated, when nearly a million persons came out into the streets of Santiago to celebrate "their" victory.

This support is Allende's only strong card against the maneuvers of the bourgeoisie and imperialism. Yet he refuses to organize this potential power because of his respect for bourgeois democratic traditions — "social forces must express themselves through elections and the parliament" — and because of his fear of a reaction by the bourgeoisie, which would then feel threatened.

This aspect of the Chilean situation today is both ironic and tragic. The ministers and leaders of the Unidad Popular, especially the Socialists, are expounding through all the communications media the idea that anything is possible in Chile, every hope is justified for "the people," since "the people" are in power. But *necessarily* and in the near future they must expect a reaction by the bourgeoisie and imperialism. Therefore, they must prepare themselves, these leaders repeat insistently, sometimes citing the examples of Spain, Brazil, or Indonesia, to back up their arguments. But prepare how?

For the Chilean Communist Party the answer is clear. They have already begun to put it into practice. Their solution is not to organize, not to develop a framework for leading the masses, still less arming them, since this would frighten the bourgeoisie and "open the door to adventures" (*sic*). To the contrary, in the framework of the present bourgeois democracy, their answer is to beef up their apparatus to the maximum (four months ago they had 2,500 paid functionaries; today they have 5,000 — for 40,000 members!) and place as many men as possible in key positions in the bourgeois state, especially in the Ministry of the Interior. In a way, this is bringing an old tradition up to date.

For the Socialist Party, the response is less clear. The Chilean SP today has no equivalent anywhere in the world. By its very loose structures and weak apparatus, it is related to classic Social Democratic parties, but the Social Democratic current in its ranks seems to be greatly outnumbered, even almost nonexistent.

For a long time the party was really dominated by a centrist-type tendency that held to a reformist perspective in Chilean domestic politics but was linked internationally to revolutionary currents in the rest of Latin America (it participated in the OLAS conference for example). Allende was one of the most typical representatives of this tendency, and it has furnished the bulk of the Socialist ministers in the present government.

Since the Unidad Popular came to power, the situation inside the SP has changed to a large extent, reflecting the profound process of radicalization and politicalization of the Chilean masses now going on.

At the party's last congress in January 1971, the left wing, representing unquestionably revolutionary currents, increased its strength notably. Thus, the ELN [Ejército de Liberación Nacional — National Liberation Army], a current of Castroist origin which today advocates arming the proletariat to struggle effectively against the threats of the bourgeoisie and imperialism, won sixteen seats out of forty-five on the Central Committee. The resolutions of the congress reflected this evolution rather faithfully as regards the general analysis of the situation and the measures to be taken. They posed the problem clearly of mobilizing and arming the Chilean workers in the framework of the Unidad Popular committees.

But the SP is also a "government party." That is why, at the request of Allende and his ministers, the passages dealing concretely with these problems were not made public in their entirety, in order not to provoke the bourgeoisie! This is a strange way of educating the Chilean masses politically in order to mobilize them.

In these conditions, the revolutionary tendencies, essentially the ELN, are working on their own behalf outside the party. But they are torn between maintaining minimum discipline toward the party and taking up the far-from-resolved problem of concretely arming the Chilean workers, as called for by their strategic analysis — and that's without mentioning the organizational weaknesses inherent in this kind of ambiguous situation. These difficulties narrow the actual practice of the ELN, and its political vision as well, to arming and training small networks of sympathizers, which, when the time comes, threaten to be only a drop of water in the ocean.

These tendencies have, nonetheless, to their credit the important accomplishment of opening up debate on these crucial questions in the SP, and thus in the Unidad Popular as a whole, with all the public discussion this involves. This achievement is far from negligible in the context of a situation where the mobilization and politicalization of the masses are growing.

Of course, the CP is playing a considerable braking role in the process and stands as the chief defender of the present order. It was this party, for example, that condemned the peasant land occupations in the most unrestrained language, while in many cases the Socialists and Minister of Agriculture Chonchol, a dissident Christian Democrat, saw them as a good way of prodding a reluctant bureaucracy committed to serving the most reactionary bourgeoisie. The fact remains that today, even though the masses are unorganized, their support of the Allende government is too great and the process of politicalization too rapid for the bourgeoisie and the imperialists to take the risk *at this time* of a confrontation which, moreover, is not justified by the measures taken so far by the Unidad Popular.

The tactic of these reactionary forces is clearly more subtle and of longer range. The daily harassing maneuvers of the Christian Democrats in parliament and the provocations organized by extreme rightist elements must not be taken at face value. Their objective is much more that of creating a climate of permanent instability, plotting, and scandals, than of launching a real battle against Allende and the Unidad Popular.

The bourgeoisie and the imperialists are already waging a real fight on the economic level. Their method is not a ruthless blockade, as in Cuba, which would involve the risk of seeing the regime turn abruptly toward the USSR and the East European countries, with all the dynamic that implies. Moreover, a blockade would cut both ways. Chile is the world's main exporter of copper, which has become quite scarce on the international market because of the needs of the American army in Vietnam. Blockading Chile would bring on a considerable rise in the price of copper on the world market, from which the United States would be the primary loser.

On the other hand, measures severely restricting credit, banning loans, and limiting or halting investment are already in force. And they will quickly put the Chilean economy, which is very dependent on the world market, in a difficult position, forcing Allende to resort to austerity measures which will cut down the prestige and popular support he enjoys. Such a perspective is all the more likely if the masses are not prepared politically and organizationally for this new situation. That is when the bourgeoisie and the imperialists will step in — when they have been able to show that the experiment was a failure. Whether this intervention is a hot one, in the framework of a military and police operation, or a cold one, through an electoral victory of the Christian Democrats, is not the essential thing today.

What is important is that, at any price, as its strategy proves, imperialism is trying to avoid creating the conditions for a confrontation, and thus, in the present context, an almost inevitable mobilization of the masses.*

This only highlights still more the suicidal side of the Unidad Popular's policy regarding mobilizing and arming the Chilean workers, and the criminal irresponsibility this represents in conjunction with the illusions it is cultivating in the Chilean masses.

In the present political context in Chile, if a revolutionary organization, standing in independence from the Unidad Popular, correctly posed the problem of mobilizing and· arming the proletariat, and had the minimum base among the workers and peasants enabling it to lay the first foundations for carry-

---

* This strategy does not, however, protect the Chilean regime from a coup d'état carried out by some sector of the army, for example, with the encouragement of one or another service of U.S. imperialism. Such a development, of course, owing to the dynamics entailed, would greatly alter the situation.

ing out such a policy on a mass scale, this would change the situation entirely. Unfortunately, this is not the case.

Many vanguard nuclei exist today in Chile. But their extreme organizational weakness and their almost total lack of a working-class base prevent them from influencing the development of the situation, even though some of them have a highly lucid and correct analysis of the problem.

With its organizational base, its influence in the shantytowns and poor neighborhoods of Santiago, Concepción, and other Chilean cities, its influence in some important sectors of the poor peasantry, and its prestige and real influence in the student milieu, the MIR could have been a key element in forming this revolutionary rallying point, if not itself serving as the rallying point.

Unfortunately, this organization's great political weaknesses and its apparently divided leadership did not prepare it to play this role. A high degree of schematism in their analysis and thought led its leaders to believe that it was impossible for Unidad Popular to win in the elections. When Allende was elected, they didn't know what to say or do.

Some ambiguous statements suggest that the MIR leaders are giving critical support to the Unidad Popular, but on a basis that has not been clarified. They seem to have direct personal relations with Allende, to the point of assigning several MIR members to guard him. The organization has already vanished from the *poblaciones** around Santiago where it had mass influence. On the other hand, it is very active in the southern part of the country trying to organize the Mapuche Indians and politicalize them so as to make the agrarian reform a reality in this area and convert the region into a revolutionary "bastion." In the absence of other statements and analyses, these scattered items make it difficult to assess the role and perspectives of the MIR.

One thing is certain, however — *so far* it has failed in what should have been its role at this time: *to be a revolutionary mobilizing center to the left of the Unidad Popular.*

Atomized and scattered in the SP left wing and the MIR, for the most part, as well as in numerous groups. the Chilean revolutionists have an immense task to accomplish in an ex-

---

* Shantytowns around Santiago and the main Chilean urban centers. In Santiago, between one-third and one-half of the population of 1,800,000 live in these *poblaciones.*

tremely short time. On their capacity to organize themselves, to sink roots even in a limited way into the decisive sectors of the workers and peasants, and to organize them, will depend essentially the capacity of the Chilean masses to counter the maneuvers of their own bourgeoisie and the imperialists and to achieve a real socialist revolution.

One Year of the Unidad Popular

This article was translated from the October 8, 1971, issue of La Gauche, *a weekly newspaper published in Brussels by the Ligue Révolutionnaire des Travailleurs (Revolutionary Workers' League), the Belgian section of the Fourth International.*

It has been a year now since the election of Salvador Allende as president of Chile, on September 4, 1970. This period, although short, is rich enough in experience to allow us to draw up a necessarily tentative, yet essential balance sheet.

The recent Bolivian events, the hardening of the stance of the governments of Brazil and Uruguay towards Chile, the campaign unleashed by the U.S. press — leading up to the tense discussions over compensation for the copper mine nationalizations — these are but the most obvious elements of a situation that is proving to be an ever growing threat to the "Chilean experience."

The Allende government is striving to put its program into practice — "the first step towards the construction of socialism," the regime calls it. "A Chilean socialism," President Allende hastens to add.

The economic program of the Unidad Popular envisions the creation of three forms of corporate ownership: private, mixed, and state-owned.

The relative share of the economy to be operated under each of the three forms of ownership has not yet been spelled out. At present, the state-owned sector, nucleus of the future socialized economy, comprises a "nationalized" half of the banking industry, a few "expropriated" textile and food industries, and the iron and saltpeter deposits — as well as the copper mines, which will be "nationalized" as soon as the compensation rates for the North American corporations are set.

Concerning the private sector, the government has launched the "battle for production," which seeks to encourage workers to increase production ("for the people's government and nation"), and has advised the owners to run their factories at full capacity so as to reap "normal" profits in spite of the salary raises and price freeze. Here is Allende's description of the process:

". . . The firm should absorb the wage increases. . . . The profits per unit of production will decline, but this decline can be offset by producing a larger number of units, by using installations that are currently operating below capacity. . . ." (He argued thus, like a good bourgeois economist, last February 4.)

This battle for production is running into obstacles, as the capitalists don't always see eye to eye with the "people's" government, and the workers have been asking themselves the following questions: Can such agreements be made with the same bosses who are mixed up in rightist plots for a coup d'état? And why don't we take control of operations for ourselves?

Here, for example, are the words of the workers at a steel cable factory: "In the present situation, we are willing to increase production, on condition that it be clearly established that control over production is exercised by the workers and not by the bosses."

"Produce more, but under workers' control!" This was the slogan of those striking workers, a slogan that is beginning to spread among the most militant sectors of the working class.

Up until now, the government has intervened in the labor disputes in two ways:

● When the bosses openly abstain from producing, and a factory is in bankruptcy, the government "expropriates" the industry and puts it under state control.

● In other cases compromise formulas are worked out that don't satisfy the aspirations of the workers, who demand expropriation. All of this is couched in abstractions such as "the national interest," and the like.

It is in the countryside that the government has encountered the greatest difficulties in applying its program, which is limited in this area to the agrarian reform law promulgated by the Frei regime. The boycott and active resistance offered by the big landowners to government agents responsible for carrying out the expropriations have given rise to unrest among the agricultural small-holders, workers, and unemployed, who have responded with a wave of "illegal" land occupations. These actions have laid bare the limitations and inadequacy of the measures provided for by the law, to which the government agents strictly adhere.

The timeliness and effectiveness of the organizational and agitational work carried out by the MIR among the peasants have turned these actions into an example that is spreading, like an oil slick, from the south towards the center and north of the country.

What has been the official response to the problem of the "*tomas de tierra*" [land seizures]? Let us give the floor to a peasant leader from Linares province, who at a public meeting addressed Allende as follows:

"Comrade President, we don't want to provoke clashes. What we are interested in is production, particularly on the plots smaller than 80 hectares [one hectare equals 2.47 acres] not covered by the agrarian reform law, where cases of abandonment, poor utilization, and violation of social legislation are most common. This forces us to occupy the lands in order to increase production."

Allende's answer: "We are not in a position to expropriate all landholdings. Besides, there are many proprietors with no other means of subsistence. Beyond that, occupations of land pose a threat to property rights."

Allende went on to ask, "Are you a member of UP?"

"I am a sympathizer," replied the peasant.

"There you are," Allende continued. "You are under no obligations. But I have to confine myself to the UP program. I remind you that the question of land expropriations had not been raised for twenty years. This time, you are fortunate in that there is no repression."

On his part, the minister of the interior stated in a communiqué published last February 13:

"The government has confidence in the good intentions of Chilean workers and peasants. This is why it has not unleashed repressive action, which is by no means a sign of weakness."

The Communist Party's general secretary, Luis Corvalán, declared in his turn on February 17: "We do not approve of land occupations because we have an obligation to the country, and because we are going to carry out agricultural development within the limits of the law."

On April 21, Carlos Altamirano, the Socialist Party's gen-

eral secretary, declared: "We must put a stop to the bound-
less, opportunist demands, to the unofficial occupations of
lands and factories."

We shall give the final word to the MIR, through one of its
leaders, Nelson Gutiérrez, who stated on May 30:

"To limit peasant activity to the letter of the present agrarian
reform law signifies abandoning the mobilization of the most
important sector of the peasantry and the agrarian proletariat.
In fact, it signifies the fragmentation of the peasant movement
and the weakening of the entire process. . . . The conflict is
reaching the most important urban industrial centers, and the
workers are insisting with growing firmness on the need to
extend the expropriation process to industry by developing
workers' control over production."

The Crisis in the Government Parties

UP's basically equivocal and vacillating character is shared
by its component parties and movements.

The April municipal elections showed strikingly the real weight
of the parties belonging to the coalition, which won 49.73
percent of the votes cast, plus 1.05 percent from the Socialist People's Union [Unión Socialista Popular], a group outside of the UP which gave it critical support.

The percentage breakdown was as follows: Socialist Party,
22.89 percent; Communist Party, 17.36 percent; Radical Party,
8.18 percent; Social Democratic Party, 1.38 percent. (The MAPU
did not run any candidates.) The Radical ministers, confronted
with these results signaling a spectacular decline of their party,
immediately offered their resignations, which were rejected by
Allende.

But the full impact of the April elections was not felt until
August, when the polarization reflected by the gains of the
traditional workers' parties and the conservative National Party,
and by the repercussions inside the petty-bourgeois UP parties, became fully apparent.

The Radical Party, which wound up its twenty-fifth conven-
tion on August 31, adopted political resolutions in which it
described itself as socialist and revolutionary, acknowledged
the class struggle and historical materialism, and called on the
workers, peasants, and students to join its ranks.

This stance provoked a split by an important group of par-
liamentarians — five senators and seven deputies, among them
Baltra, a possible contender for the head of the next UP electoral slate — who formed a new group, the Independent Radi-

cal Movement [Movimiento Radical Independiente — MRI]. Despite efforts by Allende to reunify the Radical Party, the split was formalized. The new grouping continued to support the government while making important reservations about possible excessive measures the latter might undertake in the future.

Simultaneously, the Christian Democratic Party (which lost 100,000 votes between September 1970 and April 1971) underwent its second split in two years. Once again, a "left wing" seeks to collaborate with UP. And this time it was MAPU that lost the bulk of its top leaders, including Agriculture Minister Jacques Chonchol, who rallied to the new Christian Left [Izquierda Cristiana] movement, which was due to hold its founding congress in October.

The arguments given by Chonchol and his friends to justify their departure were spelled out in a letter to the MAPU general secretary, in which they said they were joining the Christian Left because they supported the "humanistic and Christian values" it embodies, and not the Marxist-Leninist positions allegedly adopted by the existing MAPU leadership. Allende retained Chonchol in his cabinet post even though he was no longer part of the UP. MAPU still has two cabinet members of its own, however, in the ministries of Health and Family Affairs.

The revolutionary left has seized upon the maneuvering room opened up by the UP victory to strengthen its position and to carry out intense organizational activity among the masses of students, peasants, and workers. This work is moving ahead despite the tensions between the MIR and the UP. The hostility that surrounded their relations prior to the elections subsided following the efficient performance of the MIR security apparatus in detecting the activities of networks of conspirators who were preparing a coup d'état, which culminated in the assassination of General Schneider.

A month later, during elections in the Santiago University Student Federation, the MIR decided to support the UP candidate, in light of an alliance between the National and Christian Democratic parties which threatened to take over this important organ of agitation within the university.

At the beginning of December, the focus shifted to Concepción University (an important center in southern Chile), where the MIR had held a majority for three years. The CP refused to support a MIR candidate. The electoral campaign thus became a dangerous arena of confrontation within the left, marked by provocations initiated by the Communist Youth. The tragic outcome of this campaign was the gunshot death of one student and the serious wounding of another, both of them members of the MIR.

These events left public opinion in a daze, and furnished the right with invaluable ammunition for launching an offensive against the government. The gravity of the situation forced the CP leaders to make a public self-criticism, acknowledging the MIR as a group that is also struggling for socialism, and with which it disagrees mainly over tactics, etc.

Thus the MIR appeared for the first time to the CP rank and file not as "allies of the bourgeoisie in the pay of im perialism," but as revolutionists.

The rural agitation of January and February and the penetration of MIR slogans within the ranks of the workers provoked violent disagreements with the CP, but the latter could no longer indulge in its traditional, antiquated arguments.

The funeral services for one of the MIR's most important leaders, Luciano Cruz, who died in an accident on August 14, provided the occasion for a gathering of over 30,000 people in the capital city — refuting those who predicted that the MIR would disappear if it didn't join the ranks of the UP.

The Role of the Army

The transformation of a prerevolutionary situation such as Chile is experiencing into a resolute struggle for power must be accompanied by the military organization of the workers. On this question, so essential to the triumph of the revolutionary forces, the UP is content to avoid the issue by openly opposing the creation of people's militias, and by expressing confidence in the bourgeois army.

The government seizes every opportunity to praise the army for its "professionalism" and "patriotism," while calling upon it to defend Chile's "economic frontiers." In short, it perpetuates the mystique of the army's loyalty to the "people's government."

This supposed loyalty has never prevented the army from firing on its own people. In 1907, more than 2,000 workers, women, and children were massacred at Santa Maria School in Iquique. In 1921, 130 died in the north in the San Gregorio saltpeter mines. On April 2, 1957, many demonstrators, students, and workers were killed in the streets of Santiago. On March 11, 1966, eight died and sixty were wounded in Salvador's copper mines.

As the venerable labor leader Clotario Blest — whose memory is keener than that of other "representatives of the workers' interests" — recalls, "These are but a few of the aggressions perpetrated by the army against Chilean workers."

The revolutionary left, meanwhile, is engaging in penetrating the army's lower echelons, and has been involved for some time in creating a military infrastructure on various fronts.

But the right is more advanced in this arena. Beyond the proliferation of fascist groups such as "Patria y Libertad" [Fatherland and Freedom], "Grupo Anticomunista" [GRACO — Anticommunist Group], "NECH" [We Won't Sell Out Chile], etc., the assassination of General Schneider and its repercussions show clearly that the right is not wasting time and that it has great influence within the top ranks of the army — an influence that is hardly a new phenomenon.

Capitalism can only be abolished through a socialist revolution. This time-tested axiom of Marxism is being forgotten by certain leaders. But the Bolivian masses remembered it recently when they told Torres, "nationalism no, socialism yes," and "enough of promises, we want arms."

In Chile, some sectors of the urban and agricultural proletariat, led by their vanguards, are confronting the same problem. Thus we see factory workers counterposing workers' control to the "participation" offered by the government, and peasants countering rightist sabotage and government vacillations with their own mobilizations under the slogan of "*Pan, Tierra, y Socialismo*" [Bread, Land, and Socialism].

The Bolivian experience provides a clear-cut lesson concerning the arming of the workers. As long as they are denied arms, as long as measures that strike seriously at the bourgeoisie's interests are not accompanied by the systematic mobilization and arming of the workers, aren't all such measures merely pious promises, or in reality pure and simple treachery?

Here once again, the history of the labor movement shows us the efforts made by the Social Democracy to keep the proletariat bottled up by "patriotic" compromises that benefit only the bourgeoisie. Allende, and with him the Socialist and Communist parties, are simply binding the proletariat's hands and feet while giving a dangerously free hand to reaction, which has already demonstrated its capabilities in Bolivia, in the Sudan, and long before that, in Indonesia.

The Chilean revolutionists have before them an extremely difficult and urgent task: to put the workers, peasants, and students into motion towards the socialist revolution, unmasking

the fraud of "the Chilean path to socialism" being perpetrated
by the Social Democrats and their Stalinist allies. They will
thereby join in the struggle of revolutionaries throughout the
world, reinforcing it while learning from its previous ex-
periences.

Chile— The Coming Confrontation
Statement of the Fourth International

*This statement was issued by the United Secretariat of the
Fourth International, the world revolutionary party founded
by Leon Trotsky in 1938. It was passed unanimously at a
meeting at the end of December 1971.*

*Organize Democratic Councils of the Workers, Peasants, Slum
Dwellers, and Students!*

*Struggle for the Arming of the Proletariat and the Formation
of a Popular Militia!*

Build a Revolutionary Party!

Fourteen months ago, as a result of the September 4, 1970,
elections and an agreement between the parties of the Unidad
Popular and the Partido Demócrata-Cristiano [PDC — Christian
Democratic Party], Salvador Allende was inaugurated as president of Chile and formed a popular front government. This was
a major event that all formations both within the country and
in the Americas as a whole had to take a stand on. From the
beginning it served as a touchstone, revealing the concepts
and attitudes of the various currents in the workers' movement. The experiment in Chile is being watched throughout
the world, particularly as a test of the efficacy of the electoral,
parliamentary, and peaceful road that has been advocated
by the reformists as a way of achieving socialism.

In a setting of vigorous mobilizations of opposing social
and political forces, the crisis in Chile is becoming increasingly acute. Particularly since the defeat suffered by the masses
of Bolivia last August, the contradictions and the struggle

in Latin America have come to a focal point in Chile. Thus
it is imperative for revolutionary Marxists to grasp the nature
of the events, to understand the tendencies that are developing
and the issues that are coming to the fore, and to define their
position without any ambiguity so as to be able to intervene
effectively.

1. The victory of the Cuban revolution—which coincided
with the irreversible crisis of the bourgeois or petty-bourgeois
revolutionary nationalist movements that marked an entire
stage of the political struggle in many Latin American countries—led U.S. imperialism and the indigenous ruling classes
to reexamine where they stood. On the one hand, the imperialists stepped up their military preparations, with an eye to
the possible danger of revolutionary struggles inspired by the
Cuban example; on the other hand, they projected a reformist course the aim of which was to reinforce certain economic
sectors considered to be the most dynamic, to favor a shift
in the relationship of forces within the ruling classes toward
the "new" bourgeois layers, and to broaden, even if but a little, the mass base of the system. This attempt—to which Washington, however, allotted only derisory funds under the so-called
Alliance for Progress—ended in total defeat. Within this context, the reformist experiments, or those tending in that direction (for example, Goulart in Brazil, Belaúnde in Peru) were
either crushed in the egg or soon ended in bankruptcy. One
of the consequences of this was the proliferation of military
regimes, most of them reactionary, and the tendency to use
the army on an increasing scale as a substitute for the traditional political mechanisms that had proved incapable of
carrying out their tasks.

The dictatorship of the Brazilian *gorillas* was one of the
variants adopted to establish a relative political equilibrium
and to revive the economy through increased exploitation of
the working class and the toiling masses as a whole. Another
variant was an expansion of reformism that aimed at modernizing and rationalizing the economic and social structures,
at imposing a new balance within the ruling classes themselves at the expense of the traditional oligarchy, and at establishing better and more active relations with the masses or
considerable layers of them. The pilot experiment in this was
the military regime set up in Peru by Velasco Alvarado in
October 1968.

The relative success of the Peruvian regime, combined with
the defeats suffered by other governments or the dead ends in

which they found themselves, favored analogous reformist tendencies — military or civilian — stepping forward in other countries, even if they remained only incipient. As a whole, these
currents raised the question of modernizing the agricultural
structures through agrarian reforms directed against the most
conservative landholding layers and designed to foster the
formation of layers of small and middle peasant owners. They
sought a more substantial displacement of capital toward the
industrial and urban sectors of the economy in general with
the idea of breaking the direct imperialist domination of the
traditional raw materials sectors. Against the old setup, as
partisans of a more vigorous intervention in the economy by
the state, to which they assigned an increasing role as a sta-
bilizer, they favored "collaboration" with the so-called modern
industrial sectors. Such an orientation, as they saw it, would
make possible an improvement in relations with the masses,
which, within strict limits, could play a role in supporting the
new regimes against the resistance and counterattacks of the
ultras.

2. The events in Chile in recent years come within this more
general tendency. It must not be forgotten that the Frei regime
itself began as a reformist experiment that sought to modernize
socio-economic structures, particularly through an agrarian
reform, increased intervention by state, and the final displacement of the former oligarchical ruling layers. Thus in a general
way, the Popular Unity government stands as a continuator
of the government that preceded it. It was not accidental that
in the period before the September 4 election, sectors of the
Popular Unity and the Christian Democrats did not exclude
running a common candidate and that the Christian Democrats stood on a program analogous to that of Allende's front.
Even more significantly — the new president did not project
a new agrarian reform, but limited himself to applying the
reform adopted by Frei.

The essentially reformist character of the Allende government
conforms, moreover, with the program presented before and
after the elections. Basically this program projects carrying
out the Christian Democratic agrarian reform, ending the direct
imperialist grip on the exploitation of raw materials, the statization of a series of industrial sectors, and the nationalization
of the banks. This program, if it were carried out in its entirety,
would greatly alter Chile's economic structure, bringing about
considerable modifications in the relationship of class forces,
in the division of the national income, and in the political

role played by the different forces. But it would not involve a qualitative change—Chile would not cease to be a capitalist country dominated by the law of profit and still integrated in the imperialist world structure. In the countryside, agriculture would be marked more and more by the growth of capitalist enterprises and layers of land-owning small and middle peasants that would act as stabilizing elements, at least for the time being. The industrial bourgeoisie would still be the strongest and most dynamic class economically, it would retain and even strengthen its links with international capitalism, and, in the final analysis, it would be the main beneficiary of the new economic and political equilibrium and of the rationalization of the system, including through the presence of a very important sector controlled by the state.

Maintenance of the basic economic structure of capitalism is guaranteed all the more by the fact that the Popular Unity fought for the presidency not only on a strictly electoral level but committed itself to work within the framework of the pre-existing state apparatus (parliament, administrative apparatus, constitutionally authorized bodies of control such as the police, the army). That is why Alessandri and Tomic, who were supported at the time by virtually all the bourgeois voters, agreed to abide by the electoral outcome and permit Allende to take office (the factions favoring a coup d'état consisted of only very small groupings even within the army).

3. While the events in Chile fall within a more general context of analogous tendencies that are either potential or already operative in other Latin American countries, they are nevertheless marked by very important specific traits that clearly differentiate the Allende regime from any other regime in Latin America.

First of all, while Peruvian reformism is being carried out by a military leadership that has displaced the traditional bourgeois parties, in Chile guidance is being undertaken by a coalition whose base is to be found essentially among the workers, the peasants, and the slum dwellers, and in which the two workers' parties exercise unquestionable preponderance. Thus Chilean reformism is being conducted under the leadership of a workers' bureaucracy.

The question arises as to whether the Allende government is a popular front government in the traditional sense of the term. It has been argued that the bourgeoisie as such, represented politically by the Christian Democrats and to a lesser degree by the National Party, is not directly represented in the government. But, even leaving aside the fact that at least one of the parties in the coalition was traditionally a bourgeois party, the bourgeoisie exercises its influence through the petty-bourgeois parties that were included in both the Popular Unity and in the government. In addition, Allende is continually obliged to negotiate with the majority bloc in a parliament dominated by the Christian Democratic Party, which permitted him to be elected and which can paralyze anything he undertakes whenever it chooses. Finally — and this is decisive — the class-collaborationist nature of the coalition was determined by its acceptance of the fundamental economic framework of the capitalist system and the bourgeois state apparatus.

Such a characterization should not lead one to identify the movement of the masses with the coalition nor even to simplify too much the problem of the relationship between Allende and the masses. Allende's victory was the outcome of a long history of hard battles, of many ups and downs, of the slow ripening of a proletariat that is among the oldest and most homogeneous in Latin America. In the eyes of the workers, the peasants, and the plebeian layers of the slums, the September 4, 1970, election represented a victory over the bourgeoisie, a historic step forward in the struggle for the elimination of capitalist exploitation. It expressed a new relationship of forces, more favorable to the masses than ever before. All this became translated after September 4 into an extraordinary upsurge, a broad mobilization of the working class and the peasantry, a radicalization of layers of the petty bourgeoisie, a rise in political consciousness among the plebeian sectors of the big cities. Broad layers of the vanguard, inspired by the mobilization of the masses and confronted by immediate political necessities, began discussing the main themes of revolutionary strategy and the problem of how to get from capitalism to socialism.

4. One of the fundamental factors in the situation in Chile is the inevitable tendency of the mass mobilization to break through the framework of reformism and class collaborationism prescribed by Allende. This, in the final analysis, is what provokes the sharpest conflicts and alarms the indigenous bourgeoisie and the imperialists. Out of fear of being overwhelmed, they raise the question of an inevitable confrontation.

In other words, the bourgeoisie, understanding its necessity, was inclined to accept and even to foster a reformist operation. After the defeat of Frei, this could only be attempted under the leadership of the workers' parties. But it fears the dynamics of a mass movement that could break through the framework of reformism, precipitating a genuine revolutionary crisis and placing on the agenda the question of power. In the same way, imperialism fears that the dynamics of the situation in Chile could have explosive effects on a continental scale, inspiring new upsurges of the proletariat and the peasantry.

In fact, in the period since the election, the workers and peasants have not at all limited themselves to supporting Allende and waiting for the government to act. They have often taken the initiative, obliging the government to approve the things that have been done. More importantly, the practical actions undertaken by the masses have often gone beyond the limits of the program of the Popular Unity. Peasants have taken over land without waiting for formal decisions and have even seized properties that could not be touched, according to the law. Workers have undertaken actions along the same lines, accelerating the process of statization and hitting enterprises that in principle were to be left in the sector of privately owned property. For the bourgeoisie this involved a crucial question — a substantial extension of expropriations beyond the projected limits raised the danger of gravely weakening its social weight, of more profoundly altering the relationship of forces. This could prevent it from effectively carrying out the projected restructuring of the economy to its own benefit. The bourgeoisie recognized at the same time that as this course gathered headway, the working class and the peasantry, by force of circumstances, would more and more be compelled to deal with the question of power by cutting through the limits of the constitution and forming qualitatively new bodies of proletarian power.

In the currently developing conflicts, the contending forces are mobilizing and reacting more and more sharply in relation to issues that must be decided in a relatively short time. The masses — at least the layers in the forefront — are not ready to give up their offensive and are seeking to bring to bear the greater social and political weight they have gained. The bourgeoisie is combining defensive operations and sallies designed to encourage its troops. For the bourgeoisie, it is essential to gain exact delimitation of the three economic "areas" (state, private, mixed) and to maintain the political structures of the system. The latter is required as a guarantee against any tendency to go beyond the framework of the reformist experiment. Allende and his coalition, unable to accede to measures that might provoke a break with the masses or even considerable sectors of the masses, are compelled to reply to the attacks of the bourgeoisie; but at the same time they continually seek to hold back the masses and to counter the pressures exerted from the left. They need to maintain an appreciable margin for maneuver and to avoid or to postpone any major confrontation. This is the meaning of the widely applied measure called *intervención*, which, by designating a manager to act in the name of the government, offers a certain satisfaction to the workers while at the same time not necessarily implying expropriation, thus maintaining capitalist property relations. This is also the meaning of the projected single chamber parliament, which, if it is accepted, would permit the government to carry out its program more rapidly and would better reflect the existing relationship of forces in Chile while on the other hand guaranteeing to the bourgeoisie the preservation of parliamentary structures completely within the bourgeois tradition.

5. In a situation like the one in Chile today, the different forces are not always in position to strictly pick and choose what they will get into or to act in accordance with a thought-out overall plan. The contradictions and potential conflicts accumulate from day to day, and events that are insignificant in themselves, and difficult to anticipate, can precipitate dramatic confrontations at practically any moment. This must never be forgotten, and it would be a grave error for the workers' movement to lull itself with the illusion of a painless unfolding of events.

However, it is unlikely that a decisive confrontation will occur in the immediate future. The government, for its part, is seeking to keep the initiative while carrying on a balancing act and putting the brake on actions from below that it considers to be dangerous from its point of view. As for the bourgeoisie, it is provoking multiple tensions both to create difficulties for the Popular Unity and to make it modify its course more (it knows from experience that reactions of this kind are typical of reformists and centrists). But it is not able to precipitate an immediate showdown, nor does it want one.

It must be remembered, first of all, that the Chilean bourgeoisie has a rather long democratic-parliamentarian tradition and that its political personalities were shaped in that school. This corresponds with the existence of a series of structures and flexible, efficacious mechanisms that make defense and counterattack genuinely possible. The solution of a "strong state," of a military coup, presupposes in any case preparations that the army itself has hardly begun. The forces that are already voicing *"golpista"* [coup-ist] or fascist inclinations and who are preparing the means to carry forward such an orientation are at present completely in the minority, even if they are gaining ground. Finally—and this is the most important—the bourgeoisie and its most representative party, the Christian Democrats, are very much aware that they can hardly visualize a confrontation without having a considerable mass base. Recent events have shown that time can play into their hands thanks to the weaknesses and contradictions of the Popular Unity and the economic difficulties these have helped foster. In fact the Christian Democrats have gained or consolidated positions that are far from negligible among the peasants, have regained influence among the students, and widened their margin for maneuver, including within the working class (particularly among sectors that, misled for a long time by the blind economism of the reformists, have fallen for the bait of certain demagogic bids); and, as the events in Santiago in November and December have shown, the reactionaries are able to mobilize considerable forces in rather aggressive street demonstrations.

Nevertheless, a postponement of the decisive battles is not necessarily injurious to the cause of the working class, which needs to strengthen its positions, to organize an offensive, to face and resolve the decisive problem of arming itself. But this holds true only to the degree that every tendency to limit and to channelize the mass mobilizations, and to give priority to political operations at the top level of the bureaucratic machines and state institutions is resolutely combated; to the degree and rapidity with which economic sabotage is counteracted; to the degree that the working class feels it has no obligation to carry the burden of the economic difficulties without being able to defend itself, to intervene actively, and exercise control; and to the degree that the illusion is rejected that "moderation" and loyalty to the norms of a bourgeois constitution constitute the best way to avoid a reactionary counteroffensive and a fascist coup.

6. It is a prime necessity at this stage of strategical rearmament that the working class free itself completely from any kind of reformist ideas and parliamentary cretinism of whatever form. It must understand that Chile will not prove to be an exception.

In a country whose economic and social structures are very advanced in comparison to the average level in the neocolonial

world, it is clearer than ever that the perspective of a bour-
geois-democratic revolution, separated from a socialist revolution, does not have the slightest objective justification. The
only possible revolution in Chile is a revolution with a socialist dynamic without any break in continuity and at a relatively rapid rate. And emancipation from imperialism — in view
of the close symbiotic relation between imperialism and the
national bourgeoisie — can be achieved only by the complete
expropriation of the indigenous ruling class. Any ambiguity,
any slurring over on this subject could have disastrous consequences, disarming the basic revolutionary forces, who need
to gain a clear understanding of what they grasp intuitively
and try to carry out empirically.

To believe in the idea that a revolutionary dynamic of this
kind can unfold completely to a victorious outcome without
breaking the political framework of the old society thanks to
a "peaceful" evolution and not by breaking up the old state
structure, including both the administration and the military
establishment, and starting afresh is to deliberately delude
oneself, to forget the lessons of the long history of the workers'
movement, to be incapable of grasping the implacable logic of
the situation that is developing in the country. Far from being
a theoretical innovation, as claim the charlatans of all stripes
and those who trample on the Marxist method out of empiricism or opportunism, the concept of a "Chilean road" is
only a new version of the reformist ideology that Marxism has
fought since the turn of the century and that at crucial stages
has ravaged the workers' movement in other parts of the world.
The essential point is that in Chile the problem of taking power
has not been solved at all nor even begun to be solved. It
can only be met and actually solved on the revolutionary
road.

From all the preceding, it follows that any form of class
collaboration with the bourgeoisie or with sectors of the bourgeoisie must be resolutely rejected. This implies that the masses
in Chile must struggle to replace the coalition government of
the Popular Unity with a workers' and peasants' government
that excludes any participation by parties or groups that represent, if only indirectly, the interests of the bourgeoisie and
other layers of the exploiters. This means that the revolutionary
process must be deepened and stimulated by the creation of
bodies of dual power, by bodies of genuine proletarian democracy formed directly in the plants, the fields, the *campamientos*
[shantytowns], and schools, in which the members are elected,

subject to recall at any time, and enjoy no material privileges. These bodies will represent the proletariat and the peasantry as a whole and constitute the means of mobilizing the key sectors of the masses in the revolutionary struggle for the conquest of power. The unions will remain separate and apart, continuing to play their specific role, on the basis of the widest internal democracy for all tendencies in the workers' movement and in complete independence from the government and the state.

The revolutionary Marxists are conscious of the difficulties involved in forming and extending such bodies of a soviet type; but if they are not built, one of the essential elements for the conquest of power will be lacking and the revolution in-gestation can be aborted. In the battle for workers' and peasants' councils, the sharpest line of demarcation must be drawn between the exploiting classes and their political machines while this is coupled with an uncompromising defense of the broadest democracy for the masses and all the organizations and tendencies of the workers' movement. The defense of proletarian democracy is all the more necessary in view of the fact that the concept has become obscured after the decades of Social Democratic and Stalinist preponderance. It is an imperious practical necessity that unfortunately has not been absorbed and understood by the organizations that are struggling against the opportunistic, bureaucratized parties. A continual, very broad, thoroughgoing mobilization of the masses is the condition sine qua non for a positive development of the revolutionary crisis in Chile. It is precisely because the reformist leaderships — which the working class and peasant masses in their great majority continue to accept — have sought to limit and channelize these mobilizations and to impose decisions taken exclusively at the governmental and parliamentary level, that the movement became weakened, opening the way for the foe to take the initiative and partially set in motion layers whose interests do not coincide in principle with those of the reaction. If this short-sighted policy is continued — still worse, if the government cracks down on sectors of the vanguard of the proletariat and the peasantry, as it has already done on certain occasions, this could strengthen tendencies toward confusion and demobilization. The conditions thus created would enormously facilitate a reactionary counterattack and a rightist coup d'état.

7. A strategy of revolutionary struggle for power must single out several key objectives. Without pretending to provide answers to all the problems that have arisen and that will arise

at different stages, the revolutionary Marxists stress the following:

(a) The poor peasants and agricultural workers cannot accept the framework of the agrarian reform set by the Frei government, that is, by a bourgeois political leadership. The transformations in the agrarian structures must include the total expulsion of the landlords and the expropriation of the capitalist entrepreneurs. The limits on holdings must be set at a level designed on the one hand to avoid forming a layer of rich peasants, dangerous to the revolution, and on the other hand to guarantee the necessary resources to peasants who want to own an individual plot. Very precise norms must be established (particularly with regard to the buying and selling of land) so as to achieve the equivalent of nationalization of the land and to block any tendency toward a new concentration of property. If the agrarian reform refrains from touching the capitalist enterprises, complete domination over the most dynamic sector of agriculture will be left in private hands and the agricultural workers will turn away from the revolutionary process. It is necessary to inscribe in the program of the workers' and peasants' government the expropriation of the agricultural capitalists and the formation of collective farms. The latter, thanks to their technological level, play a central role in developing the economy during the period of transition.

(b) In the domain of industry, it is necessary to reject the concept of three "areas" that reserves a sector for private capital. Such a sector, embracing the most modern and dynamic fields in the existing capitalist system, would inevitably become the nerve center of the process of accumulation and the meeting place of national and foreign capital. Through general expropriation it is necessary to break the backbone of Chilean capitalism, thereby breaking at the same time the indigenous support on which imperialist penetration depends. It goes without saying that to the degree it controls entirely and directly all the key sectors of industry and agriculture, the workers' and peasants' government would have no interest in breaking up small business and craft industry nor feel any urgent need to do so.

(c) The nationalization of the banking system and the establishment of a state monopoly on foreign trade must be carried out to the end. These measures are all the more necessary because of Chile's position as a semicolonial country subject to imperialist exploitation.

(d) Workers' control plays a key role in a revolutionary

strategy for the conquest of power. It fosters the formation
of dual power, the active participation of the masses and a
deepening grasp of what is genuinely at stake. Through workers' control the proletariat mobilizes in a concrete way at the
point of production, thus helping broader and broader layers
to understand in practice the need to pose the problem of power.
Any form of "participation" by the workers, subordinated in
reality to the power of the bosses or of government technicians,
or any form of "comanagement" must be rejected. It is necessary to demand workers' control of production, exercised by
democratic bodies, directly elected by the workers. The problems of workers' management and self-management will not
become real until after the qualitative revolutionary jump, until after the overturn of bourgeois power and the birth of proletarian power.

At the same time, workers' control enables the workers to
bring all aspects of job relations under surveillance. They
are able to challenge the organization of work imposed by
the bosses, to intervene actively in setting work rates, dividing
of jobs, work breaks, etc. It also makes it possible in already
nationalized industries to avoid having a technocrat simply
step into the shoes of the boss or the capitalist manager. Workers' control can likewise represent a school in which to learn
the technical tasks of administration and management which
the working class must be able to carry out after the seizure
of power lest bureaucratic tendencies gain headway.

Finally, workers' control can serve as an instrument of struggle against the economic sabotage of the foreign and Chilean
capitalists. In connection with this, general measures involving planning and control must be pushed for government adoption along with abolition of trade secrets, opening of the books,
and strict control over all banking operations as well as prices,
rents, etc. The flight of capital, the closing down of plants,
and the hoarding of goods give extreme urgency to these
measures.

(e) The struggle for a workers' and peasants' government,
for the conquest of power, must be conducted above all through
forming and constantly mobilizing organs of proletarian democracy rising out of the masses. The building of these organs is an absolutely central task at this stage, and the very
fate of the revolution hinges, in the last analysis, on how it
is carried out. As a transitional slogan, it is necessary to raise
against Allende's project of a single chamber parliament —
which fits in with bourgeois parliamentarism — the slogan of

a popular constituent assembly whose task would be to lay out new political and administrative structures. This assembly must be elected in such fashion as to assure the workers and peasants the preponderant representation to which they are entitled because of their specific social weight, thus putting an end to the fraudulent present electoral system with all its dupery.

8. The strategy and orientations outlined here would be completely abstract and not free from the danger of spontanéist deviations if two essential items were left out — the absence of which up to now has constituted the main weakness of the Chilean proletariat, that is, arming the workers and peasants and building a revolutionary party. To struggle for a correct strategy thus means struggling to arm the proletariat, and struggling to build a revolutionary party as the only means of assuring the masses conscious leadership and effectively carrying out the strategy and tactics required to win.

The experience of other countries, above all in Latin America — from the invasion of Guatemala in 1954 to Banzer's coup d'état in Bolivia last August — has shown that the working class must consider its own self-defense as an elementary task. The lesson is written in letters of blood — the blood of workers, peasants, and students. Any illusions in the "good will" of the foe must be rejected as suicidal. In view of the nature of the government and the relations between the Unidad Popular coalition and the broad majority of the masses, the task facing the workers and peasants is to arm themselves, to form political and military instruments of self-defense, to organize a genuine popular militia, to disseminate revolutionary propaganda among the soldiers. Not to begin along these lines would mean in practice depending on the "democratic loyalty" of the army and the specialized repressive bodies. It would mean incapacity to respond to the need felt by increasingly broad sectors of the masses, alerted by the events in Bolivia. Allende's proclamations, according to which the Popular Unity will meet any reactionary violence should it occur, constitute nothing but demagogic bragging, since they involve nothing practical. In place of relying on spontanéism and improvisations, the necessary instruments must be put together now to prevent the class enemy from achieving a crushing material superiority when the inevitable confrontation comes about. Against any possible misunderstanding, the revolutionary Marxists stress that it is not against Allende, but against the threats from the right, and to answer any attack from the forces of bourgeois repression, that the workers and peasants must place on the agenda the crucial problem of arming themselves.

9. In another way, Chile will not prove to be a historic exception — the capitalist system in Chile will not be overturned without the decisive intervention of a revolutionary party, the conscious vanguard of the masses. The tasks pertaining to such a party cannot be left to the Chilean Communist Party to carry out. This party, bearing the stamp of a long Stalinist tradition, is the instrument of an indigenous labor bureaucracy and relatively conservative layers of the proletariat that have not been mobilizing in the current crisis with the same dynamism as the younger generation. It has maintained all its traditional concepts, not cutting in the least way the umbilical cord tying it to the Soviet bureaucracy. The tasks of the revolutionary party cannot be left to the Socialist Party either. While the SP has gained a wider hearing, particularly among the younger workers, and has, in the organizations it controls, adopted positions to the left of those of the Communist Party — a genuine cesspool of reformism — it does not have the structure of a combat party, it does not have solid and continuous links with the masses it influences, and is more a conglomeration of tendencies and groups than a homogeneous formation, and, in the final analysis, bears the characteristic traits of a centrist organization. In any case, it is necessary to reject any concept based, explicitly or implicitly, on the hypothesis that thanks to the dynamism of the revolutionary process and the power of the mass movement and thanks to the weakening of the bourgeoisie and its very likely continuing decomposition and a situation in which imperialism would be compelled to renounce military intervention, the proletariat can come to power even without a genuine revolutionary Leninist party. It is likewise necessary to reject the variant derived from the hypothesis that an ersatz revolutionary party might prove sufficient, that is, some kind of front in which the revolutionists assemble together, or a cartel in which different organizations of the far left join up.

The task of building a party is indubitably difficult even in an objective context that is very favorable from a number of angles. But it must absolutely be accomplished. At this stage of the class struggle in Latin America, the speed with which the revolutionary crisis in Chile develops to its outcome depends, in the final analysis, on the speed with which the party is built.

10. The tense and dramatic course of events will inevitably

provoke growing differentiations among the masses and bring to maturity considerable layers of the vanguard, who will come to understand the nature of the reformist regime, the contradictions in the workers' organizations, and the necessity to work out a revolutionary strategy. In fact this line of development is already becoming clearly visible.

Since his inauguration, Allende has had to face mounting pressures from the left and sometimes sweeping demonstrations. There has been a considerable growth of dissatisfied tendencies that have come into conflict with the reformist restrictions. Concrete evidence of this is to be seen on the class level in the moves made by sectors of the workers and peasants that have gone beyond the programmatic guidelines of the Popular Unity and confronted the government with accomplished facts. On the political level it is to be seen in the increasing influence of the organizations standing to the left of the Communist and Socialist parties. It is in relation to these differentiations and these objective tendencies that the problem of building the revolutionary party must be posed, and not on the absurd hope of being able to solve it through declamations and half-hearted moves.

It is not by accident that an organization like the Movimiento de Izquierda Revolucionaria, the only one of its kind in Latin America at the moment, should arise in Chile. The MIR has considerable influence. Originating in student and petty bourgeois circles, it has succeeded, as the demonstrations of the past period have clearly indicated, in winning authority among the peasant forces that mobilized in land occupations and among several sectors of the workers who no longer accept the lead of the reformists. It is probable that this tendency will grow in the period now opening which promises a rise in political consciousness among rather broad layers controlled up to now by the Popular Unity.

The influence of the MIR is explained by its capacity to link up with the most dynamic layers of the student movement during its initial phase, of appearing as the most consistent and effective organization of the far left in putting together a rather solid organizational framework, based on cells of professional militants, despite the ultraleft deformations that marked it for an entire period up to the spectacular turn of September 1970. At the same time the MIR knew how to capitalize on the influence wielded in Chile by the Cuban revolution since the beginning of the sixties.

The contradictions to be found in the MIR lie in its incapacity to reach an overall, rigorous definition of the problems of revolutionary strategy on a world scale; in the empiricism that often characterizes its orientations and that has led to sudden oscillations from ultraleft to opportunist positions; in its concept of the party, which is far from Leninist democratic centralism, particularly in practice; and in its bureaucratic concept of relations between the party and the mass organizations. This took form in the period after September 1970 in a very clear tendency to adapt to the concepts and needs of the Popular Unity; in almost total silence with regard to international events, even those of first-rate significance (the MIR, for example, has published no analysis of the policies of Moscow and Peking); in a *"verticalista"* organizational practice that reserves important decisions for the top level (it is significant that no congress has been held for years); in efforts through administrative means and without consultation to impose decisions taken by the party apparatus on organizations considered to be vehicles for reaching the masses.

The consequence of this has been friction within the organization, the departure of groups of militants, particularly among the students, and the loss of important positions in the *campamientos*. In view of its influence the MIR, because of the weaknesses of its orientation, bears the responsibility in large measure for the crisis in the student movement. For the past year the student movement has not been able to play a major role; instead, it has provided recruits to reactionary provocations.

The forces organized or influenced by the MIR will unquestionably play an important role in building the revolutionary party that is the condition sine qua non for the victory of the Chilean workers and peasants. But other forces that still belong to the traditional parties will participate in this. The Socialist Party, because of its present composition and structure, constitutes a seedbed of militants and combative and politically conscious cadres who will have a lot to offer in the process. It must not be forgotten either that a decisive change in the relationship of forces in favor of the revolutionists also presupposes a deep differentiation among the working-class layers that still represent the main base of the Communist Party.

In carrying out their elementary task of constructing a Leninist party, the revolutionary Marxists must avoid both sectarian dogmatism and opportunist adaptation, integrating themselves in the real movements and advancing their program in an audacious way as an autonomous organized force in confrontation with all the other tendencies of the left.

This involves attacking without any ambiguities or concessions the reformist nature of the regime and the forces backing it. Complete independence must be maintained with regard to the popular front coalition. Revolutionists cannot participate in such a coalition even by offering it electoral support. (Revolutionary Marxists can, in certain situations, vote for a labor candidate but not for a candidate of a front that includes petty-bourgeois and bourgeois parties.) They must, however, support progressive measures undertaken by the Allende regime and maintain a united front against the attacks of the reactionaries.

The necessary criticism of the contradictions and weaknesses of the MIR must not at all stand in the way of recognizing the important role the MIR is playing as a catalyzer at the moment, or of appreciating the programmatic rectifications or advances it makes (as, for example, in the speech of Miguel Enríquez last November).

A continuous tenacious struggle must be conducted to concretize the revolutionary strategy outlined above and to advance the transitional slogans flowing from it.

11. The outcome of the crisis in Chile will be determined not only by the dynamics of the domestic situation but by powerful international forces. This must be kept in mind all the more attentively in view of the fact that the thesis of Chilean "exceptionalism" goes hand in hand with a confirmed and striking underestimation of these forces. Underlying this attitude, in reality, are extremely dangerous illusions and inveterate opportunism.

It is obvious that imperialism, if need be through its satellites, will do everything in its power to influence developments in Chile and block Santiago from becoming the capital of the second workers' state in Latin America. Through its international weight and its links with the Chilean Communist Party, the Soviet bureaucracy will also exercise powerful pressure. The Chinese bureaucracy has played only a completely secondary role in Chile and this will hardly change. As for Cuba, its influence takes contradictory forms. Fidel Castro's visit was symbolic in this respect. On the one hand the masses turned out in huge demonstrations to greet him and pay tribute to the Cuban revolution. On the other hand Castro's almost unconditional support of Allende and his adherence to the verbiage of the Popular Unity created obstacles to the development of understanding among the masses of the necessity to build a Leninist party and to develop a revolutionary strategy for the conquest of power.

Thus it is imperative for the revolutionists to grasp the relationship between the world situation and what is happening in Chile and to bring it out clearly. The need for an international revolutionary perspective has become more acute than ever. That is why the battle now unfolding in Chile concerns not only those who stand for revolutionary Marxism in that country but the Fourth International as a whole. In this stage, so important for Latin America, it must bring to bear its theoretical tradition, its political analyses, its experience, and its world organization.

III

THE OCTOBER 1972 BOSSES' STRIKE AND ALLENDE'S TURN TO THE MILITARY

ITT and the CIA Plot Against Allende

By David Thorstad

It is common knowledge that the Central Intelligence Agency and U.S. big business cooperate closely throughout the world to subvert and attempt to overthrow governments the U.S. capitalists do not like. From the overthrow of Mossadegh, to the Bay of Pigs invasion, to the war in Indochina, their cooperation has become a well-known secret, impossible to deny. At times, when their cloak-and-dagger operations succeed, as in the 1954 coup in Guatemala, even they themselves admit it.

The March 21 and 22 reports by syndicated columnist Jack Anderson, revealing that the CIA and the International Telephone and Telegraph Corporation have been devoting their attention to Chile, provide only the most recent example of the sinister scheming that is the stock-in-trade of the imperialists.

"Secret documents which escaped shredding by ITT show that the company maneuvered at the highest levels to stop the 1970 election of leftist Chilean President Salvador Allende," Anderson wrote. "The papers reveal that ITT dealt regularly with the CIA and, at one point, considered triggering a military coup to head off Allende's election."

The revelations were dramatic confirmation of charges made by leftist forces in Chile at the time that the CIA was plotting to prevent Allende from taking office. They also prompted the Senate Foreign Relations Committee to decide to conduct an inquiry into what committee Chairman J.W. Fulbright termed "the role of multinational corporations in the formulation

From *Intercontinental Press,* April 3, 1972

of foreign policy." Fulbright said the committee will have to examine the notion that foreign investments by U.S. corporations are "a good thing, not only for the United States but for other countries."

Anderson (who set off a political bomb on February 29 by publishing excerpts from an ITT memorandum to the effect that the company would pay $400,000 to the 1972 Republican national convention in return for an agreement by the Justice Department to quash three antitrust suits against the company) said he obtained the secret materials "despite the wholesale shredding of files, which the company has admitted took place in the Washington office Feb. 24 in an attempt to keep 'embarrassing' documents out of our hands."

Anderson said the documents show that ITT officials were "in close touch" with William V. Broe, then director of the Latin American division of the CIA's "Clandestine Services." "They were plotting together to create economic chaos in Chile, hoping this would cause the Chilean army to pull a coup that would block Allende from coming to power." At one point, Broe even personally visited ITT Vice-President E.J. Gerrity, Jr., in his New York office to discuss the CIA plan.

Involved in the plotting was ITT Director John McCone, himself a former head of the CIA. On October 9, 1970, he received a confidential report from William Merriam, vice-president in charge of ITT's Washington office, in which Merriam wrote: "Today I had lunch with our contact at the McLean agency (CIA), and I summarize for you the results of our conversation. He is still very, very pessimistic about defeating Allende when the Congressional vote takes place on Oct. 24. Approaches continue to be made to select members of the Armed Forces in an attempt to have them lead some sort of uprising — no success to date. . . .

"Practically no progress has been made in trying to get American business to cooperate in some way so as to bring on economic chaos. GM and Ford, for example, say that they have too much inventory on hand in Chile to take any chances and that they keep hoping that everything will work out all right. Also, the Bank of America had agreed to close its doors in Santiago but each day keeps postponing the inevitable. According to my source, we must continue to keep the pressure on business."

Anderson reported that ITT was given "a generally polite but cool" reception by the White House and the State Department, "although Edward Korry, ambassador to Chile, is reported to have been militantly anti-Allende and friendly to ITT's cause." The campaign was so enthusiastic that one ITT representative took the trouble to buttonhole Attorney General John Mitchell about the matter at a wedding reception in the Korean embassy. The company also presented the White House with an offer to "assist financially in sums up to seven figures," if it would help prevent Allende from taking office.

Two ITT officials in Latin America, Robert Berrellez and Hal Hendrix, sent a report to ITT Vice-President Gerrity indicating that the White House was backing the anti-Allende campaign. "Late Tuesday night (Sept. 15)," they wrote, "Ambassador Edward Korry finally received a message from the State Dept. giving him the green light to move in the name of President Nixon. The message gave him maximum authority to do all possible — short of a Dominican Republic-type action — to keep Allende from taking power."

The two asserted that the "key" to the ITT campaign was former Chilean President Eduardo Frei and "how much pressure the U.S. and the anti-Communist movement in Chile can bring to bear upon him in the next couple of weeks. . . ." Korry, they said, "has never let up on Frei, to the point of telling him how to 'put his pants on.'"

By October 16, eight days before the Chilean parliament was to vote on Allende's election, reported Anderson, "ITT was pinning its waning hopes on a military coup led by former Brigadier General Roberto Viaux." According to a report from Berrellez to Gerrity on that date, Viaux was told by Washington to "hold back last week. . . . As part of the persuasion to delay, Viaux was given oral assurances he would receive material assistance and support from the U.S." Viaux and twenty-four other people are currently in jail awaiting sentencing for sedition for their role in the right-wing plot in which General René Schneider was assassinated on October 22, 1970.

The plotting against Allende did not cease when he was allowed to take office. "Some of the purported ITT memorandums, discussing possible ways of dislodging Dr. Allende from power, were written after the inauguration," wrote Ted Szulc in the March 24, 1972, *New York Times*.

ITT, predictably, has denied any attempt to interfere in Chile's politics. But it has no comment on the authenticity of the documents that escaped destruction.

The State Department attempted to stand on both sides of the question at the same time. On the one hand, it asserted that the

Nixon administration had reached a decision not to block Allende's inauguration, and on the other hand, it did not deny that Korry had received a "green light" from Washington to do everything possible short of military intervention to prevent Allende from taking power.

What prompted ITT to launch its scheme was fear that it would lose its highly profitable control over the Chile Telephone Company. "This telephone company, the largest in Chile with 360,000 telephones," wrote Juan de Onís in the March 24 *New York Times,* "was one of the biggest earners in the ITT world system, regularly earning over $10-million a year."

The concession contract ITT signed in 1930 to operate the telephone company guaranteed it a 10 percent annual profit on its investment. ITT, however, in effect sold itself the equipment necessary for maintenance and expansion. According to a *Washington Post* dispatch from Santiago, a spokesman for the company, now under state control, estimated that "these sales, largely by European plants of ITT, raised the company's recent annual profits to about 25 percent of its investment."

On March 12, Allende warned, "We are being attacked both from without and from within." The Anderson revelations certainly add weight to such a warning and show the extreme measures the imperialists are willing to undertake in order to defend their interests.

A recent measure, reported by Pierre Kalfon in the March 17 *Le Monde,* is the pressure now being exerted by Braden Copper and the Anaconda Copper Company for an embargo to be placed on Chilean capital and goods in the United States, "in particular on the stocks of spare parts that are indispensable for the proper functioning of the North American mechanical equipment that has been used up to now in all the Chilean copper fields."

A Simmering Crisis in the UP

By David Thorstad

Two events of considerable significance occurred in Chile at the end of May: an emergency closed-door session of the National Committee of the Unidad Popular coalition, and elections to the CUT, the trade-union federation.

From *Intercontinental Press,* June 26, 1972

The UP "conclave," as it is being dubbed, has been going on for more than two weeks in an effort to find a way out of the crisis confronting the coalition. The crisis came to a head over the police assault on thousands of workers and students demonstrating in Concepción May 12. The Associated Press reported from Santiago June 12 that the thirteen ministers in Salvador Allende's cabinet had handed in letters of resignation. The purpose of the move, it said, was "to facilitate any changes planned by President Allende in his Popular Unity coalition." Allende can accept or reject the resignations.

Luis Corvalán, general secretary of the Communist Party, one of the major parties in the coalition, told a news conference May 24 that the situation was "very serious." He called it a "crisis in political orientation, a crisis of political leadership."

The crisis involves serious differences within the coalition over how to meet the growing threat from the right and over what course the government should follow in implementing the program of the Unidad Popular. The dispute has been brewing for months and has taken the form of several sharp polemical exchanges between the CP on one hand and the Movement of the Revolutionary Left on the other.

The MIR, which is not in the UP coalition, insists that the government should mobilize the working masses in a struggle that will ultimately destroy the bourgeois state apparatus and replace it with socialism. It calls on the coalition to fight for planks in its own program that have been abandoned, such as dissolving the Grupo Móvil, the special riot unit of the Carabinero Corps, and replacing the bourgeois parliament with a popular assembly. It has taken the initiative in mobilizing peasants to take over farm land and workers to take over factories.

The CP, on the other hand, accuses the MIR of "ultraleftism" and provocation. It insists on strict adherence to bourgeois legality. Corvalán summed up his party's position as follows: "We feel that it [present institutional legality] is a brake, that it is an obstacle to the developing revolutionary process, but not an insurmountable obstacle because up to now it has been shown that things can be accomplished within the bounds of legality and that what it is possible to accomplish depends not so much on the law as on the struggle, on the organization and mobilization of the masses, on the relationship of forces at a given moment. On the other hand, we think that no possibility exists today, at this moment, to modify this legality, this institutionality — not by any means, neither by legal means nor by extralegal means."

The MIR charges that the CP is trying to reach an accommodation with the opposition Christian Democrats as a way out of the apparent dead end facing the government coalition in the opposition-controlled legislature, and that in order to do this it needs to hold back the developing revolutionary process. The CP denies this.

Although the MIR is not in the UP coalition, its criticisms are shared, at least in part, by certain UP elements, particularly the left wing of Allende's Socialist Party. These elements do not agree with the CP's proposals to pull back from applying the program that brought the coalition to power. The pro-government magazine *Mayoría* May 31 described the differences as focusing on "a choice between moving ahead at a faster pace in applying the program or taking a breathing spell in order to consolidate what has already been won."

It was the decision of the regional leaderships of five of the UP parties in Concepción to join with the MIR in organizing the May 12 demonstration that brought the differences to a head. The differences became a crisis when the Carabineros, on direct orders from the Communist mayor, opened fire on the demonstration. The UP parties in Concepción have maintained their united front with the MIR despite official reprimands from their national leaderships.

In his state-of-the-nation speech to Congress May 21, Allende asserted that "the big question posed by the revolutionary process, and one which will decide the fate of Chile, is whether or not existing institutions will be able to open up the way for a transition to socialism." One of the aspects of the current crisis appears to be that the CP and the reformists are answering this question with an unequivocal yes, while the far left, with the support of some elements within the UP coalition itself, says no.

"We believe that the position of the MIR is hardly realistic in that it does not take into account the peculiarities of the Chilean revolutionary process," said Minister of Housing Orlando Cantuarias, a representative of the Radical Party, in an interview in the April 10 issue of *Universidad*, a student newspaper at the University of Costa Rica. "We believe that we can move toward socialism legally, staying within the system of bourgeois democracy."

The week-long elections to the CUT that ended June 6 were considered especially important because it was the first time in the almost twenty-year history of the labor confederation that its officers were elected on a one-member, one-vote basis. More than 700,000 workers, nearly one-quarter of the entire electorate, took part. The purpose of the elections was to choose seventy-three members of the National Executive Council of the CUT and thirty-five provincial representatives.

The parties in the UP coalition ran separate tickets in the elections. In addition, candidates were presented by the Christian Democrats and various leftist organizations not in the government, including the Front of Revolutionary Workers (FTR — Frente de Trabajadores Revolucionarios), which is affiliated to the MIR.

Although not all the results have yet been tabulated, the total vote for the UP parties was reported to be more than 70 percent, with the CP and SP together receiving approximately 65 percent. The June 6 issue of the Socialist Party's newspaper, *Posición,* called the elections a "vigorous defeat for the right wing within the working class."

The results were far from completely rosy, however. The opposition Christian Democrats received a surprisingly high vote, especially among public employees. But they also received a majority of the votes in the key nationalized Chuquicamata copper mine, as well as the Chilean State Bank and the state steel works at Huachipato.

Toward a Confrontation?

By Gerry Foley

"This mass of people has gathered together to tell the president of the republic that nothing and nobody can divide the democrats of Chile. We want to tell the president and the Unidad Popular Party that we are going to win two-thirds of the congressional seats in the next elections so that we can take power and tie the hands of the individuals who are destroying the Chilean nation. We will use all our legal rights to fight the government because it is incapable of giving us bread and it is incapable of giving us peace. Let this mass rally be a gigantic cry of warning to the Marxist spiders that are weaving their webs with the idea of dominating the people, let them know that we will regain power for liberty, for bread, for justice, and for the freedom of Chile."

From *Intercontinental Press,* September 11, 1972

In its August 27 issue, the reactionary Chilean daily *El Mercurio* quoted this passage from the speech of the rightist congressman Sergio Diez. Diez was speaking at a rally in Valparaíso organized to express "an energetic condemnation of the government and its economic policy that is producing scarcity."

In another passage, Diez denounced the popular front government in even more provocative terms: "You can't play games with the patience of the people or with their hunger by subjecting them to ration cards and the dictates of the Communist Party.

Immediately below its report on the Valparaíso rally, *El Mercurio* published the answer of the Political Committee of Unidad Popular to the wave of reactionary agitation that has been sweeping Chile:

"We are duty bound to advise the public that the country is experiencing moments of the most extreme gravity in which not only its institutions are in danger but even the lives of its citizens. The activity of the right and in general of all the opposition parties has reached such extremes that we can no longer have any doubt that they are seeking a real confrontation.

"Parliamentary obstruction, insults, slander, and distortion of the facts in all the news media, the incitement to violence of the rightist armed groups continually in action on the streets and in the rural areas throughout the country, and the sabotage of the government's measures are designed to produce chaos to enable the social classes that have traditionally exploited the national wealth in open partnership with imperialism to regain power. . . .

"We have avoided violence and we will not permit the right to use it with impunity. As we have repeatedly stated, the people will support revolutionary violence against reactionary violence. We condemn the Phariseeism of the right which makes democratic declarations while it organizes armed groups.

"The government and the people cannot tolerate any more murders of worker *compañeros*. We will repel outrages and assaults against our ministers. We will confront the struggle on all levels because we are sick of the cynicism and arrogance of the enemies of the people."

The events of the past weeks seem dramatic enough to justify a strong response from the popular front regime. Under the fire of imperialist reprisals and capitalist economic pressures, the government of Salvador Allende is facing a serious campaign of sabotage by the local business community as well as attempts to organize reactionary mass campaigns against the regime that could pave the way for a military coup or civil war. In an editorial August 23, the authoritative Paris daily *Le Monde* commented:

"The present situation should worry the ruling left coalition. Right-wing commandos have seized on the general strike of the shopkeepers—who have mobilized in protest against tax agents and police searching determinedly for hoarded goods and professional black marketeers—as a pretext for going into the streets.

"The authorities cannot avoid trying to impose this kind of controls, since they are faced with a growing scarcity of food-stuffs. But besides generally proving futile, these controls have shown that the government is increasingly losing its grip on the economy of the country.

With a galloping inflation following on the heels of the major wage increases won by the workers in the upsurge that brought the Unidad Popular to power and impelled the early nationali-zations, the cost of living has increased by 33 percent in the past year. In order to limit the erosion of the workers' wages, the regime has tried to impose price controls. The shopkeepers have resisted, backed by the right-wing parties and their sup-porters in the state bureaucracy.

The shopkeepers' associations seized on the death of a store owner, who died of a heart attack while his store was being searched, to declare a national strike of retailers. In answer to this call, most shops reportedly closed throughout the coun-try on August 21. In retaliation, the government ordered the police to open the shops by force. Right-wing groups took ad-vantage of these incidents to create disturbances:

"The public reacted violently against the agents sent to open the doors of closed shops," *El Mercurio* wrote, "and they were prevented from carrying out their task, being forced to flee despite police protection. . . . The public almost unanimously condemned the order to open the stores as unreasonable. Be-cause of the late hour, they said, no one could buy anything, and the situation, moreover, threatened to provoke worse dis-orders than those that caused the storekeepers' strike."

Violent incidents continued through the night of August 21-22, resulting in 300 arrests and the declaration of a state of emergency in Santiago. A dispatch in the August 23 *Le Monde* gave this description of how the fighting started: "It was toward midnight when groups of young people belonging to the extreme rightist organization Patria y Libertad came onto the streets of the capital, armed with clubs and iron bars, and tried to block traffic. Shortly afterward, groups of women and young girls from the residential areas gathered at corners beating rhythmically on pots and pans to protest against rising prices and the lack of certain consumer goods on the market."

A report in the August 23 issue of the Buenos Aires daily *La Prensa* gave some additional details: "Groups of demonstrators built barricades in some streets and lit bonfires to block traffic. Frenzied individuals tried to burn two trolleybuses; they took the seats out of one and burned them in the middle of the street."

Other groups of demonstrators tried to get at members of the government: "During the clashes, the groups roaming the streets tried to get to the homes of the minister of the economy, Carlos Matus, and the minister of labor, Mireya Baltra, but were halted by the police." Baltra, the sole woman member of Allende's cabinet, complained, however, that the rightist mob had stoned her car.

At the same time as the apparently coordinated actions of the women protesters and the rightist goon squads, the Christian Democratic-dominated student government of the University of Santiago called a strike over a campus issue.

In the meantime, farm owners, rightists, and police seemed to be stepping up their violent attacks on the workers, peasants, and homeless people who have been pressing their demands by direct action. In Puerto Montt in the far south of the country two farm owners and a bailiff invaded a peasant settlement on August 25 to take back an expropriated pump and other agricultural implements. In the course of the operation they killed a sixteen-year-old boy, Luis Hernán Rivas González, as well as a forty-seven-year-old peasant, Alberto Rivas González. Six other peasants were wounded. "The farm owners were unhurt," the August 27 *El Mercurio* reported.

In Los Angeles, another town in the south, one peasant was killed and four wounded on August 23 when rightists attacked the office of MAPU, one of the far left parties in the UP.

"The violence unleashed last Monday [August 21] following a national storekeepers' strike . . . has spread to the provinces, where the opposition has been organizing 'hunger' marches and clashes between peasants and farm owners have taken the lives of three agricultural workers," a UPI dispatch reported in the August 28 issue of *El Diario,* a Spanish-language daily published in New York.

More violence in the Chilean capital was reported September 2 in a UPI dispatch from Santiago: "Communist and Socialist militants fought rightist elements with flaming gasoline bombs, bamboo poles, rocks and fists . . . and dozens of storefronts were smashed."

In reporting the events of the fourth week in August, *El Mercurio* made it clear that the right intended to defend its interests by paramilitary force. It defended the ultrarightist goon squads in almost the same language that was used to justify the activity of the Brownshirts and the Blackshirts during the rise of fascism in Europe: "These organizations arose precisely at a time when the streets were completely dominated by the extreme left and the countryside was at the mercy of land seizures organized by the revolutionary groups of the ultraleft."

The right was clearly defying the authority of the government. And on August 25, Allende's minister of the interior, Jaime Suárez, threated to outlaw the Patria y Libertad organization and the Comando Rolando Matus of the National Party as paramilitary groups. Thus at the end of August the arena of political and social conflict in Chile seemed to be shifting rapidly from the parliament to the streets.

Unfortunately, the left government's strong words about suppressing ultrarightist provocations and paramilitary activity were contradicted by its actions. It was ironic, for example, and probably did not go unnoticed by the right, that in the very same issue in which *El Mercurio* reported the Unidad Popular's ringing evocation of "revolutionary violence," the article directly above on the reactionary rally in Valparaíso concluded with this succinct note: "As the rally ended, sections of the left provoked disturbances in the Plaza Victoria sector and the Barrio del Puerto. Large numbers of riot police acted promptly and cleared the areas where incidents occurred with tear gas and mobile water cannon."

In its August 15 issue, the MIR's biweekly, *Punto Final*, asked a pertinent question: "Who Controls the Police?"

"The events of the 'Moncada Attack' camp of homeless people have gravely disturbed the working class, showing dramatically the contradiction that exists when a government proposes to begin building socialism and at the same time retains the repressive apparatus of the bourgeois state. This repressive apparatus moves by its own weight. It was created to intimidate the dispossessed classes. Only a little push is needed, a judicial or administrative order, for its ferocity to be unleashed against the working people.

"In fact, this tendency inherent in the police apparatus operates without regard for the desires of any authorities in the
government. This tendency of the police forces aggravates
the dangerous deviation affecting the entire process. We are
referring to the counterrevolutionary factor of reformism. Those
who want to put a bit and bridle on the working class to
prevent it from moving forward have made a dogma of the
need for repressing what they disparagingly call the 'ultraleft.'

"Alien to the process of class struggle, the reformists who
occupy high positions in the government rage against anything that constitutes a defiance of their policy of imposing
their authority over everything and conciliating the bourgeoisie.

"In May, for example, they unleashed a repression in Concepción, killing one student, when the mass organizations of
almost the entire left mobilized against the reaction. The pretext
was the need to smash the 'ultraleft.' Today in Santiago, fired
up by their main preoccupation, their desire to physically
combat the revolutionary sectors inside and outside the UP,
they have murdered a worker in a fascistlike police raid."

The police raid on the Moncada Attack camp in the district of Lo Hermina in Santiago occurred August 5. *Punto
Final* described the events on the basis of accounts by the
people living in the area. "It was not yet 6:00 in the morning
when René Saravia [the peasant who was killed] left his hut
in the 'Lulo Pinochet' camp to go to work. He washed himself
at the pump. He had 2,500 escudos [equal to U.S. $12.50
on the black market]. 'He was thinking about asking permission to get off early because he had just gotten paid and was
going to get married on the eighteenth,' his cousin said.

"He was walking along the rubbish-strewn streets which were
still in semidarkness. 'It was 6:00 in the morning when we
heard the loudspeakers,' Carlos Sánchez, the delegate for Block
No. 9, explained. 'They said that as an organized camp of
homeless people we should go out to defend the government,
which was in danger, and that we had to line up outside. And
so the *compañeros* started to leave their houses, and as they
were going out the police started shooting.'

"Machine-gun bursts were sharpened by the crack of explod-
ing tear-gas grenades. With flares, the police lit up the streets
to invade the homes of the squatters, while they arrested those
who had gone out into the road." The police said that they
were looking for stolen property and weapons.

Sánchez commented: "They fired a grenade at my hut, it

broke through the roof, and the liquid fell inside. They didn't pay any attention to the fact that there are infants only a few months old in some of those huts. If the people are the government and the privileged ones are the children [as the UP slogans claim], then they [the police] don't know about it."

The August 15 *Punto Final* carried the following headline on its cover: "Only the Communist Party Approved the Atrocity in Lo Hermina." In an article entitled "Reformism Stymies the UP," the editors explained: "Reformism needs not only to assure the bourgeoisie an acceptable rate of profit and to hold off the imperialists by giving them concessions. It also needs to hold back the classes that historically are struggling for socialism, that is, the exploited. Therefore, the reformists have invented the derogatory term of 'ultraleft' for those sectors that are fighting to go forward. . . .

"It has become sufficiently clear after the tragic incident in the 'Moncada Attack' camp that reformism engenders repression, that it is capable, as a result of this, of dragging the government into the most complete isolation and leaving it at the mercy of its enemies.

"On the other hand, the peasants of Lautaro and the workers of Concepción, rising above the sorrow and rage inspired by repression under a people's government, have shown the way forward clearly — revolutionary unity. President Allende's government has legitimate claims for remaining at the head of the masses. But it must see the lesson of its errors in time. It must acknowledge that conciliating the enemies of the workers is leading it to break with the workers themselves."

The rightist offensive has come at a time when it is clear that the UP government is losing popular support. It has done badly in recent legislative by-elections, and the Christian Democrats and rightists have succeeded even in winning a third of the votes in the elections in the country's largest union, the CUT.

In answer to arguments from the CP and other reformists about the need for conciliating the "middle strata," *Punto Final* wrote in its June 6 issue: "The so-called 'middle strata,' where the Christian Democrats and its right-wing allies get most of their electoral strength, tend to support the forces that hold the power. In the last period the firmest political line presented to the masses has come from the conservative opposition led by the Christian Democrats.

"In the period from September 1970 to April 1971, when the UP was moving ahead, taking over industries, banks, ranches, nationalizing copper, nitrates, etc., these social sectors gave their support to the government. The main beneficiary of the elections was the Socialist Party. The Radical Party, a reliable political barometer, did not hesitate to call itself Marxist. The Christian Democrats suffered a new split, with the formation of the Izquierda Cristiana [Christian Left]. In a nutshell, new contingents coming from the 'middle strata' joined a current that seemed irresistible."

The main result of the government's increasingly conciliatory line, according to *Punto Final,* was that now not only had the "middle classes" moved away from the UP government but "the opposition grouped behind the Christian Democrats has shown important strength among the workers. There could not be a graver symptom of the way the reactionary strategy is winning the masses."

In the July 18 issue of *Punto Final*, Pedro Felipe Ramírez, the deputy secretary of the Izquierda Cristiana, argued that the UP leadership's course of trying to reach an agreement on a common program with the Christian Democrats was increasing the strength of the right: — ? important if true!

"Thus far the UP has wavered between the masses and the superstructure in seeking the political strength that it needs to carry the process of change forward. Many of the enterprises today in the hands of the workers were won fundamentally by appealing for the support of the masses. The institutional conflicts with the parliament, the courts, and the supervisory agencies have tended, however, to lead to confrontations in which the government has not based itself on the masses but has sought a superstructural solution. In general this confuses the masses. They can't understand why the right-wing liberals are friends one day and enemies the next.

"One day they attack the Christian Democrats and the next day they praise them. One day they say that the Chilean courts defend the interests of the ruling class and the next day they condemn the peasants who rebel against a rightist, provocative judge. How can the people know who their friends are and who their enemies are? And if the most conscious sectors of the masses are confused, what can you expect of the peasants, the shantytown dwellers, and the workers who, victims of their alienation, support the Christian Democrats and even the National Party?"

A sharp demarcation in political lines thus seems to be developing in the UP and among its supporters. The left forces in the coalition are calling for mobilizing the people and forming organizations directly representative of the masses to combat the rightist offensive. The Communist Party opposes this. One of its most sophisticated spokesmen has argued, for example, that "dual power exists in the form of a dividing line in the state apparatus." That is, the executive branch (that must mean Allende, since it obviously does not include the police) is revolutionary, while the other branches are counterrevolutionary. (See *Chile: Una Economía de Transición?* by Sergio Ramos Córdova.)

For his part, Allende has denounced the attempt to form a mass revolutionary united-front organization in Concepción as "divisive." The solution, he says, is a big vote for the UP in the 1973 congressional elections: "To overcome the roots of this political conflict, the most important thing is to win the general parliamentary elections in 1973. A popular majority in Congress will make it possible to give impetus to the institutional and legal changes necessary for freeing the country from underdevelopment and ending the power of the revanchist opposition to engage in obstruction."

The Deepening Political Polarization

By Gerry Foley

"Two years ago, on September 4, 1970, the victory of the Socialist Salvador Allende in the presidential elections seemed to have marked a turning point in the history of Latin America," *Le Monde's* correspondent Pierre Kalfon wrote from Santiago in the September 5 issue of the Paris daily. "The ballot seemed to have won out over the bullet. Now this euphoria is completely forgotten."

Kalfon gave this gloomy assessment even taking all the Unidad Popular reforms at face value. He gave Allende credit for nationalizing copper and other natural resources, eliminating the *latifundios* (large landholdings), and asserting state control over a large proportion of the monopolies and banks. All of these achievements, he claimed, were now endangered by a mounting right-wing offensive.

From *Intercontinental Press*, September 18, 1972

"A large part of the political power still eludes Allende's grasp. He controls neither the courts, the military apparatus, nor the most influential newspapers. Furthermore, economic difficulties have so tarnished the government's image that more and more people think the time has come when a final rightist offensive could be decisive."

The right-wing campaign coincides with a sudden dramatic increase in the prices of essential consumer goods. In a two-week period in August, according to the September 3 *New York Times*, the cost of cotton goods rose 90 percent and the price of cigarettes 110 percent. Chicken and sugar went up 100 percent, milk 90 percent, and beef disappeared from the markets. In attempting to impose price controls and fight speculative hoarding, the government came into a head-on clash with shopkeepers, who formed the spearhead of the rightist offensive.

"This situation," Kalfon wrote, "explains the present strategy of the Opposition, which, sensing a favorable relationship of forces, is deliberately seeking a violent confrontation."

In the sharpening polarization, the government is trying to maintain a balance between the left and the right. At the very moment the minister of the interior, Suárez, was in Concepción in the south, paying his last respects to a policeman killed during an attack on antirightist demonstrators, the reactionaries were running amuck on the streets of the Chilean capital.

"Taking the pretext of a demonstration by high-school students that took place in the morning, young extreme rightists, reinforced by lumpenproletarian elements, took over the center of the city for several hours, blocking automobile traffic, beating up passersby, stoning the windows of shops and apartment buildings, demanding that the residents 'bang their pots' as a sign of support."

The exploited masses that brought the popular front government to power demanded that Allende let them defend themselves against the ultraright thugs. "'Let us make a little expedition to teach those rich boys a lesson,' the building workers asked. 'Give us arms to defend ourselves,' the peasants demand." (They are being intimidated by gangsterlike raids by expropriated landlords.)

But the government seems to be taking another course. "Some members of the presidential entourage have confided on their personal authority," Kalfon noted, "that Allende was going to form a new cabinet where all political forces 'without any discrimination' would be represented. One of the tasks of this new cabinet would be to organize free elections after calming the tempers of the people." The French journalist commented: "The chief of state's accepting such a proposition would simply be a form of abdication."

Political "abdication," however, seemed to be exactly where Allende's conciliationist line was leading him.

"Two years after his election by a slim plurality, President Allende took the occasion of a strategy speech last night to renew his commitment to holding regular elections and abiding by the results," *New York Times* correspondent Joseph Novitski cabled from Santiago September 6. "He declared that a political solution was the only way out of the crisis and rejected the possibility of a civil war."

The "political solution" Allende seemed to mean was a UP victory in the March 1973 legislative elections. A September 6 UPI dispatch from Santiago published in the Lima daily *El Comercio* quoted the popular front president as saying: "The parliament must be in the hands of the people. It cannot be an obstacle to actions favoring the workers. . . . We must write a constitution for this stage of the revolutionary process, a constitution that would enable us to advance toward socialism."

The dispatch summarized Allende's scheme for a new constitution: "He said that it must provide for job security, must include the right of workers to run their plants, equal rights for women, the right of workers to work for the progress of the country, organize a new financial and tax system, and provide for the formation of neighborhood committees."

According to Novitski's September 6 dispatch, the reformist president also specified: "We cannot make a bourgeois constitution nor a socialist constitution. We must write a constitution that opens the road to socialism, that consecrates rights and makes it the workers who govern this country." Since a UP majority in both houses of Congress would be necessary for adopting such a constitution, Allende said: "The coming election campaign must not be seen as just another campaign. It must be kept in mind that victory would enable us to draft a new agrarian reform, a new tax and labor code. . . ."

To the supporters of his government, to the working people who are threatened by counterrevolutionary terror at the hands of rightist gangs and the police of the regime itself, who are being denied the basic necessities of life right now by the capitalist and imperialist masters of the economy, Allende offered no solution but again voting for the UP more than half a year in the precarious future. In face of the rightist offensive, even the parties of his own coalition — with a notable exception — are increasingly unwilling to accept such a passive posture.

As a result, Allende has come more and more to rely on the one reliably reformist force in the coalition, the Communist Party. In June, the president reshuffled his cabinet, strengthening the position of the CP at the expense of his own Socialist Party. In an editorial June 20, the voice of U.S. imperialism, the *New York Times*, commented:

"President Allende has moved to resolve a severe crisis within his Popular Unity coalition in Chile by rejecting the radical counsel of his own Socialist party and adopting the more moderate and conciliatory approach urged by the Communists. In thus shifting back toward the center of Chile's political spectrum, Dr. Allende has reduced the danger of large-scale civil strife and given his revamped Government its best chance to revive a sagging economy."

The editors of the *Times*, who have always presented themselves as "moderate" opponents of "Communist extremism and totalitarianism," obviously felt some embarrassment in having to praise their traditional bugaboo as the champions of "moderation" in Chile and as the best hope for restoring a "healthy business climate." But, they explained, there were much more dangerous "extremist" forces in the field, against which the Communists were proving a valuable first line of defense.

"In most countries it would be a contradiction in terms to speak of moving toward the center by adopting the Communist strategy. In Chile, however, the major Socialist faction has long been attracted to the ideas of Mao Tse-tung and Fidel Castro, and one splinter group, the Revolutionary Left Movement (M.I.R.) is openly cynical about Dr. Allende's attempt to lead the country to socialism by democratic, constitutional means.

"The Communists hurl such epithets as 'infantile' and 'elitist' at the M.I.R. and condemn its illegal seizures of farms and factories. They urge consolidation, rather than rapid extension, of the Allende Government's economic and social programs, negotiations on constitutional reform with the opposition Christian Democrats and a working relationship with private businesses. Dr. Allende has now taken this road in an effort to curb unemployment and inflation and to boost production."

In fact, the *Times* editors evidently hoped that Allende's

turn toward the CP's "conciliatory approach" had opened the way for crushing the "extremist" troublemakers.

"This decision may force the President to crack down hard on the M.I.R. in areas where it has built formidable strength; but this is infinitely preferable to a continuation of drift and polarization that carried a genuine threat of civil war or a military take-over. It should always be the objective of Chile's now-united democratic opposition not to force Dr. Allende out of office but to make his Government play by well-established rules."

The main conservative party in Chile, the Christian Democrats, appears to understand very well the strategy recommended by the editors of the *Times*. At a party meeting in March, Christian Democratic Senator Benjamín Prado said: "We are not interested in overthrowing Allende; we are interested in winning him over. And in order to do that it is essential that he remain in his post until 1976 but be left without any popular support."

Allende's turn toward a "conciliatory approach" seemed to represent a major victory for the conservatives' strategy. The price rises that opened the way for the recent rightist offensive were part of the payoff: "This month, after devaluing the escudo, Dr. Allende began authorizing price increases 'to settle the economy at a realistic new level,'" Joseph Novitski wrote in an August 24 dispatch to the *New York Times* from Santiago.

The price increases were very effective in alienating popular support from the regime.

"'Support is one thing, but making a living is another,' said a truck driver who recalled that he and his union had supported Dr. Allende for President," Novitski reported. "He had been complaining that new shock absorbers for his truck were available only on the black market at four times the official price."

But relaxing economic controls does not seem to have had any effect in pacifying the profit-hungry retailers. If anything, it seems to have strengthened their determination to defeat the government's price policy. When Allende was forced to take desperate measures against hoarders and profiteers, the shopkeepers called a "general strike of commerce" on August 21 that opened the way for the latest rightist offensive.

On the other hand, the regime's shift to the right has forced it to attack the revolutionary left, as the *Times* editors noted. And it is on this front that the decisive battle seems to be developing that will determine the future of the popular front government.

At present most of the reformists' fire seems to be centered on the MIR, which has increased its influence in the past two years. Like most of the revolutionary groups that have developed in Latin America under the impact of the Cuban Revolution, the MIR was founded on the premise that guerrilla warfare was the only effective way of fighting for national liberation against increasingly repressive forms of rule by imperialism and the native capitalists. As a corollary, the group tended to de-emphasize the importance of specific political and economic demands, stressing broad anti-imperialist slogans.

In keeping with this approach, the MIR favored voting for Allende's popular front ticket while at the same time expressing a very pessimistic view about the possibilities of his being either elected or inaugurated. When Allende did win and was allowed to take office, the MIR was confronted with a problem. Should it support the government or continue preparing for guerrilla war?

At first the MIR seemed to want to do both, and it provided Allende's bodyguard, among other things. Recently, however, the MIR has been raising sharp criticisms of the reformism of Allende and the CP and trying to offer an alternative line. Thus a very acute confrontation has been developing.

This split came into the open dramatically on May 12, two days after CP legislator Volodia Teitelboim gave a speech in the Senate blaming the "ultraleft" equally with the right for the increasing violence in the country. "There is an extreme right that traffics in arms and is aiming for a civil war. But there are also 'ultra' groups that call themselves 'left' who are following the same course, playing the role of partner in a mad waltz with their political opposites. They feed on each other. . . ."

But the Communists "are against any form of violence that might unleash a fratricidal struggle in this country. However, it takes two to make a fight and likewise you need at least two to prevent a quarrel. And in this respect we think that this is the responsibility not only of the Unidad Popular but also of the Christian Democratic Party and of all those who think deeply about the dilemma of Chile and believe that just men can save this country from being plunged into a catastrophe."

The May 23 issue of *Punto Final*, the biweekly of the MIR, described the clash that came two days after Teitelboim declared war on the "ultraleft."

"Forty-eight hours after Senator Teitelboim's speech, the governor of Concepción, Vladimir Chávez, a member of the Central Committee of the Communist Party, authorized the Grupo Móvil of the Carabineros to use force to break up a demonstration called by the workers and students of the city of Concepción. The action of the Grupo Móvil, whose dissolution was point No. 37 in the first forty points of the Unidad Popular program, cost the life of a seventeen-year-old student, Eladio Caamaño Sobarzo, and left about forty wounded, some of them seriously. Many persons were arrested, all of them activists of the left parties.

"How did it happen?

"While the registrars in Santiago were receiving signatures of electors for the formation of the Partido Viauxista de Chile [Viauxist Party of Chile, a group of supporters of the former general Roberto Viaux] — another one of the rights that the constitution grants to the rightist conspirators — in Concepción a new 'march of the empty pots' had been organized." (The first "march of the empty pots" was in Santiago in December 1971. Scarcities were used as the pretext for organizing a rightist demonstration threatening to overthrow the government.)

"As is usual in these cases, the Christian Democratic Party helped to provide a legalistic facade for the National Party and Patria y Libertad. The PDC applied to Governor Vladimir Chávez for a permit to hold an Opposition rally on Friday, May 12, and this was granted. In view of the fact that the streets and squares of Concepción, like those of other cities, were going to be taken 'legally' by the fascists, the parties of the Unidad Popular (except the CP and the API) applied for a permit to march the same day. The MIR made the same request. In what seemed a logical decision, aimed at preventing incidents, Chávez authorized only one demonstration, the march of the fascists hiding behind the PDC.

"Faced with this situation, the Socialist Party, MAPU [Movimiento de Acción Popular Unitaria — United People's Action Movement], the PR [Partido Radical — Radical Party], the Izquierda Cristiana [Christian Left] (all of which are in the UP), and the MIR met and decided unanimously to build a popular mobilization for Friday . . . that would prevent the fascists from adding the city of Concepción to their list of successes in seizing the streets. This bloc won the immediate support of the provincial council of CUT, the university and high-school student federations, the Consejo Provincial Campesino [Provincial Peasant Council], and the Comando Provincial de

Pobladores [Provincial Command of the Homeless People], of the textile and coal miners' unions, as well as other groups.

"Shortly before the fascist march began, the government ordered the permit granted to the PDC by Chávez suspended. But in any case, resorting to the 'civil disobedience' advocated by the rightist leadership of the PDC, groups of demonstrators started a march on the streets of Concepción. Advised of what was happening, the workers and students, who were holding a rally on the university grounds, came out to make their own show of force on the streets. It was then that the Grupo Móvil attacked the people with a brutality that has not been seen in Chile since the 'golden age' of the Frei government."

The Communist Party minister of the interior, Daniel Vergara, supported the action of his comrade Chávez. The Political Committee of the Communist Party issued a statement blaming the "ultraleft" for the violence. The Political Committee of the Socialist Party also opposed the united-left bloc in Concepción, expressing its disapproval of the attitude of the SP regional committee in the area.

Despite these pressures, the united-left front held together and decided to form a broader body, a People's Assembly (Asamblea del Pueblo), that could mobilize the masses of the region against the rightist offensive. The new body immediately came under heavy fire from the CP. But it was defended by a member of the Socialist Party Central Committee, Guaraní Pereda da Rosa, in an article in the August 4 issue of *Ultima Hora*, the Socialist weekly.

"On the day the body was organized, the Communist Party publicly characterized the People's Assembly as a 'masquerade' dreamed up by the 'ultraleft,' which allegedly wanted to deny arbitrarily the presence of the people in the government."

Pereda da Rosa argued that the People's Assembly did not challenge the authority of the government but proposed "by organizing the masses to offer a solution to the most acute problems facing the working people every day, problems which the people's government is prevented from dealing with effectively by the existing state institutions." He denied that the body was an "artificial creation," pointing to the popular support it had won.

"Besides the support of the four UP parties already mentioned (the SP, PR, MAPU, and the IC) and of the MIR, the People's Assembly has the support of sixty unions, including the Sindicato Unico de la Compañía de Acero del Pacífico

[Pacific Steel Company United Union], the four textile workers' unions, various coal miners' unions, the brewery workers, various lumbermen's unions, public health workers, the coopers, and others. Five peasant organizations have joined, thirty-one camps of homeless people, sixteen student organizations, and twenty-seven mothers' cooperatives. In all there are five political organizations and 139 mass organizations representing workers, peasants, homeless people, and students.

"Was this an 'arbitrary' act as the Communist student leader said, or a 'fiction' as it is called by the daily *Clarín*, or a 'harebrained notion' in the words of Senator Montes? These words are aimed at tens of thousands of workers, students, and housewives, represented by the 5,000 persons who packed the Teatro Concepción July 27 to confirm the authority of the assembly.

"Of course, it cannot be denied that the People's Assembly organized in Concepción was not all that it could have been. One people's party, the Communist Party, which represents a substantial sector of the working class in this area and in the country, which has unquestionable weight and responsibility in the revolutionary process Chile is experiencing, did not participate in this event. No Chilean revolutionist, no people's organization can accept this, or still less, be gratified by it. This is why the regional leadership of the SP and the other UP parties have repeatedly appealed to the Communists to come into the assembly.

"But neither can we allow the majority of the UP to be called 'splitters' because they did not agree with the CP's negative view of the People's Assembly. As the Regional Secretariat of the SP maintains, 'when one party thinks it is in command of the process it is very difficult to preserve unity.' "

Despite such statements from leading members of his own party, Allende followed up the attacks of the CP, launching a violent denunciation of the People's Assembly in a statement issued July 31. He seemed to have borrowed his style of argument from his allies:

"The people of Chile are facing a powerful enemy who uses modern techniques against them. And every member of the Unidad Popular, as well as every sympathizer of the national cause not active in the parties of the UP, must realize this. The enemy studies our weaknesses and exploits them. He is able, for example, to give indirect financial aid to any adventure, or exercise a psychological influence on any person who, impelled by impatience that comes from a low ideological level, splits away from the collective struggle to carry out individual actions. . . .

"For the second time in three months in the province of Concepción a divisionist phenomenon has developed, disrupting the unity of the Unidad Popular movement. I do not hesitate to characterize it as a deformed process that is aiding the enemies of the revolutionary cause. . . .

"The enemy has sought and insists on creating an artificial confrontation dividing the country in struggles whose ramifications the participants themselves cannot foresee. Nothing would suit him better for this purpose than an artificial confrontation within the Unidad Popular.

"I have said that there is no clash between the branches of the Chilean government, and that the executive branch is facing a political conflict created by those persons who from the positions they hold in the other branches of government are exceeding their powers and violating the constitution in order to block our historic mission. . . .

"To overcome the roots of this problem I have set the main objective as winning the 1973 general elections for parliament. . . .

"People's power will not come from a divisionist maneuver by people who are using political romanticism to create a lyrical mirage, which, out of touch with all reality, they call the People's Assembly."

Some elements in the UP responded very strongly to Allende's attack. The reply of the IC (Christian Left), for example, was published in the August 6 issue of *La Nación*: "The government and the parties must recognize the dynamic of the masses themselves who are struggling to defend their interests and to press for changes in the bourgeois state institutions."

The most consistent supporters of the People's Assembly seemed to be the MIR. They proposed not only to use the assembly as a means for mobilizing the masses to resist rightist intimidation and pressures; they also presented a concrete program around which the assembly could organize the people to smash the power of the bourgeoisie and the imperialists and begin fighting immediately against the reactionary sabotage of the country's economic life. The main points of the MIR program were:

"1. Expropriation of the big industrial, commercial, and financial bourgeoisie. Incorporation into the nationalized sector of all companies with a capital of more than 14 million escudos [the official rate is 49 escudos per dollar; the black-market rate is 200]. Unconditional defense of the confiscations, interventions, and nationalizations already carried out.

"2. Expropriation without compensation and in the shortest time possible of U.S. capital in industry, finance, and commerce.

"3. Expropriation without compensation, without leaving any 'reserves' or loopholes, of all the estates of the big agrarian bourgeoisie.

"4. The establishment of workers' control in big private industry, in medium and small industry, and on the estates of the middle bourgeoisie.

"5. Workers' control and management in state enterprises, in the public services, and in the rest of the economy.

"6. Support of all kinds, under the conditions of workers' control, to the small and middle bourgeoisie in the countryside, in the cities, and in commerce.

"7. Organizing the people in the local areas to form Local Workers' Councils [Consejos Comunales de Trabajadores] in the countryside and in the cities.

"8. Preparing the conditions for dissolving the parliament and creating a People's Assembly in its place."

To organize the fight against capitalist economic pressures, the MIR raised the following immediate demands: Payment of a special bonus semiannually, or every time the cost of living rises by more than 5 percent, as a means of readjusting wages and salaries. Immediate payment of the retroactive cost-of-living increases. The adoption of measures that would make it possible to eliminate unemployment and underemployment in the countryside and in the cities.

The MIR program was published in late July. Facing the escalation of the rightist offensive and the catastrophic price increases of August, the National Secretariat of the MIR updated these demands. On August 28, it issued the following demands:

"(a) Immediate readjustment of wages and salaries by 100 percent to cover the increase in the cost of living, with preference given to the most poorly paid workers. Readjustment of wages every time the cost of living rises more than 5 percent. It is to be understood that this does not limit the legitimate struggles of the workers to win increasing shares of the profits from their bosses. Moreover, we call for establishing state outlets at which the basic necessities would be sold at subsidized prices, giving preference to the poorest strata who lack stable employment.

"(b) Workers' control in the companies of the private sector, on the basis of opening the books of businesses and banks. Workers' management in state enterprises.

"(c) Control by the people over supply and prices, including, if necessary, rationing of the basic necessities. This control should be applied by the unions, the JAPs [Juntas de Abastecimiento y Control de Precios — Supply and Price Control Boards], neighborhood groups, and other mass organizations represented in the Local Workers' Councils.

"(d) The establishment of a consumer market basket of basic products whose prices would not be allowed to rise. Discriminatory price rises on those products consumed by the well-to-do strata. A price policy that would effectively transfer resources from the private to the nationalized sector.

"(e) Immediate expropriation of the big wholesalers and big retail traders.

"(f) Expropriation of the industrial big bourgeoisie. Only the people can produce for the people.

"(g) Expropriation of ranches of more than forty hectares without leaving any 'reserves' or loopholes, with the land being handed over immediately to the peasants, under the direction of the Local Peasant Councils [Consejos Comunales Campesinos].

"(h) Workers' control over the means of mass communication in order to stop the campaign of terrorizing the people by creating fears about scarcities.

"(i) Immediate suspension of payment on the foreign debt to the U.S. and the opening of bilateral negotiations with those countries ready to cooperate with Chile. We need our dollars to feed the people."

The MIR program ended with an appeal for worldwide support: "We call on all peoples and in particular the socialist countries to show internationalist solidarity with the struggle of the Chilean people."

Allende Declares a "State of Emergency"

By Gerry Foley

"At about 3:00 a.m. on an ordinary day, the telephone rang in a house in the Pedro de Valdivia section of the well-to-do Barrio Alto residential area of Santiago. A housewife heard a voice at the other end say that a 'No. 3 alarm' had been issued. The sleepy woman left her bedroom and immediately began to fill the bathtub with water, while she shouted to wake up the rest of the family. She reminded her husband that a 'No. 3 alarm' called for getting the car ready to leave immediately.

"An hour later, while the house was kept in semidarkness, according to the instructions, the telephone rang again. The same voice said: 'The danger is over.' The woman went to empty the bathtub, and the household quickly returned to normal."

An article in the October 10 issue of *Punto Final*, the biweekly magazine of the MIR, explained the meaning of this incident: "The voice on the telephone belonged to one of the home vigilance squads of Proteco, the acronym for the fascist organization Protección a la Comunidad [Community Protection], which is the cover for one of the apparatuses that have been created in Chile to organize those actively opposing the Allende government."

The MIR organ described how middle-class areas have been tightly organized and whipped up to a fever pitch of anticommunist fanaticism by well-organized gangs:

"The terror imposed by the fascists is so great that some people are firing their maids, in the first place because they are afraid that they're 'giving information to the enemy,' and secondly because they are turning the servants' quarters into refrigerated places to keep hoarded food. 'We are prepared for civil war,' these people say."

Since August the right-wing opponents of Allende, both inside and outside the state apparatus, have mounted increasing pressure on the popular front regime. In this campaign they have been able to exploit popular discontent created by rising prices

From *Intercontinental Press*, October 23, 1972

for consumer goods and shortages of essential items. Faced
with imperialist economic reprisals and the sabotage of local
capitalists, retailers, and big farmers, the government has found
itself in worsening economic difficulties.

Trying to remain within the framework of capitalist legality,
Allende has been unable either to take decisive measures
against rightist subversion or to meet the demands of
the masses whose hopes for a better life were aroused by the
popular front's victory on September 4, 1970, and who have
been hardest hit by rising prices and shortages. This September alone, prices rose by more than 22 percent.

In the second week of October, the pressures on the Allende
government jumped to a new level. A nationwide truck strike
beginning October 10 brought serious shortages of gasoline
and flour, forcing the regime to declare martial law in an area
from Valparaíso province, 85 miles north of the capital, to
Bío-Bío province, 315 miles to the south. About 70 percent
of the population lives in this belt.

The truckers' strike was touched off when the government
refused to meet the demands of the Confederation of Truck
Owners for higher cargo rates. According to an October 12
UPI dispatch, the owners were also unhappy about a state
trucking company being set up in the south of the country.

In an effort to stop the strike, which threatened to halt the
supply of bread, among other things, the government ordered
the arrest of Leon Vilarín, the president of the confederation,
along with 160 owners and drivers. In this case, the undersecretary of the interior, Daniel Vergara, invoked the internal
security law against subversion.

On October 12, the small businessmen's, retailers', builders',
and large farmers' associations declared a strike in sympathy
with the truckers. "Jorge Fontaine, president of Chile's Confederation of Production and Commerce, speaking on behalf
of all the sympathy strikers, said the walkout would begin
tomorrow and continue for an indefinite period," UPI reported
October 12 from Santiago. It was a small businessmen's strike
that provoked the last crisis of the regime in August.

During the night of October 13-14, the government seized
all of the radio stations in the country, reportedly to prevent
the rightists from spreading alarmist rumors. The regime and
its supporters have often complained about right-wing stations
and commentators inciting fears of coming shortages and of
"Communist atrocities."

Just after midnight on October 13, Allende broadcast a message denouncing fascists and profascists who, he said, were trying to paralyze Chile. But "he also called on the Government's left-wing supporters to abstain from any moves — such as the occupation of factories, communications centers, or public buildings — that could be interpreted as a 'provocation' and cause the army to stand against the Government," an AP dispatch reported.

Allende had good reason to worry about the attitude of the army. The state of emergency decreed by the under secretary of the interior, a member of the Communist Party, put the military in effective control of the country. "Gen. Héctor Bravo, the commander of the Santiago garrison who is in charge of the state of emergency in the capital, warned that any public meetings or disorders would be dissolved 'with utmost energy,'" AP reported October 13.

In its anxiety to defend itself by "constitutional" means, the popular front government denied freedoms not only to the militant right but to the left and to the workers' and people's organizations. Moreover, since the state apparatus remains fundamentally under bourgeois control and the right is already well organized, these restrictions can be expected to be much more effective against the left than against the reactionary opponents of the regime. In fact, by ordering harsh administrative measures against the rightists and at the same time repressing the masses and preventing them from taking control of the society, Allende risked infuriating the petty-bourgeois layers supporting the paramilitary right and, in the last analysis, leaving himself defenseless against them.

One of the dangers facing the country was pointed out by Edgardo Enríquez, a member of the Political Committee of the MIR, in the October 10 *Punto Final*: "Historical experience shows that while fascist movements develop in prerevolutionary situations, or situations with prerevolutionary features, it is no less true that fascism can only grow and spread in a situation where there is a prolonged and persistent working-class upsurge but where, because of a vacillating and conciliationist policy by the reformist political leaderships of the popular movement, the workers fail to take power into their own hands."

Another danger facing the popular front government was pointed up by a speech of Senator Benjamín Prado at the March leadership meeting of the Christian Democratic Party: "We are not interested in overthrowing Allende, we are interested in winning him over. And in order to do that it is essential that he remain in his post until 1976 but be left without any popular support." The Christian Democratic strategy expressed by Prado corresponds to what seem to be the main objectives of Washington, to wear down and discredit this unstable leftist regime without at the same time destroying the credibility of the "peaceful road to change."

The Army Moves to the Fore
By David Thorstad

"'Has Chile's moment of truth arrived?' In Santiago, this question is being asked with some uneasiness in all political circles," Pierre Kalfon reported in the October 18 *Le Monde*. "The truckers' strike launched last week is, in reality, a political strike against the government much more than it is a simple trade-union strike; by now, this is admitted.

"From the very beginning, this movement, marked by highway barricades, has been severe, and it has had spectacular effects: no more gas, and therefore no more shipping of goods in a country where the railroad network is not very developed and where the highway, which stretches out over 3,000 kilometers from the north to the south, plays an economic role of the first order. The scarcity of basic food products — milk, sugar, rice, etc. — has suddenly increased, and lines have appeared in front of bakeries as well as gas stations.

"The tactic being followed by the opposition is to spread this strike to the point where the entire country will be paralyzed and the helplessness of the government demonstrated."

Luis Corvalán, general secretary of the Communist Party, the strongest member of the Popular Unity coalition, stated that "the patriotic task is to keep the country going." Thousands of Allende supporters, Kalfon reported, have responded to this appeal from the government. "While the government anxiously wonders how far its opponents will go," he continued, "all the parties of the left are in a state of alert. The CUT has asked its members to work more than ever to prevent the bosses from closing the factories. More than 17,000 volunteers — among them many students — have offered to drive or unload the 400 trucks loaded with goods that the government has already requisitioned."

From *Intercontinental Press*, October 30, 1972

For the activists of the MIR the slogan is: "Turn every factory, every farm, and every shantytown into a stronghold of struggle against fascism."

On October 12, two days after the truckers' strike plunged Chile into the most serious crisis since the Allende regime took office, the main opposition party, the Christian Democrats, issued an official statement blaming the government for anything that might happen: "At the moment, the country is going through an extremely tense situation for which the government is responsible. The facts show categorically that it will not be possible to return the country to calm unless the serious errors reflected in the present regime's conduct are rectified." The Christian Democrats stated their "support for the just demands of the truckers' union" and warned that failure of the government to yield could "precipitate a conflict of incalculable proportions."

"The statement said that Allende's declaration of a state of emergency — announced the same day — revealed the political weakness of his regime and its need to rely on the army: "The government has chosen to heat up the conflict through repression, and it is once again masking its incompetence by shifting the responsibility for maintaining public order onto the armed forces while, at the same time, persons in official positions are crudely inciting certain sectors of the population to disrupt it."

The Christian Democratic Party could hardly claim to be a mere commentator on the mounting crisis, however, for the Confederation of Truck Owners, which initiated the strike, is affiliated to the party. And any strike that threatened to halt the flow of goods, including the supply of bread, could be expected to upset "public order." Even the right-wing, anti-Allende daily *El Mercurio* noted this in an editorial in its October 9-15 international edition. The paper admitted that "under the circumstances, it cannot be considered strange" that the government invoked the state internal security law and arrested more than 200 truck drivers and union leaders. Indeed, it added, the truck drivers' leaders "had anticipated the government's reaction." By week's end, a thousand truck drivers had been arrested.

On October 13, a sympathy strike by small businessmen began, further heating up the crisis. The strike was called by the Confederation of Production and Commerce — also controlled by the Christian Democratic Party.

The opposition decided October 15 to step up its campaign. The Christian Democratic unions announced their intention to continue the strike, and the party itself issued a virtual declaration of war against Allende. Renán Fuentealba, the head of the Christian Democratic Party, called on its members to "pass from a state of alert to a state of mobilization." In the unions, a call to "resistance" was issued.

The opposition is demanding that the leaders of the truck drivers be freed and that the government accede to the demands of their confederation. These include granting higher cargo rates and giving up plans to set up a state trucking company in the south of the country.

As the crisis unfolded, the state of emergency, originally applied to thirteen of the country's twenty-five provinces, was extended to include others. On October 17, Brigadier General Héctor Bravo Muñoz, the commander of the Santiago garrison, declared a curfew from midnight to 6:00 a.m. in the capital of 3,000,000 and the surrounding province.

The strikes continued to pick up momentum, reported *New York Times* correspondent Joseph Novitski October 17. "Civil engineers, some bank employes, some university and high school students and the officers and crews of Chile's largest private shipping line joined the wave of strikes that began with a nationwide work stoppage by truck owners early last week.

"Doctors and dentists announced a 48-hour strike beginning tomorrow and the country's shopkeepers kept the metal shutters down on most urban stores except food stores, pharmacies on duty and occasional automotive repair shops."

Many shops that stayed open were forced by street disturbances to close anyway, according to United Press International.

While Allende has appealed to the left to refrain from any actions that might "provoke" the army to take a stand against the government, the opposition has kept tensions high by ignoring the ban on demonstrations. On October 16, for instance, police in Santiago used tear gas and water hoses to break up a demonstration led by former President Jorge Alessandri, leader of the right-wing National Party. "Although drenched, Mr. Alessandri continued walking to his destination, the building housing both the United States Embassy and his own company, a paper-manufacturing concern," reported the Associated Press. "The incident drew a large crowd, and Mr. Alessandri was loudly cheered. He was also showered with ticker tape from offices above the street."

The strike wave was joined October 20 by owners of private

buses in Santiago and by pilots of the national airlines. At the same time, the movement was given greater political focus by a joint statement by the five opposition political parties endorsing all the protest strikes and blaming the government for what they called "total chaos" in the economy.

The government was able to avert a strike in public transportation October 18, Novitski reported, but it owed this victory to the fact that the agreement was "reached under army auspices." By forcing Allende to fall back on the army for support, the opposition appears to be succeeding in its aim of further undermining the strength of his Popular Unity regime as the campaign for the March 1973 legislative elections gets under way. Although some elements in the opposition may be hoping to provoke the army into toppling Allende, this does not appear — right now at least — to be the aim of the Christian Democrats. They seem to prefer for the moment to force Allende to "rectify his errors" and reach some kind of agreement with the opposition to go even slower on implementing the Popular Unity program.

"This is a middle-class movement, with support from the upper class," Jaime Castillo, a political analyst for the Christian Democratic Party, told Novitski. "It does not extend to the proletariat." He said that the aim of what one paper called "a strike by the bourgeoisie against the workers" is not, for the time being, "to overthrow Allende, or make him renounce his program, but to put him back in his place: within the Constitution and using only laws to carry out his program. We're giving him an opportunity to manage the situation, to talk to the Opposition." Some opposition strategists appear reluctant to stage a showdown at this time for fear that Allende's support is still too strong and that the role of the army might be unpredictable. "It's absurd to think of overthrowing Allende now," one opposition politician told Novitski. "It would be all out of proportion with the causes of the crisis, and an attempt might put the army on his side once and for all."

Government supporters are concerned, however, and have described the strike wave as part of a concerted effort to overthrow Allende. "We all agreed that this is an escalation of sedition, a coup d'état in the making," Luis Corvalán said October 16. He added that this "will not bear fruit, because the armed forces are faithful to the law and to the legitimately constituted government."

Allende finds himself in a rather tight bind as a result of his dogged adherence to the norms of bourgeois law. Thus, while on the one hand his government issued an appeal to "the people" to "respond with organization, unity, and mobilization to the provocations of the seditious right," on the other hand it stripped the working class of its right to mobilize by placing the country under a form of martial law. Meanwhile, the right continues to mobilize in open violation of the law, and the popular front government urges the working masses to trust not in their own strength, but in the generals who command the bourgeois armed forces.

In an editorial October 16, the *New York Times* warned that if Allende wants to weather this latest storm, it will be necessary for him to make important concessions to the opposition. Allende, the influential imperialist newspaper advised, "should stand up to the extremists in his camp, relax the repression and revive political dialogue with the Christian Democrats and other democratic forces. That course will inevitably involve major compromises on the Popular Unity program; but it offers the best insurance both of his own survival and the survival of Chile in freedom and peace."

The current anti-Allende campaign was launched at the same time that the American-owned Kennecott Copper Company was opening up an offensive against sales of Chilean copper in the international arena. The offensive, noted *Le Monde* in an editorial October 13, "seems to enjoy at least the tacit approval of the United States government."

Kennecott (whose subsidiary, Braden Copper, was part owner of Chile's largest copper mine, El Teniente, before it was expropriated by a unanimous vote in the opposition-controlled Congress in 1971) claims that the $80 million it was paid was inadequate compensation for its holdings. It is seeking court orders in Europe blocking payment by European customers to the Chilean Copper Company, Codelco. It has already won one such order in Paris, and is threatening to seek another in Sweden, where a delivery of 1,500 tons of copper is expected in November. The Paris court order barring payment of $1.3 million to Chile for 1,250 tons of copper originally scheduled to arrive in Le Havre October 15 amounted to legal piracy with a bourgeois touch. Not only has no bourgeois court ever handed down such a ruling preventing, say, the shipment of U.S. weapons to Vietnam, but it came at a time when the bourgeoisie is mounting a hue and cry over air piracy. Chile is appealing the ruling.

Out of solidarity with Chile, Le Havre dockworkers refused to unload the copper from the West German freighter *Birte*

Oldendorff. In view of this the ship proceeded to Rotterdam — where the Dutch Transport Workers Union instructed its dock workers to also refuse to unload the ship. "The instructions are to follow the example of the dockworkers of Le Havre, France, who said they would not touch the tainted copper," announced Martinus Loef, a spokesman for the longshoremen in Utrecht.

Kennecott's legal offensive, noted Clyde Farnsworth in the October 17 *New York Times,* "has been timed for what is known in the trade as 'the mating season,' when buyers and sellers get together to make their contracts for the following year. Kennecott is thus challenging not only present deliveries but also future contracts."

Allende's Concessions
Fail to Halt the Crisis

By David Thorstad

Faced with a continuing nationwide crisis that erupted when truckers went out on strike October 10, President Allende decided the night of October 17-18 to grant three concessions to the strikers. According to a report in the October 19 issue of *Le Monde,* these were: to return requisitioned trucks to their owners; to withdraw charges of subversion against the main leaders of the Confederation of Truck Owners, thus releasing them from jail; and to recognize the "private nature" of the transportation companies. The last concession appeared to remove the bone of contention that had helped set off the strike wave — the government's plan to form a state trucking company in the south, whose competition the private companies feared.

But the government's concessions failed to induce the opposition, spearheaded by the Christian Democrats, to call off its attempt to engulf the country in chaos and paralysis. On the contrary, on October 21 a whole series of new and explicitly political demands were raised, clearly revealing the ultimate aim of the opposition: to force Allende to abandon his policy of nationalization and to turn him into a captive of the opposition and the army.

From *Intercontinental Press,* November 6, 1972

The escalated list of demands was presented to the government by a "national command" representing a whole series of organizations: truck owners, merchants, associations of manufacturers and construction magnates, professional groups, landholders, taxi drivers, Catholic University students, students in private educational institutions, etc. The list included most of the demands the opposition has been raising over the past few months, among them the following: return to their owners of all factories taken over by the state since August 21; elimination of the Juntas de Abastecimiento y Control de Precios (JAPs—neighborhood watchdog committees on food supplies and price controls) and the Committees for the Defense of the Revolution; adoption of the opposition's constitutional reform measure forbidding any state take-over without prior approval from Congress; expulsion of foreign "extremists" from the country; a promise not to create a unified banking institution; a lifting of the price ceiling imposed on Papelera, the newsprint producer controlled by the right wing; and an end to the silencing of radio stations (the government has closed down more than a dozen for six-day periods for broadcasting "alarmist" information).

"The government is pretty much being asked to retreat and in large part to abandon the legal means it still has at its disposal in its attempt to begin the 'passage to socialism' called for in its program," wrote Pierre Kalfon in the October 24 issue of *Le Monde*. On October 27, Allende announced that he had broken off talks with leaders of the middle-class unions involved in the continuing strike because "they want political concessions that would limit his constitutional powers," according to the Associated Press. "I cannot accept that," Allende said in a nationwide television address.

The opposition has resorted to other methods than escalating its list of grievances in order to maintain the momentum of its movement. On October 24, for instance, it called on the Chilean people to stay at home and observe a "day of silence." "With our silence we want the government to hear the loud voice of the malcontents," said a spokesman for the Democratic Confederation. The confederation consists of the five center and conservative parties in the parliamentary opposition: the Christian Democrats, the National Party, the Party of the Radical Left, the Democratic National Party, and the Radical Democracy. United Press International reported that the call for the day received a "mixed response" but "failed to paralyze" activity in Santiago.

On October 29, the Democratic Confederation made public its decision to bring a motion of censure against four ministers in Allende's cabinet. It is taken for granted that the motion will be passed, since the opposition controls both houses of Congress. In that case, the four would have to resign. The ministers, who are being charged with "repeatedly infringing the constitution and the law," are Jaime Suárez (Socialist), minister of the interior; Carlos Matus (Socialist), economics minister; Jacques Chonchol (Christian Left), minister of agriculture; and Aníbal Palma (Radical), minister of education. It has already been announced that Palma and Suárez plan to resign before November 4, the deadline to declare candidacies in the legislative elections scheduled for next March.

Although the strike has continued, with daily incidents of street violence provoked by demonstrating opposition forces, Allende seemed optimistic at a news conference for foreign journalists October 21. A major reason for his optimism was no doubt the response of the workers and broad layers of students to what the government is calling the "strike by the bourgeoisie." "No factory has closed its doors," reported Kalfon. "The railroads, the ports, the mines, and the public services continue to function normally. Workers and students, activists and the unaffiliated, have stepped forward to insure the distribution of food to the population, beginning with the poor sectors on the outskirts of the cities."

Allende's tone at the news conference contrasted considerably with his warning a few days earlier that the country was on the verge of civil war. "We are no longer on the brink of civil war," he said, "because the vast majority have understood that the seditious actions of a small group could be crushed without the use of violence. If we wanted, we could bring a hundred thousand or a hundred and fifty thousand people here. The slightest signal would be enough to bring in fifteen or twenty thousand workers from the industrial suburbs of Santiago to open up Santiago's stores. We told them not to do so. The strength of this government lies in respect for the constitution and the law."

A key "strength" of Allende's Popular Unity government at the moment, however, is the military, in whose hands he placed administrative authority over most of the country's provinces when he declared a state of emergency. This prevented any mass effort whatever by progovernment and working-class forces to combat the right-wing offensive. In the past, Allende has always denounced plots against his government by warning that "the people will answer any provocation." "But the nearest approximation of 'The people' on the streets this time were the middle class strikers who risked their civil-service jobs to demonstrate against the government that paid them," observed Lewis Duiguid in the October 26 *Washington Post.* During the previous week, he noted in a report October 25, "Allende has averaged more than one public statement per day in high praise of the Chilean military." There are persistent reports in Santiago that high-ranking military officers may soon enter the Chilean cabinet.

Although the military continues to pledge loyalty to Allende, pressures on it to act are increasing. "Sources close to Dr. Allende show signs not only of worry about the eroding popularity of his government, but more importantly about the Army and its potential for action," wrote James Nelson Goodsel in the October 27 *Christian Science Monitor.* In the city of Valparaíso, reported Everett Martin in the October 24 *Wall Street Journal,* "some people have taken to throwing kernels of corn on the steps of the local regimental headquarters — a not-too-subtle gesture to suggest that the army is 'chicken' for not acting against the government."

The Workers Move Forward — as Allende Retreats

By Gerry Foley

"We found out that a joint military and civilian cabinet had been formed. Nobody consulted us. Why? We poor people in the cities and the countryside have been good enough for some things. . . . If we had not been prepared, if we had not been ready, our *compañero presidente* would have had to pack his bags as fast as Goulart [ex-president of Brazil] did, as fast as rulers must who do not have the people behind them. But we were there, producing, transporting, guarding, distributing, organizing so that the country wouldn't shut down. We were there for the twenty-seven days of the crisis. If this isn't true, let our *compañero presidente* say so. It was the physical presence of millions of workers that kept him in power. It was we who kept him in power. The armed forces and deft maneuvering are good for many things, very significant things. But they cannot maintain a government without popular support. It was us, Comrade Allende."

This was the comment of *Aurora de Chile*, voice of the Socialist Party's left wing, on the governmental changes that ushered in a shaky truce after the "bosses' strike" against the popular front regime of Salvador Allende. It appeared in an article entitled "Letter to Ourselves" in the November 9 issue, which contrasted the triumph of the workers who mobilized to defeat the capitalist-sponsored attempt to paralyze the country, on one hand, with the surrender of the president and the Unidad Popular parties, on the other.

On the night of November 2, after more than three weeks in which the workers had mobilized to run the economy themselves, Allende announced that he was handing over three key positions in his cabinet to high-ranking military officers. The chief of the armed forces, General Carlos Prats, was given the Ministry of the Interior, and with it direct authority over the police and local government. The Ministry of Public Works and Transport was handed over to Admiral Ismael Huerta, and the Ministry of Mines to General Claudio Sepulveda. Both are vital to the economy. At the same time, the Ministry of Agriculture went to Rolando Calderón, the general secretary of the country's main union federation, the CUT, and the Ministry of Labor to Luis Figueroa, a CUT leader and a member of the Communist Party. The Ministry of Justice portfolio is held by Sergio Insunza, another member of the Communist Party.

Thus the most politically sensitive posts went to representatives of the government parties, while the positions of real power were taken by the military.

The Socialist Party reportedly opposed giving the Ministry of the Interior to General Prats. But this rumor was denied by Party Secretary Carlos Altamirano who said, according to the November 17 issue of the Montevideo weekly *Marcha*: "The Socialist Party has never objected to the presence of uniformed men in the cabinet. That is a prerogative of the president."

The weekly magazine *Chile Hoy*, which reflects the "main-

stream" of the UP coalition,* saw the new cabinet as the product
of a deft and rather exciting new political combination. *Chile
Hoy* quoted a statement by Radomiro Tomic, the 1970 presidential candidate of the Christian Democrats, and noted ap-
provingly that that moderate standard-bearer saw a possibility
of the Chilean military following the "Peruvian path." "It was
Radomiro Tomic who was to cool the illusions of a section
of the reactionaries. . . . He recalled in the same statement,
widely published in the press, that 'there are already strong
governments in our America that have set out on other roads
to socialism than the Cuban or Chilean. . . . What will happen
here. . . ? Who knows?'"

The same issue of *Chile Hoy* carried an interview with the
new minister of the interior, illustrated with five pictures of
the uniformed general assuming different profiles. "The incorporation of three leaders of the armed forces into the Unidad
Popular government is the most important political development since Salvador Allende assumed the presidency on November 4, 1970," the magazine wrote. "It was important first of all
because the inclusion of the military officers in the cabinet
brought an abrupt end to the strike that for twenty-six days
turned into the most serious challenge from the opposition
in the two years of the people's government."

It was noted that Prats received his military education at
the U.S. armed forces officer training school at Fort Leaven-
worth, Kansas. The magazine profusely praised the general's
political acumen, without speculating on where he received his
political training: "Not even in a country so jealous of its
'traditions of noninvolvement' of the military in politics does it
seem logical that a man could reach such a high level in the
armed forces hierarchy without possessing political gifts. In
his first acts as minister of the interior, General Prats has
shown that he has a very fine political touch. Immediately after
taking his post, he skillfully turned around the inevitable question of whether the entry of the military into the cabinet meant
a compromise between the armed forces and the UP. 'It is not

---

* *Chile Hoy* served as a weather vane for judging the thinking of the leadership of the Allende government. Its publisher
was a member of the Socialist Party right wing; her editorial
policy was very sympathetic to the Communist Party. The
magazine also provided an occasional forum for viewpoints
to the left of its editors.

a political compromise but patriotic cooperation in the interests of social peace. . . .'"

Further on, *Chile Hoy* returned to this theme: "But without doubt the moment General Prats really demonstrated his political talents was in his comments at his first press conference as minister of the interior. Before replying to reporters, he made a statement that was as precise, subtly turned, and, above all, as clear and coherent as the most experienced political leader could offer. The same was true of his answers." In its report of Prats's press conference, *Chile Hoy* wrote that the new minister of the interior had been "surprisingly hard, especially in dealing with the equivocations of the rightist press about the way the strike was settled." The magazine asked its readers to judge for themselves how cleverly the general answered its questions.

Some of the general's answers were clearly very carefully formulated, but they did not seem unprecedented for a military officer in his position. For example, when asked about CUT participation in the cabinet, he said: "This is a solution well suited to the present circumstances. The workers of the country have given an example of great civic responsibility during the strike campaign, and their social consciousness of the need for order and their dedication to production merit the respect of the military. The army has no class fixations. Its cadres reflect the social reality of Chile because they are drawn proportionately from the various levels of the national community." The magazine made no comment on this classical justification of the bourgeois armed forces playing the role of arbiter in social crises, an arbiter that has always resolved these crises in the interests of the dominant class.

On another sensitive issue, it also did not question Prats's position. *Chile Hoy* asked the general if he intended to apply the new arms control law to the right-wing groups. Prats answered: "I don't distinguish among armed groups. The spirit of the arms control law is to guarantee the public peace. It calls for removing the weapons banned by the law and taking them away also from authorized persons who do not observe the regulations for registering and carrying them, no matter who they are. Naturally, my duty is to enforce the law." Apparently this was reassuring enough for *Chile Hoy*. It did not defend the workers' right to bear arms as the only guarantee of their conquests.

In assessing the reaction of the right to the new cabinet,

the magazine pointed up what it thought was the discomfiture of the conservatives in the face of Allende's new formula. "In a public statement, Patria y Libertad called on 'all Chileans without exception to remain on the alert against this new Communist strategy.'"

The Patria y Libertad statement did say: "The composition of the cabinet does not indicate a desire to correct mistakes but rather the clear aim of pursuing a wrong and unpopular policy." But the editorial in the November 9 issue of the group's paper, also called *Patria y Libertad*, offered a more rounded view, which was apparently overlooked by *Chile Hoy* in its enthusiasm for Allende's "daring" maneuver:

"Unfortunately, the presence of the armed forces in the cabinet is no more than a temporary refuge in time of crisis. In fact, the presence of uniformed men in the new cabinet is, we repeat, a guarantee for non-Marxist Chileans. But side by side with the officers are outstanding representatives of extremist views who have gravely endangered the constitutional order. The coexistence between intransigent Marxist-Leninists . . . and high-ranking officers seems likely to be difficult and even impossible. *One group will try to continue the transitional program leading the country to Marxist socialism through expropriations, interventions, or seizures, seeking sanction only in legal loopholes or a policy of faits accomplis; the others will try to force faithful observance of the existing laws and respect for the other legitimate branches of the state.*" (Emphasis in the original. "Other branches" refers to the legislature and the state bureaucracy, which are still controlled by the right.)

In another article analyzing the new cabinet, a contributor to *Patria y Libertad* wrote: "And finally a mere observation of the facts leads us to believe that the temporary safeguard represented by the presence of the armed forces in the government can become a permanent one if the men in uniform realize fully — as we are sure they will — the responsibility that has fallen on their shoulders and that they cannot escape now by leaving the government."

Thus, if the CP seemed to have great hopes in "original" formulas, the right at least was keeping its eyes firmly fixed on the fundamental class realities.

The "Letter to Ourselves" in *Aurora de Chile* warned that Allende's new formula had solved nothing: "They [the cabinet] are going to return the construction enterprises. They are going to return the stores. They are going to return some industries. Plants that were closed and locked, plants paralyzed by their owners, are going to be returned. We opened them, we made them produce, we organized their production, we alone, without the bosses and in spite of them. Today they are going to return them. For twenty-seven days we proved that we didn't need bosses to make these plants function. And today they are going to return them. Who are the bosses? They are the enemies of the people. They are the fascists in collusion with the foreign imperialists, they are the ones who made a deal with ITT [which plotted the overthrow of the government], and now the government comes and compromises with them, and turns the plants over to them — until the next bosses' strike.

"Because we are sure that there is going to be another bosses' strike. The strike was called off but not ended, the rich said on Sunday night [November 5]. We heard them clearly. They said that this strike was only a skirmish, and that the fight is continuing. We heard them clearly over the radio. Either the drones are going to leave the honeycomb or they will come back to rule the country with blood and fire. It is us or the rich. . . . There is going to be another bosses' strike, and the government is handing the plants back to the fascists so that they can make another try. . . .

"The big problem is that we are in those plants and we are not going to give them back. The government said for us to make these plants produce, and we did, and now we are not going to give them back. What is the government going to do? Shoot us? . . . They didn't drive the rich out of the enclaves where they were holding the trucks. Are they going to drive us government supporters out of the plants? What a dilemma, *compañero presidente!*"

In accepting the new governmental formula, the Communist and Socialist parties refused to see such a dilemma. In its November 10 issue, *Chile Hoy* said: "The main parties in the Unidad Popular government, the Communist and Socialist parties, accepted the participation of military officers in the cabinet on the following premises: (1) That this . . . would conclude the sentence of death that the workers had decreed against the strike by their tumultuous reaction; (2) that it would not mean any halt in carrying out the program of the Unidad Popular or (as the Socialist Party statement stipulated) reversing the economic measures and sanctions decided during the strike."

Chile Hoy acknowledged that bringing the military into the cabinet had been "a daring move, even in a country of original political formulas with a worldwide significance such as Chile." It cautiously noted that this solution was "still open to question." But it considered that the "fruits by which the new cabinet will be known began to ripen in the period General Prats set for the end of the strike—forty-eight hours. As the conditions came to light, they seemed to have a sweet taste for the government and a bitter one for the opposition."

Chile Hoy even suggested that the situation was now safe enough for Allende to go ahead with his travel plans: "And since the right was talking about a truce, President Allende seemed to decide to make his planned trip to Cuba, Mexico, the United Nations, and Moscow. Some add to this itinerary a 'technical' stopover in Madrid. This is an extremely important trip in the political and also the financial sense. But it will be a short one. It is to last less than fifteen days, so that permission from the Congress will not be needed. The vice president? Minister-General Prats. Another loop of braid for a man who, although pledged by the constitution not to take a political position, remains in the very center of politics." In another place, *Chile Hoy* upbraided the right for trying to woo the military with flattery.

El Rebelde, the newspaper of the MIR, criticized the government parties very sharply in its November 13 issue, denouncing the claims made in particular by the Communist Party that the formation of the new government did not mean a retreat: "A few days ago, through the Ministry of the Interior, Señor Prats proposed returning various construction, industrial, and commercial enterprises that the workers had seized in the name of the people during the bosses' strike.

"Along with this, he proposed to drop the cases against the gangsters who led the strike, to restore corporate legal status to the capitalist *condottieri*, to limit the nationalization of transport and the big wholesale houses that was carried out to make these enterprises serve the people, and he threatened to repress the people's legitimate forms of mobilizing. The minister of the interior did not say one word about the terrorism of the right, or about the crimes of the bosses in trying to shut the country down and starve it into submission, in seizing the public roadways and creating a commotion in the streets.

"During the last week, the government proceeded to reprivatize CODINA [the wholesalers' combine seized by the workers during the strike], to return the trucks seized and the daily *El Sur* in Concepción, as well as other enterprises. This demonstrates beyond any of the conciliationist arguments the reformists habitually use that the measures carried out by the UP-Generals government represent an objective setback in the overall situation."

In its November 7 issue, the MIR theoretical magazine *Punto Final* analyzed the "cabinet of social peace" as representing the program of "that section of the bourgeoisie that has been trying since 1970 to reduce the UP to inaction by detaching the government from its class commitments and turning it into a moderating force in social struggles."

Following a month of the most intense social conflict since the inauguration of the Unidad Popular government, the dilemma of both the reformist government and the bourgeois opposition seemed clear. By a policy of economic sabotage and boycott, the capitalists and the imperialists have pushed the Allende government to retreat step by step from its commitments to the working class and poor people. In a desperate maneuver to sidestep the fundamental class contradictions, the UP government has thrown itself on the mercy of the general of a bourgeois army, whom the Communist Party and *Chile Hoy* are now praising to the skies as a providential statesman and patriot.

At the same time, the increasing bourgeois pressure against the Allende government touched off a mobilization of the workers that limits the maneuverability of both the bourgeoisie and the reformists. In the reaction of the workers to the "bosses' strike," the dominant wing of the bourgeoisie could see confirmed the wisdom of its cautious policy of wearing out the UP government while avoiding sharp confrontations that could trigger a mass response. In mobilizing to defend the "workers' government," the Chilean proletariat and poor strata went far beyond the real perspectives of the UP. While Allende and his allies were making a new and humiliating capitulation, they carried the attack on capitalism and bourgeois rule to a higher level.

"The masses have demonstrated a vital lesson in the crisis unleashed by the bourgeoisie and imperialism," the November 7 *Punto Final* wrote. "New forms of power have arisen in the heat of the mass mobilization, impelled by the workers themselves. *Consejos coordinadores comunales* [municipal coordinating councils] — for example — have been dotting the country. . . . Including unions, neighborhood organizations, mothers' groups, student organizations, groups of artisans, small businessmen, etc., these workers' councils have been opening up perspectives for creating a real popular power. Inasmuch as

these bodies assume concrete tasks, such as taking over the
supply of food, transport, health services, production, and if
need be, defense against fascism, they are taking a significant proportion of state power into their hands. . . .

"If they are not thwarted by paternalistic attitudes, the revolutionary organizations being created by the initiative of the
masses can overcome the narrow bourgeois limits of the present state through consistently democratic forms. In any case,
during this crisis that was touched off by the onslaught of
the bourgeoisie, the working class has successfully invaded
various prerogatives of the state. It has shown that it is perfectly capable not only of excluding the bourgeoisie from the
economic life of the country but of taking the state into its
own hands. That is the great lesson of the crisis."

Furthermore, even though they have capitulated to the bourgeois opposition, the reformists know (especially after the reactionary offensives of recent months) that they dare not demobilize the workers. "The right may be preparing a definitive
provocation today," Pio Garcia wrote in the November 10 *Chile
Hoy*. "In any case, the realization of the government program
and the revolutionary process can only be guaranteed by
mobilizing the workers and the people and developing popular power."

On November 2, the same day Allende announced the formation of his military-civilian cabinet, representatives of one of
the largest workers' groups that developed out of the struggle against the "bosses' strike" challenged the government to
accept the logic of the situation created by the popular mobilization. The assembly of the Cordón Industrial Vicuña Mackenna, representing 30,000 workers, issued the "Pliego de los
Trabajadores" (Workers' Demands) to counter the right-wing
strikers' "Pliego de Chile."

In their program, the Vicuña Mackenna workers called on
the government to "base itself on us, on the workers' coordinating committees, and above all consult us about the steps
it makes. It must not base itself solely on the legally constituted bodies, which have always served to defend the interests
of the bosses and the imperialists. We must reject a military-
civilian cabinet. We do not need one. Only socialism can solve
the problems of the working class. Only the workers and the
people, because socialism is power for the people; it is the
people made into a government."

At the same time that the workers' councils raised these demands, it was clear that the Communist Party's elaborate

scheme of a reformist government backed by the mobilized masses and moving forward irreversibly a step at a time toward socialism was getting more and more threadbare. The "dual power within the state" described by CP spokesman Sergio Ramos Cordova in his book *Chile: Una Economía de Transición?* has now assumed an even more ambiguous character. Ramos saw the executive branch under the "people's president" as a bridgehead of socialist power in the bourgeois government. In the new cabinet, there would seem, according to Ramos's theory, to be dual power within the executive branch itself.

But despite the CP's timid centrism and the repeated success of the bourgeois opposition in rendering the government more and more impotent, the mobilization of the workers during the recent crisis shows that the margins for maneuver in the Chilean situation are getting dangerously tight, for both the reformists and the bourgeois moderates. The capitalists' minds are on arms. That was shown by the gun control law that was rushed through the opposition-dominated Congress on October 21, giving the army the right to control all weapons.

The MIR and the left wing of the Socialist Party have raised sharp revolutionary criticisms of the Allende regime. The existence of substantial far-left forces is a factor that has not been present in other reformist experiments in Latin America, such as the Goulart government in Brazil; it has clearly had an effect in pushing forward forms of revolutionary mobilization and workers' power.

But it is still unclear whether any of these forces is developing the capacity for leading the workers in a decisive confrontation with the bourgeoisie. Neither the Pliego de los Trabajadores nor the Pliego del Pueblo, for example, calls specifically for arming the workers, although this demand would seem to follow logically from creating vigilance groups to guard the factories against sabotage by well-armed rightist commandos. The MIR has said that it favors an alliance with soldiers, not just generals. It seems a safe assumption, however, that the generals in the cabinet will not extend "patriotic cooperation" to the point of permitting soldiers to participate in the processes of direct democracy developing in the country. The next few months will show how effectively the revolutionists can surmount this obstacle. In any case, if there were a mass workers' militia, it is likely that soldiers and police taking the side of the people would be attracted to it.

The MIR's concept of organizing the people to take power

seems a little static. "In the factories, in the mines, on the ranches, in the villages, and in the schools. First there, then in the townships, the towns, and the cities, and finally the battle for all power." This is the way the November 6 *El Rebelde* described it. But if the delicate balance in Chile should suddenly be tipped toward a decisive confrontation, which seems a real possibility after October, it is not likely that people's power will grow regularly from the "grass roots" to the centers. The battle for power in Chile could be decided in a few rapid operations.

The bourgeoisie is capable of coordinated national maneuvers, since most of the machinery of society remains in its hands. The reformists are paralyzed by their own ambiguities. What is yet to be seen is whether a Chilean revolutionary vanguard is developing that can weld the nuclei of popular power that emerged in October into a coherent force and direct it according to a precise strategy.

Significant advances were won in October in raising the consciousness and level of organization of the workers. These cannot be obscured by the miserable capitulation of the UP parties. But more decisive tests may develop in the near future.

Chileans greeting President Allende and Cuban Premier Fidel Castro during Castro's 1971 visit.

An assembly of workers discusses the running of their firm, one of those under government intervention.

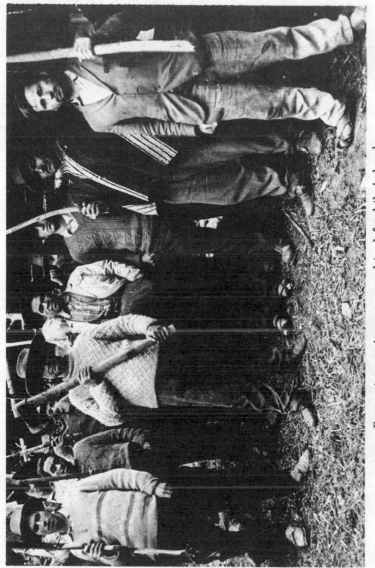

Peasant occupiers prepared to defend their land.

The junta's reign of terror.

IV

THE MARCH 1973 ELECTIONS
AND THE RISE OF THE CORDONES

The Developing Situation
of Dual Power

This article originally appeared in the February 1973 *issue
of* Revolución Permanente, *voice of the Partido Socialista Revolucionario (Revolutionary Socialist Party), Chilean section of
the Fourth International, under the title "JAPs and Comandos
Populares: Embryos of Workers' Power."* (JAPs *were* juntas de
abastecimiento y control de precios — *supply and price control
boards.* Comandos populares *were people's commands.*)

Through its finance minister, Fernando Flores, the government announced [on January 11] a series of drastic measures
to deal with the acute problem of food supplies and the black
market.

Aside from whatever conjunctural considerations — related to
the coming legislative elections in March — may have motivated
this action by the UP government, the cause must be sought
in the serious economic crisis that is causing desperation among
broad layers of the petty bourgeoisie and even of the prole
tariat and the working people as a whole, with the resulting
erosion of the government's — and ultimately the UP's — social
support.

But basically, the roots of this governmental decision lie
in the fact that the executive finds itself in an indefensible situation, caught in the crossfire between antagonistic classes in
society.

On one hand, there is an insolent and very powerful bourgeoisie engaged in a full-scale, virulent political offensive in its
desire to regain control of all the power. This bourgeoisie,
rather than being satisfied by the conciliatory attitude of the

UP leadership, demands more and more, and prepares its leading cadres and its methods for dealing the final blow to the UP. This is what the lessons of the October crisis show.

Dual Power

Facing it is a workers' movement that has not suffered any defeat as a class, that is strong and determined, and that in spite of its general support for the UP resolutely presses ahead on the road toward nationalizing industry and creating basic organs of workers' power, resulting in conflicts with the government itself.

A situation of dual power prevails in Chilean society. This cannot help but be a transitory and unstable stage. The opposing classes cannot settle the problem of power in the idyllic and peaceful electoral arena, despite the government's effort to transform itself into an arbiter of the class struggle by attempting to place itself above it in a Bonapartist role that demobilizes and ties the hands of the proletariat, leaving it at the mercy of the bourgeoisie. The question of power will be settled through class confrontation. In this regard, the death rattle of the policy of a "Chilean road" can already be heard.

What Flores Did Not Say

These are the deepgoing social causes that prompted the Flores statement. After characterizing the shortages as a problem that is political in nature and brought on by the actions of imperialism and the national bourgeoisie, the government announced a series of important measures.

What is obvious is that Flores did not unravel the underlying causes of the phenomenon, namely: the existence of a capitalist economy that prevents socialist planning but which, in view of the state take-overs and the struggle of the workers to nationalize industry and establish workers' control, does not feel motivated to increase production, and resorts to boycott; the appearance of a kind of bureaucratic layer that is beginning to have different interests and goals from those of the proletariat and that has transformed itself into a platform for a reformist policy and into an obstacle that will be difficult to salvage for the advancing revolutionary struggle; and the demobilization and resulting frustration of the working masses that have been brought on by the UP leadership. All this is what is behind the deceitful policy of the government in the face of the attack by the bourgeoisie.

The measures that have been announced will, moreover, have

no effect unless they go together with a continuing expropriation of industry and with the establishment of workers' control—both of which, furthermore, will make possible an increase in production.

Basically, what is being proposed is state control over domestic trade and the planning of distribution. In achieving these goals the needs of each family will be taken into consideration. The programming of such needs will be the responsibility of the *comandos comunales* [municipal commands] and the JAPs, which will be under the jurisdiction of the Secretaría Nacional de Distribución [National Office for Distribution]. The JAPs will not only report cases of speculation, but will have the power to take direct action to prevent it.

The organization of these basic bodies will be extended throughout the entire municipal unit and will involve the participation of all inhabitants and merchants. And although they will not be forced to, it already looks as though the merchant who does not take part will find himself deprived of certain traditional advantages, such as credit.

The Bourgeoisie Acknowledges the Blow It Has Been Dealt

No sooner had the government's statement been made than the bourgeoisie touched off a campaign of alarm. Its parties, its personalities, and its press denounced the measures proposed by the UP as the first steps on the road to the dictatorship of the proletariat. They charged the JAPs and the *comandos comunales* with being organs of revolutionary power existing outside the law and called for "civil resistance" to prevent the proposed plan from being implemented and to prepare for a confrontation.

They were quite right. The JAPs and the *comandos comunales* are, indeed, embryos of workers' power that, by consistently carrying out the policy announced by the finance minister, will take on great importance since they will involve broad layers of the working class and will press forward with the struggle against the bourgeoisie by going beyond the narrow framework of the parties belonging to the UP.

Revolutionary Conclusions

The class struggle will be intensified and the workers' movement strengthened through the application of the government's plan. We are on the right course. The decisive confrontation is drawing near.

But if they are to accomplish their tasks, the JAPs and the

comandos comunales must eliminate any trace of bureaucracy, become democratic, and seek out the criticisms and opinions of the masses, who are the ones who must decide how the supplies are to be allocated — namely, by delivering a quota of the scarce goods to the consumers by means of rationing, without requiring them to pay for those that are in plentiful supply.

The government announcement cannot remain a simple statement of intention; the masses must see to it that it is applied.

In taking on this task, the workers' movement suffers from one weakness. It lacks a revolutionary leadership. The UP has demonstrated its reformist character, its revolutionary verbalism, its scorn for action by the exploited, its weak and conciliatory attitude toward the bourgeoisie, and its inconsistencies. Revolutionists must not be content to point up the positive sides of the government's proposals, nor to warn against the limitations of the UP leadership. We must resolutely take part in the rank-and-file organizations of the workers, in the JAPs and in the *comandos comunales* in order to urge the workers' struggles forward, to form organs of proletarian power, to help form a true revolutionary leadership in the heat of the struggle, to defeat and destroy the bourgeois regime, and to unflinchingly advance toward socialism.

The Election Reflects Increasing Polarization

By David Thorstad

The social polarization that has been developing in Chile since the Unidad Popular coalition came to power in November 1970 was clearly reflected in the March 4 legislative election, the first since Allende's six-year presidential term began. The results show that the electoral base of his coalition has not only held firm but has expanded.

At stake were all the 150 seats in the Chamber of Deputies and half of the 50 seats in the Senate. The final returns indicate that the UP coalition won 43.4 percent of the vote and the opposition CODE (Confederación Democrática — Democratic Confederation), a bloc led by the Christian Democrats and the right-wing National Party, 54.7 percent. The remainder were either blank ballots or went to the independent socialist group USOPO (Unión Socialista Popular — Popular Socialist Union). The vote gave the UP an additional six seats in the Chamber and three in the Senate (one of which was won away from the USOPO), but, as anticipated, it left the control of both in the hands of the opposition. The breakdown of seats in the Chamber is now 87-63 and in the Senate 30-19, with the USOPO retaining one seat.

Supporters of both sides took to the streets following the vote to claim victory — the UP because of its definite gain over the 36 percent of the vote it won in the September 1970 presidential elections, and the opposition because it clearly retained its majority position in the legislature. Yet in terms of what each side was predicting prior to the vote, the results were pretty much what the UP expected, while they fell short of what the opposition was hoping for. The opposition, which campaigned on the idea that the election would be a "morally binding plebiscite," had set its sights on winning at least two more seats, thus giving it a two-thirds majority and the power not only to veto all major legislative bills but even to impeach President Allende. Instead, however, it lost seats in both houses. Everett Martin wrote from Santiago in the March 6 *Wall Street Journal:* "As a rule of thumb, political observers here said before the elections, anything less than 60 percent would be considered a disappointing performance by the opposition."

"My Government will be the only one in Chilean history that will increase its percentage over its presidential election," Allende predicted on the eve of the vote, belittling the opposition's chances of gaining seats. "They are dreaming with their eyes open." He observed, in rebuttal to the opposition's view of the election as a plebiscite, that in 1969 the then-ruling Christian Democratic Party headed by Eduardo Frei (currently the most prominent figure in the opposition) won only 29.8 percent of the vote in the legislative elections.

The increase in the UP's voter support is not only a reflection of the mounting polarization in Chilean society but also of the fact that the issue of economic difficulties was not the big vote-catcher the opposition had hoped it would be. Indeed, the economic problems — caused in no small part by the imperialist credit squeeze and by deliberate economic sabotage at home by the bourgeois backers of the opposition — failed to win votes for CODE among the poor and the working people.

"Despite the hardships of the middle class," noted Jonathan Kandell in the February 9 *New York Times*, "Government officials and other sources contend that in terms of general welfare—the quality and quantity of goods and services—lower-income groups are better off than they were two years ago." In Santiago, for instance, where half the electorate lives, unemployment dropped to around 3 percent from a pre-UP level of 9 percent. "A blue-collar worker knows that this Government has done more for him than any previous one," a foreign economist living in Santiago told Kandell.

The UP's showing would seem to be part of a general trend. Since it came to power, eight provincial elections have been held. Of these, the UP won half. The total popular vote in the eight provinces gave it 49 percent, compared with 51 percent for the opposition. And the UP won all but two of the elections held in 1972 in the ten major trade-union and student organizations. In the view of the editors of *Le Monde*, the March 4 results "confirmed the thrust to the left that has been going on in Chile for half a century."

Both the Unidad Popular and the opposition regarded the election as a continuation in the electoral arena of last October's three-week confrontation aptly dubbed the "capitalist strike." And the results confirmed the continuation of the polarization that came to the fore in October. "Splinter parties on both sides lost heavily as Chileans cast their votes for the big parties in the two electoral alliances—the Christian Democrats and Nationals, and the Socialists and Communists," wrote Kandell in the March 6 *New York Times*. This phenomenon was also noted by Pierre Kalfon, writing in the March 3 *Le Monde:* "Despite the attempts at moderation on the part of the more cautious sectors on both the right and the left, the economic and social order established by the bourgeoisie is being increasingly called into question. It is no longer possible to be neutral or to take a wait-and-see attitude. One is either for or against—without nuances." This polarization, of course, is reflected in the very fact that most of the political spectrum is allied into two opposing camps.

Also indicative of the increasing polarization is the fact that the right-wing National Party won an additional three seats in the Senate and a substantial number in the Chamber—partly at the expense of its ally, the Christian Democrats. The National Party consistently proclaimed throughout the campaign that it wants "Allende's head" and the elimination of the Communist Party. ("A new parliament is not enough—what we need is a new government.") The Christian Democrats, on the other hand, claim that they don't want to overthrow Allende, but only hope that he will "rectify his errors."

The crack in the opposition bloc that this difference in emphasis reflects has its counterpart in the UP coalition. Indeed, the elections increasingly drew into the open the differences over strategy that exist within the UP. The differences between the two largest parties in the coalition, the Socialists and the Communists, had already begun to surface during the October crisis. At the time, for instance, Carlos Altamirano, general secretary of the Socialist Party, supported a Socialist statement denouncing as "a victory for the reactionaries" the decision of Allende and the Communist Party to bring three military officers into the cabinet.

The differences erupted into a sharp public debate in January. The immediate cause was a proposal submitted to the legislature by Economics Minister Orlando Millas, a Communist, that would officially define the "social sector" of the economy and that entertains the possibility of returning to their private owners some industries that have been intervened.* In an interview with Kandell prior to the elections, CP theoretician Volodia Teitelboim discussed the idea in terms that the *Times* correspondent found "quite businesslike": "There must be a severe readjustment in economic planning, self-financing, quality of production, and salary demands. State-owned industries must justify themselves economically and not weigh down on the Government."

The proposed law was submitted without consulting either Undersecretary of the Economy Armando Arancibia, a Socialist, or the SP leadership. Altamirano denounced it as a "step backwards in the revolutionary process." And on January 29, the Political Bureau of the SP delivered a sharp statement to Allende—himself a Socialist—voicing indignation at being slighted, and condemning the proposed law. The statement was published in the bourgeois press.

Allende responded immediately with a statement reiterating

---

*Many factories came to be run by the government during the October crisis. Bosses refused to carry on production, workers occupied and ran the plants, and the Allende government sent interventors to supervise their operation. The owners demanded their return, and the workers demanded that they be formally placed in the social sector—i. e., nationalized. This created a dilemma for the Unidad Popular regime, which had not intended to carry out sweeping nationalizations of industries owned by Chilean capitalists.

the government proposal that the "social sector" be fixed at ninety state-owned factories and that a commission study what should be done with other industries already intervened but not on the list of those destined for the "social sector." This decision would be made, Allende said, by "taking into account the interests of the workers in these plants and of the national economy." He sought to downplay the number that might be returned to their capitalist owners.

The left-wing forces in the UP coalition do not want these plants — some of which were occupied by the workers against the wishes of the more reformist forces in the UP — returned to the private sector. The success of any postelection effort on the part of these reformists — headed by the Communists and the Radicals — to reach some "understanding" with the more "moderate" forces in the Christian Democratic opposition may very well hinge on this question.

Will the UP attempt such a rapprochement? And if so, will it require some kind of showdown with leftist forces in the UP? A number of things besides the Millas proposal would seem to point in this direction.

On March 7, for instance, as meetings among the UP parties were getting under way to analyze the election results, one of the parties that has seen an important layer of its membership move toward the left, the MAPU, announced the expulsion of fifteen of its top leaders for "ultraleftism." Of those expelled, nine were members of the Central Committee and six of the Political Committee of the organization. They were charged with "divisionist activities within the party" and with having contacts with "ultraleftist sectors that do not belong to the Popular Unity." The expulsion came less than a week after the MAPU's Political Committee issued a public statement criticizing the Millas proposal. The MAPU statement brought a severe reprimand from Allende. The statement, he said, "seems to be conceived and drawn up as if the MAPU were *outside* the government and the Popular Unity."

The CP, moreover, has apparently decided to step up its campaign against "ultraleftism." "In a recent published letter," reported Kandell from Santiago March 3, "Luis Corvalán secretary general of the Communist party, criticized the growing influence of M. I. R. among the Socialists. He suggested that through a more moderate approach, as many as 90 per cent of Chileans might eventually support the Government." Altamirano replied in a letter to the press that such an approach would involve unacceptable compromises with "parties that serve the bourgeoisie and capitalism."

The military members of the cabinet are known to be pressing for a law that would, along the lines of the Millas proposal, clarify the status of some 250 concerns that have been taken over or intervened by the government. "The generals want the law to detail which companies would become a permanent part of the state and which would be returned to the private sector," reported Everett Martin in the March 6 *Wall Street Journal.*

During a television appearance on February 25, the minister of the interior, General Prats, lumped the revolutionary forces together with the far right as extremists and characterized the remaining political forces as the "progressives." Such observations lend substance to speculation that the "neutral" armed forces conceive of their present role as one of translating their concern for "social peace" and "respect for the constitution" into a blessing upon any rapprochement among "progressives." Any such understanding would, of course, be so fraught with contradictions that it would of necessity strengthen the role of the military as an "objective" arbiter.

The Generals Leave the Cabinet
By Joseph Hansen

President Salvador Allende's announcement March 27 of the composition of his new cabinet caused some surprise internationally. He said that he had accepted the resignation of the three generals who had become a more and more prominent feature of his regime, and had named three civilians to their posts. Army Commander in Chief General Carlos Prats (the minister of the interior), air force General Claudio Sepulveda (the minister of mining), and Rear Admiral Daniel Arellano (who had succeeded Rear Admiral Ismael Huerta as minister of public works and transportation) were replaced by Gerardo Espinoza, a Socialist, Sergio Bitar, a member of the Christian Left (which split from the Christian Democrats), and Humberto Martones, a Radical.

The departure of the generals did not seem compatible at first sight with the widely held view that they were moving toward taking power in view of the sharpening class tensions in Chile and the increasing polarization in the political arena.

Does the shift in makeup of Allende's cabinet show that the danger of a military take-over has been overcome?

It is true that Allende did better in the March 4 legislative elections than the ultrarightists expected. They were counting on a two-thirds vote for the bourgeois opposition, which they thought would be proof positive of the erosion of popular support for Allende's Unidad Popular coalition, thereby justifying an immediate military coup and eliminating the need to wait for the 1976 elections for a change in regime.

Despite the UP's relatively favorable electoral showing, Allende continues to face the perspective of an intensifying class struggle in which long survival for his regime is hardly in the cards. Chilean capitalism is not viable in face of the pressure from U.S. imperialism on the one hand and the demands of the masses on the other. Inflation alone continually goads the masses into action.

Chilean democracy itself, for all the boasts of its protagonists, cannot be maintained for a prolonged period under such circumstances. The Chilean capitalists, in fact, have already been debating whether it is not beyond their economic means. Hence the appearance of ultrarightist and fascistlike bands. Concomitant with this, the uneasiness of the working class and its allies and the formation of various types of committees on the rank-and-file level in both cities and countryside—concerned at present mostly about defending their standard of living, about decent housing, distribution of the land, prices, etc.—constitute signs of the rising level of political consciousness in Chile.

Last October, the mounting tensions flared into a widespread bourgeois "strike" that shook the Allende regime. The workers began to counter this "strike" with defensive actions of their own. The rapidly increasing polarization of political forces led Allende on November 2, 1972, to bring the three top generals into his cabinet.

His action was highly revealing as to the class nature of the Popular Unity. Besides the Socialist and Communist parties and some bourgeois splinters, the army-party (as some have dubbed the military in Latin America) was included in the coalition. In the cabinet, General Prats stood next to Allende. This showed in a decisive way what influence the most powerful bourgeois party in Chile actually wielded in the regime set up by the Popular Unity. This proof that the Popular Unity is class collaborationist to the core could hardly be more convincing.

Allende called in the generals — if only temporarily — to strengthen his regime against the ultrarightists and those among the bourgeoisie who, out of fear and impatience, were provoking the masses and possibly goading them into actions that, once started, could end by bringing down the entire capitalist structure in Chile in short order.

Although the generals blocked with Allende against the right from November till March, thereby seemingly supporting the left, their real role was to dampen the class struggle. The generals, especially Prats, played the role of "savior" when the country appeared to be on the verge of civil war.

But the mere inclusion of the generals in the cabinet raised apprehensions in the far left in Chile — the left wing of the Socialist Party, the Movimiento de Izquierda Revolucionaria (MIR), the Trotskyists, and similar formations. They feared a coup d'état by the "gorillas," an outcome that was clearly inherent in the political role assumed by the generals in the Allende regime.

This fear became a new element in the polarization. Warnings about the danger of a take-over became more insistent and more widely heard. The issue began to give a keener cutting edge to the propaganda of the far left concerning the bourgeois nature of Allende's government, the need to break with capitalism once and for all, the need to carry out the socialist revolution, to prepare for a test of arms, and so on. The continued presence of the generals was beginning to compromise Allende politically.

At the same time, the vote in the March 4 elections showed that Allende's standing with the working class and masses of the people was still strong. The emergency aid rushed to his regime last November (with its implication of a further emergency operation by the military if required) could now be withdrawn.

These appear to be the main political reasons why the powers-that-be in Chile decided to shift the generals from center stage back to the wings. On the surface it appeared to be a concession to the left. Actually it was intended to allay the growing fears about a coup, induce the masses to relax, and help block the organizing efforts of those who insist that the danger is very real. From this point of view, the "withdrawal" of the generals was only a tactical maneuver.

General Prats, it should be noted, is not without guile. He owes his post as commander in chief of the army in part, no doubt, to his capacities as a military politician. He remained constantly in public attention, evoking the image of an incorruptible patriot and statesman, as he upheld the regime against the frenzied layers that sought to bring it down before Allende's work was done and the masses had become demoralized. The image makers likened him to the late Mexican President Cárdenas, who became heralded as the elder statesman of Latin America, mostly because of his role in diverting the Mexican masses from taking the road opened by the Cuban revolution.

Thus the Chilean general became widely known as a strong person able to deal blows to right and left, an upright figure on whom the entire country can depend in a crisis, a potential Bonaparte. He withdrew to the sidelines before this image had time to become tarnished.

Reporting from Santiago in the March 28 *New York Times*, Jonathan Kandell sized up the experience with the general as follows: "He has described himself as a 'simple soldier' with no political ambitions and has always indicated that his continued participation in the Cabinet was entirely in President Allende's hands.

"But his political stature has risen spectacularly in recent months and he has occasionally been considered a possible presidential candidate in 1976, when Dr. Allende's term expires."

This general bears watching. It can safely be predicted that he will be heard from again, and probably much sooner than 1976.

Why the Generals "Resigned"
By Hugo Blanco

Santiago

The major political event in the last week of March has been the change in the cabinet. It marked a milestone in the sharpening of class contradictions in the country and the reflection of these within the Unidad Popular ruling coalition. However, the new ministerial team shows that the shifts in the government's policy will not be as deepgoing as some had hoped.

From *Intercontinental Press*, April 16, 1973

The outgoing cabinet was the product of the October crisis caused by the bosses' strike, which provoked a strong response from the working class. As will be recalled, on that occasion, although the government could have based itself on the mass mobilization of the workers that was defeating the strike, it preferred to come to an understanding with the right, making concessions limiting the independent dynamic of the workers and people.

One of these concessions was incorporating leaders of the army, navy, and air force into the cabinet. Among these, General Carlos Prats, the chief of staff of the armed forces, came in as minister of the interior, thereby assuming the chairmanship of the cabinet and the post of vice-president (he served in fact as president during Allende's trip abroad). Two representatives of the workers (the general secretary of the CUT and a peasant leader) were also brought into the cabinet at that time, but this could not cover up the government's capitulation.

The right understood that while the military officers' remaining in the government offered them guarantees, it also caused them problems. If they attacked the government, they would also be attacking, like it or not, the military men, who were losing their image as "impartial arbitrators." Since the working class has not been crushed, it was impossible for the minister of the interior to restrain, as effectively as he would have liked, the push of the masses toward direct distribution of scarce items. Nor could the minister close his eyes to the excesses of the rightist groups. Moreover, the right could not claim that the March 4 elections were fraudulent. These examples show why the right needed the military men out of the government and why they themselves wanted out.

La Prensa, the Christian Democratic daily, noted: "In a prolonged meeting in the middle of last week, the Council of Generals decided to call on President Allende to meet four demands. Failure to do so would mean that the men in uniform would leave the offices they held. The demands included the right to maintain effective surveillance of the armed groups; the end of the executive's use of legal loopholes to institute social reforms; and taking a technical and nonpolitical approach to the questions related to food supply.

"Because of the pressure to which Dr. Allende is being subjected by extremist groups, it was not possible immediately to accept the demand about armed groups and to establish a new foreign policy orientation. A 'deal' was made on the question of food supply that involved maintaining General Alberto Bachelet in the post of general secretary of supply. As regards the executive's use of loopholes, it was agreed not to resort to this at least in the early period of the new cabinet."

It is clear from this "secret report" given by the Christian Democrats, with the agreement of the military, that the officers could not dream that Allende would be able to grant such fantastic demands, given the present conditions of the class struggle in the country. They realized that at this time the best course was to leave the cabinet.

The "official" reasons given, of course, were more diplomatic. In his speech, Allende noted the tasks the former cabinet had been appointed to accomplish. "The first was to enforce respect for legal norms and authority. To maintain order in the economy, which meant putting an end to the strike. To maintain public order, which was threatened by subversion. To guarantee the democratic process in national affairs and, most fundamentally, to make certain that the elections would be held — as they were this March, with the strictest neutrality on the part of the government. Furthermore, we assigned this cabinet the task of assuring the continuity of the process of revolutionary transformation, in accordance with the political program of the government and in the context of democracy, pluralism, and freedom.

"I can say with profound satisfaction that the cabinet has accomplished all the difficult tasks that were demanded of it. . . . The cycle that began in October culminated politically on March 4."

Then Allende read the following letter of resignation by the cabinet: "The recent parliamentary elections, whose result showed a strong vote for the sectors that support the government's program, at the same time constitute an excellent occasion for Your Excellency's closest collaborators, the ministers of the cabinet, to leave you freedom of action so that if you see fit you can, in accordance with your constitutional function, form a cabinet representative of the political reality expressed in this significant civic act."

While it is true that the right wing of the Unidad Popular was not able to afford the luxury of getting in some Christian Democrat or "independent" intermediary as a minister, the new cabinet reveals a clear consolidation of this wing in the government. The sharpening conflicts between the left and right inside the UP make this fact all the more evident, which in turn is increasing tensions.

The present composition of the cabinet is as follows:

Four right-wing Socialists: Clodomiro Almeida (Foreign Relations) and José Tohá (National Defense) were in the previous cabinet; Gerardo Espinoza (Department of the Interior) and Pedro Hidalgo (Agriculture) have been added. Espinoza is said to be to the right of Allende.

Three Communists, all of whom were in the previous cabinet: Luis Figueroa (Labor and Social Security), Jorge Insunza (Justice) and Orlando Millas (Economics). The latter was the author of the notorious "Millas Bill" that provided for returning some intervened plants to their owners. It was energetically rejected by the working class.

Three Radicals: Jorge Tapia (who remains as minister of education), Humberto Martones (shifted from Land and Homesteading to Public Works), and Aníbal Palma (who takes the post of general secretary of the government).

Two "left independents": Arturo Girón (Public Health) and Luis Matte (Housing and Urban Affairs). Both were in the previous cabinet. One member of the Izquierda Cristiana (Christian Left), Sergio Bitar, has been included as minister of mines. He is the least representative figure in this small party in the left wing of the Unidad Popular. One member of the API, which is in the right wing of the UP, has also been brought in: Roberto Cuéllar (Land and Homesteading). The one member of MAPU remains: Fernando Flores (Treasury).

The reason for this kind of cabinet was to give the appearance of "pluralism" in the Unidad Popular. However, as was noted, the Izquierda Cristiana minister does not reflect the views of his group. Moreover, keeping Flores in his post was very significant. This represents Allende's giving his blessing to the right wing of MAPU which, under CP prompting, recently staged a coup d'état against the party leadership elected at a congress not long ago. Thus, the UP right has quietly solved the difficult problem of recognizing the usurpers in MAPU.

The formation of this cabinet clarifies and sharpens the conflicts between the masses and their leaderships, heightening the crisis of the UP. The next important chapter in this process will probably be the congress of the Socialist Party, on which the dynamic of the workers' and people's mobilizations will have a decisive impact.

The Workers Organize Distribution

By Hugo Blanco

Santiago

Just as in production great and irreconcilable conflicts exist between the private sector and the state sector, in which there are various degrees of workers' participation and control; strong conflicting pulls have also appeared in the field of distribution, where the fundamental antagonism is growing clearer day by day.

On one hand there are the capitalists, the various levels of private traders. This sector is fighting for the return of all distribution to private hands, for complete "freedom" of commerce.

On the opposite side is the mass of consumers who every day are fighting more consciously for centralizing distribution under popular control.

In the center, in the slack between these two opposing forces, are the government and the reformists, trying to maintain an equilibrium that is becoming more and more untenable.

As for the immediate causes of the scarcity that exists, we can cite:

1. The imperialist boycott. This began even before Allende took power, and since he took office it has assumed serious dimensions. The case of Kennecott Copper (which took legal action to have exports from the nationalized mines seized) and the stopping of shipments of machinery and spare parts are notorious examples.

2. Low agricultural production. The principal cause of this is that in carrying out the agrarian reform the government allowed the landowners to remove their machinery, livestock, seed, etc., from the confiscated area. Added to this is the fact that the big ranchers who still hold their land have no interest in pushing production. Finally, the bureaucracy involved with the agrarian reform is not exactly a stimulus to developing the revolutionary potential of the peasantry.

3. Sabotage by the industrialists. Many cases of this have been exposed by the workers. The bosses don't want to modernize equipment. They don't want to repair machinery. They don't want to buy raw materials or even vital machine parts.

4. Speculation. This has become the most profitable sector

of the Chilean economy. Seeing the possibility for doubling their investment overnight, the big capitalists are pouring their funds into this field, and this includes the money the land-owners have gotten thanks to the "democratic" agrarian reform.

5. The increased buying power of the working class. Previously the workers were subjected to strict rationing, since the windows and shelves of the stores were full of goods that they could not buy because of their low wages. Now, as a result of their struggle, their wages are higher.

As for the effects of the scarcity, one is long lines, hundreds of persons in some cases waiting to buy a liter of cooking oil, a kilo of detergent, a pack of cigarettes, a roll of toilet paper, a tube of toothpaste, or something else. Some articles are sold as soon as they are made—sheets, ankle socks, refrigerators, etc. Another effect is the black market, a vast black market. There is also a lot of hoarding, some of which has been uncovered and some of which has not.

The right is taking advantage of this and waging a big campaign to discredit the government through the press, radio, and television. During the election campaign, it inundated the lines with leaflets. All this has succeeded in shifting part of the middle class to the right.

The government, which through the Distribuidora Nacional (DINAC—the National Distribution Agency) and other bodies, controls less than half of wholesale trade, has made efforts to rationalize distribution without encroaching on the businessmen. The Communist Party argues that any interference with them would mean "losing the support of the middle class."

The government has created the JAPs (supply and price control boards), which in theory are supposed to be made up of the local people and merchants in city neighborhoods. The JAPs have the task of receiving the goods sent out to each sector by the national distribution agencies and distributing them among the merchants in the area.

The power of these bodies fluctuates depending upon how much pressure is brought to bear on the government, and upon the militancy of the population. Once, the JAPs were permitted wide power. But, following this, their role was restricted, with many of their functions being handed over to the police at the same time that military officers were being brought into the top posts in the distribution system.

At their height, besides receiving the goods and taking them to the merchants, the JAPs maintained supervision over the prices and weighing of products sold over the counter. To a lesser extent, they saw to it that sales were not made to two members of the same family in a row. Once things reached this level, the consumers saw that they were "unpaid employees of the storekeepers," realizing that the merchants were unnecessary.

The shantytowns in the slum belt around Santiago and other cities were in the vanguard of this, as in other aspects. There were many reasons why this happened:

● Their proletarian or semiproletarian composition.

● The combativity and organization that have been traditional in them since their inception as a result of the fact that the land they are built on had to be taken by force, which required prior organization and facing many clashes with the police. Many of them, such as the "Nueva La Habana" (New Havana) encampment, have kept their block organizations to this day.

● Many of them are led by members of the MIR or left Socialists.

● Many of them lack any licensed merchants. For this last reason, direct distribution was "legally" authorized in these settlements. And this practice gradually spread to other areas, where there were merchants.

The restrictions placed on the JAPs by the government have been counterproductive in some areas, especially in the shantytowns. Instead of stopping the push toward direct distribution, they have led to its being taken over by other bodies, which may be called by various names—neighborhood councils, cooperative associations, etc. This has been facilitated by the existence of many lower officials belonging to the left wing of the SP, the left wing of MAPU, or other currents, who have yielded to the pressure of the masses. The most notable case was that of the Graham Agencies (Almacenes Populares de Agencias Graham—a government-run distributor).

For some time, the left wing—the SP left, the left wing of MAPU, the MIR, the Partido Socialista Revolucionario—has been demanding rationing under some kind of popular control. This has been called by various names: "the family market basket," "ration cards," "certificate of residence," etc.

Until recently the CP tenaciously opposed rationing. At present, seeing that the popular efforts for direct distribution are increasing and causing the party to lose some of its grass roots support, it is yielding somewhat on this question.

In the field of distribution, and in others, the contradiction

between the masses and the system grows more acute every day.
Every day it is more difficult for the UP government to maintain an equilibrium. Every day new scarcities occur, and this
does not augur well for the balancers.

The UP's Right Wing Consolidates
By Hugo Blanco

Santiago

The events that have taken place since the recent changes in
the cabinet indicate that a strengthening of the right wing within
the government and the governmental coalition is continuing.

The Central Committee of the Socialist Party held a plenary
session March 28-31. Nothing spectacular came out of it, but
it did unquestionably represent an advance for the party's
right wing. To be sure, general statements were reiterated on
the need to "stimulate and strengthen" the "new class organizations forged in the heat of the struggle," a reference to the
*cordones industriales,** the municipal commands, etc.; to the
effect that the "people's power must continue to develop institutional forms that differ from those of the bourgeoisie and that
in certain circumstances make possible the expression of opposition to bourgeois power"; on the deepening of revolutionary
transformations; on the need to correct bureaucratic deviations;
etc. Nevertheless, it is generally understood that all these statements were made only to soothe the party ranks and the left
wing of the leadership, represented by the eternal conciliator,
Carlos Altamirano.

The general tone of the plenum was marked by such statements as that "the popular government is the main instrument
for continuing to move forward," that the development of the
mass organizations must not hinder the government's action
but help it, that "Popular Unity fully continues to be the
political alliance that will make possible a deepening of the
revolutionary transformations," and that "the Socialists continue

---

* Organizations embracing workers in a number of factories
grouped together in the "industrial belts" in the Santiago suburbs.

From *Intercontinental Press*, April 30, 1973

to view their alliance with the CP as the basic axis of the Popular Unity."

If we compare these statements with the atmosphere prevailing in the party in January and February, we can see a rapid retreat from leftist positions.

At that time, mass mobilizations were unfolding around the direct distribution of necessary goods, in addition to the powerful mobilization by the workers (especially the Cordón Cerrillos) against the Millas plan, in which the CP economics minister proposed returning to their owners many of the companies that have been intervened. These mobilizations applied so much pressure on the SP that there was open talk about a split in the Popular Unity and the formation of a more militant left-wing front that, in addition to the SP, MAPU, and the Christian Left, which are in the UP, would include the MIR and other smaller revolutionary groups. This would have constituted an open break with the CP and the lesser groups in the right wing of the UP — the Radical Party and API.

These illusions evaporated with the latest SP plenum. Moreover, among the resolutions before the plenum — read, ironically enough, by Altamirano himself — one stands out. Toward the end, it stated: "The party takes a positive view toward the significance and importance of holding a National Congress of Popular Unity that will take a fundamental stand on the concrete application of the program, and the platform that complements it, in each front and in every part of the country." There can be no doubt that if this congress is held, it will unquestionably be under the auspices of the CP and Allende, and any agreements that are reached will revolve around how to meet the mass movement head on in close alliance with the Christian Democracy and the armed forces.

This consolidation of the right wing in the SP was reflected in changes in its Political Committee. Although these amounted to nothing spectacular that might provoke a split — Altamirano remains general secretary, for instance — two pro-Allende figures, both graduates of the governmental apparatus and both softened by their tenure, were gently eased onto the committee. They are Hernán del Canto, former general secretary of the government, and Rolando Calderón, former minister of agriculture. Another important addition is that of the right-wing cabinet member Clodomiro Almeyda.

The groundwork has now been laid for a triumph of the right wing in the next party congress, all the more so in view of the scattered state of the left and the absence of an organized tendency.

If the plenum of the SP turned out to be less heated than expected, the Communist Party plenum, also held at the end of March, unfolded in the usual touching atmosphere of angelic harmony.

There was some mention of workers' participation in managing the factories, which has been going on for some time now, and of other "revolutionary" topics. But the main theme and axis of the plenum was the "battle for production." The CP is not concerned about leaving a major part of the economy in capitalist hands. As the masses are struggling day after day to increase their power in the countryside, in production, and in distribution, it is getting to the point where the CP is not only putting a brake on this struggle, but is actually fighting it. It is doing this by putting forward as its main slogan the exhortation to produce more: "The main thing is, and will continue to be, to increase production and productivity in copper, in mining as a whole, in industry, and in agriculture, in order to increase exports, reduce what we need to import, and reach the point where there is an abundance, not a shortage, of consumer goods on the domestic market."

The CP is understood to be pleased with the coup that was recently carried out inside MAPU and with the progress made by its friends inside the SP. New attacks on the left are being prepared.

Another sign of the strengthening of the right that is presently occurring within the government coalition is the fact that General Alberto Bachelet, once he received confirmation as head of the National Office for Food Distribution and Marketing, proceeded to clean out the left-wingers. In line with his stated aim of "implementing a new plan to rationalize distribution," he asked for the resignations of the directors and assistant directors of the state distribution agencies. It is rumored that military men will be appointed to fill these posts.

The general director of the Graham Agencies, Sergio Juárez, offered resistance: "Concretely, with regard to your request that I resign my post — which was from the outset an inadmissible and legally ineffectual request — I am complying by notifying you that, in accord with instructions that I have received and in compliance with an elementary disciplinary duty, I am informing the Socialist Party about this matter."

Graham Agencies has taken some of the most audacious measures with regard to direct distribution. It enjoys the sympathy of popular sectors, such as marginal shantytowns and *cordones industriales*. Bachelet had already removed its director once before, but mass pressure forced him to relent and appoint Juárez, who has followed the same approach as his predecessor. It appears that Bachelet now feels that he is in a stronger position and is attempting to strike a heavy blow.

The Socialist Party rejected the path that Juárez had chosen, and Allende stated in a speech that "it must be very clearly understood that it is only the government that can determine which officials should retain their posts and which ones, for reasons that, moreover, need not be explained, must be changed.

War has also been declared on *"tomas"* (take-overs). The first act of the new minister of the interior, Gerardo Espinoza, after taking office, was to state that no more *tomas* would be permitted.

The *toma* is a form of mass mobilization used by various sectors. The workers take over factories, the peasants take over land, students occupy high schools, squatters take over distribution agencies, and everybody takes over roads, blocks avenues, etc. Up to now the "People's Government" had not moved directly against this form of mobilization, which is not directed against it. With the naming of the new cabinet, it began to do so.

The *tomas* continued after the minister of the interior's speech. Allende himself felt the need to speak out, and on April 3 he devoted an entire speech to attacking the *tomas* and directing threats at the workers' and people's movement. The *tomas* are still going on, however. A breach has opened up between the masses and their reformist leaderships, and the UP is beginning to appear to the masses as a defender of the rights of the bourgeoisie. The police attack, using clubs and tear gas, and leaders of the *tomas* are arrested and put on trial.

The battle against the *tomas* has begun but it has still not been won. The popular movement recognizes that it must become better organized.

The Fascist Threat Mounts
By Hugo Blanco

Santiago
Along with the strengthening of the right wing inside the Unidad Popular government, a strengthening of fascism is also occurring.

From *Intercontinental Press,* May 7, 1973

Of the two best-known organizations that represent fascism in Chile, Patria y Libertad and "Rolando Matus," it is the former that might have pretensions of being respectable.

Its full name is Frente Nacionalista Patria y Libertad (Nationalist Front for Fatherland and Freedom). It was formed two years ago. Its founder and general secretary, Roberto Thieme, died in an accident last February 23 while (in the words of his cothinkers) "carrying out a patrol in the province of Concepción." Another of its "heroes," Héctor Castillo Fuentealba, is honored as having been "murdered by a socialist activist in Chillán on December 20, 1972."

This group has a higher degree of organization, discipline, armed preparation, and determination than any other Chilean party, whether of the left or the right.

In spite of its small size, it has public headquarters (no one knows how many clandestine ones) and a newspaper, *Patria y Libertad*. Its "swastika" is a stylized spider.

It has already carried out many "actions," primarily against squatters in marginal areas, in cases where hoarding of goods has been uncovered, or when homeless persons have taken over unused land. In these cases, or when certain factories have been occupied, members of the group have functioned as shock troops for the capitalists. They also carried out a great deal of activity during the election campaign, storming the headquarters of left-wing parties or using firearms to attack propaganda teams of these parties. On such occasions, they were joined by members of other right-wing parties, such as the National Party and the Christian Democracy.

Patria y Libertad feels that "there is no political solution" for the present situation in Chile.

At the end of March it stated: "With this second anniversary, we are holding the first national gathering of our leaders, with provincial heads from the entire country also in attendance. This will be the best opportunity for us to redouble our faith in nationalism and to prepare ourselves, with greater self-sacrifice than ever, for the great battle that awaits us in the immediate future. Every day brings the day of liberation closer. This is a day not to be waited for but to fight for. It will be we nationalists who will return dignity, freedom, and a future to our captive fatherland." The gathering was dubbed the Expanded National Council. The main agreement reached was operation SACO (Sistema de Acción Cívica Organizada — System of Organized Civic Action).

The internal document explaining this operation could not be kept secret — or (more likely) Patria y Libertad "leaked" it so that it would be given wide circulation. The following are the main points of the "black commands," as they are now known:

● For professionals who work in the social sector of the economy (companies that have been taken over by the state):

"Make a brief report on the firm's financing and the banks where money is deposited, as well as the persons in charge of the depositing, and to the extent possible on the firm's monthly financial status. . . . Draw up a list of stocks and supplies, and the names of the respective importers and the usual suppliers. . . . Draw up a list of the kind of machines that are used, detailing the sources of energy, water, or fuel and the emergency electrical plants. . . .

"Do not teach their technological methods or their codes. . . . Do not report their experiments to the UP. . . . Do not train anyone in the UP. . . . Remove plans and manuals dealing with their projected and present operations and maintenance, and in cases where this is not possible, create chaos in the archives. If you are involved in planning, raise the margin of certainty for every estimate and quantity. . . . Increase the personnel involved in 'dead work,' administrative aides, day laborers, and service personnel, without rationalizing activities or mechanizing the work that is performed. . . ."

● For private contractors:

"Under legal pretexts, let the contracts of Marxist workers or employees lapse if they are constantly attempting to form cells that are preparing to take over the company. . . . Industrialists will have to win over their workers through *pledges* that involve small cost to the company. . . . Lunch, coffee break, etc., and small breakfasts for those who live furthest away. . . . Work shoes, vacation retreats, emergency funds, scholarships for children of the most outstanding workers, free time for going to school, help in paying for books and for enrolling to obtain training. . . .

"The industrialist will have to do business preferentially, and later exclusively, with the democratic clients included on the list provided by the coordination center. . . . In cases where state-run companies exert pressure to bring about sale of a product, payment in cash will be required, partial deliveries of the goods will be made, and increased prices will be charged. . . . The distribution of products will be entrusted only to democratic distributors; in case of state repression, only products of lower quality and in lesser quantity will be delivered to the social sector, and this will be done with delays and dragged-out negotiations over the matter. . . .

"In case of illegal take-overs of plants, the owner will notify the coordination center in advance of all details and the names and addresses of the leaders, etc., and the appropriate protective mechanism will be provided. . . ."

● For ranchers:

"Draw up a sketch with the location of the property and access roads, paths, crossings, and tracks that can be used as alternatives in blocking roads. . . . Lists of their own available means of transportation, or hired trucks capable of carrying freight (preferably with fully licensed drivers). . . . Reports on the type, frequency, and schedule of stations for overhauling and repairing the same. . . . Volunteers for organizing a system of signs and road patrols that can facilitate the moving of transport. . . . Attempts could be made to enlist the cooperation of private planes and ham radio operators in perfecting the system. . . .

"Produce basic foods — beans, lentils, chick-peas, potatoes, corn, etc. — in the best soil and in small plots that are not liable to be detected, but that produce a high yield and high quality. . . . Furnish SOCOAGRO [state distribution agency] with false reports on the yield per plot and the possibilities of the property. It will be necessary to give the impression of cooperating in order to obtain allowances and other credits, but the major part of what is produced will be delivered through SACO. . . .

"Form self-defense nuclei and an information system by means of loyal workers who infiltrate the peasant settlements and the estates that have been expropriated throughout the zone. Reinforcement nuclei will be set up in the towns together with a warning system involving the cooperation of civil servants in financial bodies. . . . Activists in the UP . . . will be identified, and they will be subjected to constant surveillance and possible psychological or physical intimidation."

● For neighbors:

"Fathers will instruct their children in detail about the meaning of totalitarianism, using oral and graphic examples of it throughout the world, and they will indicate to their children who the Marxist totalitarian agents are so that they can avoid physical contact with them and isolate them. . . . On a permanent basis they will make them read about or will call their attention to the daily brutality of Marxism, using a wide number of examples to teach them about the unsuitability of the dogma. . . .

"SACO section heads will get from their neighbors the location of cells and the meeting places for pro-UP businessmen, for the JAPs, and for distributing rationed goods; the names and nicknames of militants and their movements, places of operation, etc. . . .

"Sustained campaigns involving psychological intimidation will be carried out, using slogans and propaganda aimed at UP militants, as well as rumors and scare stories aimed at UP women and their children; these will be furnished by SA-CO. . . . Follow a policy of ill will: offer no transportation to UP people; give no aid to UP people; do not lend to, obtain from, speak to, compete with, or maintain friendly relations with UP people. . . . Boycott the directives of the UP Neighborhood Boards with perfectly organized groups whose aims are clear and precise."

As can be seen, fascism is formulating its line of action with ever-increasing clarity. In its lexicon special meaning is given to concepts like "democracy" (i.e., the international right) and "totalitarianism." UP means the entire left and every individual worker, student, or squatter in the vanguard. "Unionists" are those who participated in the bosses' strike last October. The front page of the latest issue of *Patria y Libertad* carried the following headline: "Nationalism, Unionism, and Armed Forces: The Only Alternatives for Power."

The Christian Democracy bemoans the "irresponsibility of Patria y Libertad" and whiningly asks a few questions: "1) If the political process is blocked by the institutional deadlock, what are their feelings about continuing to adhere to democratic principles? 2) If the political process becomes blocked, do they propose straightforwardly a coup d'état against Allende? 3) Are they in a position to perform such a coup by themselves, or do they expect the armed forces to take part in it? 4) Do they believe, if they are in their right mind, that the armed forces would carry out a coup d'état in Chile? And if they do believe this, do they think that the armed forces would do it on behalf of their movement?"

This sniveling is not preventing the Christian Democracy's members from being polarized in the direction of Patria y Libertad, which they definitely feel is more "in its right mind" than Frei or Tómic.

Although the UP denounces certain attacks by Patria y Libertad on inhabitants of marginal shantytowns, its position is confusionist. The government's general secretary, Aníbal Palma, for instance, denounced the attitude of squatters and workers participating in occupations as a plot by the MIR and Patria y Libertad. Statements of this kind confuse the people and can only work to the advantage of the fascist groups.

Only the strength of the organized workers, continuing their struggle without letting themselves be held back by vacillating and traitorous leaderships, can force fascism to retreat. The real accomplices of Patria y Libertad are not the workers who are mobilizing in defense of their interests. On the contrary, they are the worst enemy of fascism. The true accomplices are those who hold back and vilify this mobilization of the masses.

The Sharpening Struggle
By Hugo Blanco

Santiago, May 4

During the past two weeks, Santiago and other cities have been the scene of street demonstrations that reflect the sharpening social and political tensions in Chile.

Daily, the right wing brought hundreds of secondary-school students into the streets to demonstrate against the government's proposed educational reform, the ENU (Escuela Nacional Unificada — Unified National Education). Behind the students followed shock troops of the right. They stoned buildings, such as the offices of the leftist dailies *Puro Chile* and *Ultima Hora*, the headquarters of the Socialist Party, the home of left-wing legislator Mireya Baltra, and finally the governmental palace. The street demonstrations were combined with student strikes.

Public Works employees took over the offices of that ministry, and highways were blocked in support actions. Their struggle is around economic demands, but it also has important political ramifications. In response to the accusation by Allende and such reformist sectors as the Communist Party that the strike action was inspired by right-wing sentiments, the president of the National Association of Workers in the Ministry of Public Works, Alberto Gálvez, made some strong statements: "Let there not be the least doubt that if the president calls us, we will go over the heads of not only the Congress and *El Mercurio* [a right-wing newspaper], but also of the Contraloría [federal control office], the courts, and the armed forces. Even though we reach a state of civil war, the workers will not be held back by these reactionary institutions. . . . Our movement has arisen out of· the workers' need to increase their income, given the fact that Public Works is one of the most neglected sectors."

He stated that between 50 and 60 percent of the Public Works budget goes to private contractors, who are doing a fantastic business at the expense of the workers.

In addition, he denounced the bureaucracy: "It is the managers who enjoy a kind of all-embracing authority. A government of the workers must be based on the power of the masses. We demand not only a raise in wages, but also that the power of the people be exercised from the bottom up and that decisions affecting the ministry be taken by the ranks."

He added that the workers are demanding that the social sector be expanded, that private contracting be eliminated, that the workers have the right to supervise the managers and remove them, and that there be an end to the payment of incorrect wages. Finally, he said that if the necessary funds are lacking, payment should be stopped on the foreign debt, and on the stocks of private companies and state-run industries. "If this is done, there will be enough money to pay the workers," he said, speaking for the 30,000 workers he represents.

After several days of continuous right-wing demonstrations, leftist students decided to counteract them by also taking to the streets. In Santiago, they held a meeting in Caupolicán theater to discuss the problem of the ENU. Upon leaving the meeting to stage a demonstration, they had to confront the right-wing bands that were operating in the central part of the city. Similar clashes also occurred in other cities. The rightists, who up to that point had been operating with impunity, saw their path blocked.

On April 27, the CUT called a workers' demonstration in support of the government. As one of the branches of the march was moving through downtown Santiago, it was attacked by gunfire from the headquarters of the Christian Democratic Party. The result was several workers wounded and one killed. The dead man was José Ricardo Ahumada, a construction worker and member of the Communist Party. The police charged the workers. At a rally shortly afterward, Allende made a speech in which he attempted to pacify the workers.

The funeral was held on April 30. It drew an impressive hour-and-a-half parade of 150,000 persons in a repudiation of fascism. Together with the tepid, reformist slogans of the CP could be heard others, chanted by the revolutionary left: "Create, create, people's power," "Create, create, a popular militia," and "Workers to power."

The left staged another gathering on May Day, although this time the turnout was smaller — around 80,000. The explanation for the difference in size lies in the fact that the funeral was an outraged rejection of fascism, whereas on May 1 the workers were to be treated to the reformist talk of Jorge Godoy, president of the CUT, and Salvador Allende. Both the Communist leader and the president of the republic appealed for calm and passivity, and even went so far as to make more or less veiled attacks on the workers' vanguard and the revolutionary left. In spite of this, militant slogans were still in evidence, occasionally chanted in direct response to the reformist ideas that were being aired. A demagogic reference to Cuba and Vietnam, for example, prompted the chant "Move forward without compromising, as in Cuba and Vietnam."

The reformist point of view was represented essentially by the CP. The revolutionary left consisted of the left wing of the Socialist Party, the MIR, and, on a lesser scale, the left MAPU and the Partido Socialista Revolucionario, a Trotskyist party belonging to the Fourth International.

It is worth noting that after a long absence the Trotskyist movement is again making its presence known at the May Day demonstrations this year. It took part in the demonstrations in Santiago and Valparaíso. Its banners — the only ones in the Santiago meeting — carried slogans like "Workers' Control," "Nationalize the Banks," "Workers' Militias," and "Workers' Government." A few incidents occurred between reformists and revolutionists during the meeting, but nothing serious.

Tensions are continuing to mount, with reports of clashes between fascist bands and squatters or workers. Santiago is currently affected by an urban transport strike, and although this one is qualitatively different from the bosses' strike last October — this time it is the workers themselves who are paralyzing transportation in support of their demand for higher wages — the interference of the right wing in the present strike cannot be denied.

And while the dynamism of the fascist bands has led to an intensification of activity by the revolutionary left, the serious organizational weaknesses of the working class nevertheless remain.

Fascist Provocations
and Labor Unrest

By Hugo Blanco

Santiago, May 15

The government declared Santiago Province an "emergency zone" on May 5. The reason it gave for this was the "seriousness of the events of the past forty-eight hours."

After the murder of a Communist worker on April 27, the revolutionary left partially broke with the passivity that the Popular Unity leadership urged in the face of the provocative bluster of the fascist bands. Clashes occurred between leftist and rightist groups. The most serious clash took place May 4 in downtown Santiago. It left Mario Aguilar dead and four persons wounded — all members of Patria y Libertad. One of the wounded was Ernesto Miller, who holds a top post in that organization.

Another important event that Patria y Libertad was behind was the "resurrection" of Roberto Thieme, the general secretary of the organization. Thieme had been pronounced dead approximately two months earlier; his "death" was handled in the proper way, with a mass for the dead, speeches, and all the appropriate ceremonies. Now he has turned up in Mendoza, Argentina, along with Juan Sessa, another leader of Patria y Libertad. They were arrested after they secretly landed a plane there May 2. It appears that since his "decease," Thieme has been busy transporting weapons from Argentina to the big landholders in southern Chile. The Argentine government granted both fascists asylum on May 8.

Subsequently, some Patria y Libertad weapons dumps and contraband trade were discovered near the Argentine border.

There is no question that these ostensible reasons for declaring Santiago an emergency zone are important. But it is no less certain that behind the move were other serious reasons that were not mentioned.

A protest rally of four Santiago municipalities (Providencia, Nuñoa, La Reina, and Las Condes) had been called for May 5. It is true that all four are led by the right wing and that they contain rich neighborhoods, but the reason for the mobilization was the problem of food shortages, which is the main problem in Chile these days. This demonstration could have developed into the first link in a chain of mobilizations around the question of food distribution. And although the demand being raised by the four municipalities was freedom of trade, the subsequent demonstrations that it might have kicked off would probably have raised the demand for direct distribution of goods, bypassing the merchants altogether.

The demonstration was canceled after the area was declared an emergency zone, but this does not eliminate the fact that the problem of the distribution of goods continues to be the big time bomb that becomes more explosive the longer it takes to blow up.

As a result of the high cost of living and the wretched distribution of goods, the problem of wages also takes on an increasing importance.

A "readjustment law" for workers in state companies is presently under discussion. The executive branch is proposing that only the wages of the lowest-paid workers be raised and that the readjustment be financed through direct taxes being levied against those who have the most money. The parliament, which is in the hands of the opposition, says that the readjustment should not be limited only to the lowest categories, but the demagogy of its position stands out clearly owing to its refusal to approve any way of financing the proposal.

Besides giving its support to the government in this interminable discussion, the working class is beginning to indicate its concern over its economic situation in more expeditious ways. Direct struggles around economic demands have been begun by public works employees, truck drivers in collective transport, and miners.

The extension of the emergency zone to O'Higgins Province on May 10, in fact, was the product of a strike begun twenty-seven days earlier by the workers in El Teniente mine, which employs around 13,000 workers. The purpose of the strike is to defend the sliding scale of wages already won by the workers, which the government now wants to do away with. This strike was supported by a forty-eight hour strike by the workers in Chuquicamata mine; they are discussing the possibility of launching an indefinite strike. In addition to this, a nationwide strike in the copper mining industry appears probable.

The government and the news media that support it are attempting to minimize the problem by pointing out that "the majority of the workers have gone back to work" and that it involves "only a strike by white-collar workers." In addition, they are trying to grotesquely distort the character of the movement by depicting the workers as vulgar pawns of the right wing that have been carried away by their "economism."

The right wing is trying to make hay out of the problem by giving it publicity and by giving verbal backing to the strikers. The president of the Senate, for instance, went to the zone, and the leader of the rightist organization of secondary-school students made a speech to the miners in which he voiced "solidarity" with them.

The government attempted to intimidate the workers with 500 Carabineros and two tanks, but the miners offered resistance and blocked access roads to the mine. When it was over, thirty people had been wounded. At that point, both sides adopted a more restrained attitude, but the strike is continuing.

In view of the dizzying rise in the cost of living, it is possible that these conflicts among layers of workers that are not fully under the control of Popular Unity might be the beginning of a wage struggle on such a broadened scale that it would not enjoy the demagogic support of the right wing. The public works employees already showed clearly that the struggle against the government for wage increases does not amount to playing into the hands of the right wing. The government came off very badly when it made this insinuation in the case of these workers; actually, it gave the workers a chance to demonstrate their antirightist determination, in contrast to the timidity of the Popular Unity.

In turn, the government's antipopular attitude will become clearer to the workers each time and will have the effect of making them less reluctant to struggle against it.

Workers Organize to Meet
the Rightist Threat
By Hugo Blanco

Santiago, May 18

A superficial glance at Chile might lead one to conclude that everything is moving to the right. Among the parties of the right, the fascist movement Patria y Libertad is becoming stronger. In the Christian Democracy the right wing has carried the day. The right wing of the Unidad Popular is getting stronger. Even the left wing of the Socialist Party and the left MAPU are softening their line, and the MIR itself goes so far as to defend General Bachelet, the official who has brought about a retreat from the distribution of goods under popular control.

Yet the workers' vanguard is boldly moving into action in the face of the right-wing escalation. This is clearly shown by the Cordón Vicuña Mackenna. (This is a concentration of factories along a certain avenue in Santiago.)

The working class is organized into unions on a factory basis, and these unions are grouped into federations of the various industrial branches; these federations in turn belong to the Central Unica de Trabajadores (CUT). The leadership of the CUT is bureaucratized and serves as a brake on the workers, though to a lesser extent than in other countries, owing to workers' mobility. The main political force in it is the Communist Party, though it also includes even Christian Democrats.

As in every prerevolutionary process, the masses are beginning to create new organizations that are more responsive to their struggle, though for the moment they are not abandoning the old ones. The *cordones* are a partial innovation in the sense that they continue to make use of the unions, but they are linked by zone, by *cordón*, rather than by industrial branch.

At first the top leadership of the CUT refused to recognize the *cordones*, and the CP called them illegal bodies. Today this position is no longer tenable, and the reformists now reluctantly recognize them in view of the fact that their own rank and file has refused to heed their effort to ignore the *cordones*. At the same time, they are demanding that the *cordones* subordinate themselves to the CUT leadership. The *cordones* are paying no attention to this demand.

Going back, the history of the spread of the *cordones* began with the "Workers' Command of the Cordón Cerrillos" in June 1972. It was formed in connection with three serious workers' struggles in the zone at the time. The second was the Cordón Vicuña Mackenna, which was formed in August 1972 but reached its high point during the bosses' strike last October.

The big advantage of organizing by *cordones* lies in their ability to quickly assemble the masses and leaders, which is something that federations by industrial branch cannot do. In a period of "emergencies" such as the present one, this is a quality of no small value. Their big weakness is also tied to "emergencies," since it is only during such periods that they surge forward in a demonstration of workers' power.

During periods of relative calm, the workers' representatives who continue to attend *cordón* meetings are overwhelmed by petty-bourgeois elements, who are also allowed to attend because the vanguard workers are not sectarian. In these cases, interminable "high-level" discussions can be heard, heavily flavored with personal recrimination and superficiality. "Fishhead stupidities" is the way the Chilean worker describes this. And along with all this are MIR-ist proposals for artificial "mobilizations" that are not prepared at the rank-and-file level.

But now, when the workers sense an imminent threat from the right or the capitulation of the reformists, they are returning to their *cordón* and calling a gentle but firm halt to the behavior of their generally well-intentioned petty-bourgeois friends.

This can be seen very clearly in the case of Vicuña Mackenna. In face of preparations for a new strike by the bosses in the transportation industry (in spite of the fact that the government is rewarding their strength by offering them 2,000 vehicles); in face of the escalation of the right wing in the political and economic spheres, especially as regards the problem of distribution; in face of the escalation in activity by the bands of Patria y Libertad; in face of the threat of seditious actions by the right during the [May 21] ceremony opening the next session of the national Congress, at which Allende will be speaking; in face of this entire offensive by the bourgeoisie, the *cordón* is stirring like a colossus awakening from slumber.

Unlike previous meetings, during which the *cordón* languished with little worker representation, the workers' vanguard from the zone was strongly represented at the last one. It got right to the point and some important concrete agreements were arrived at:

1. It was agreed that in case of a strike by the bosses, the workers in the *cordón* would organize transportation in a centralized fashion so that the workers will be able to reach their factories. This is to be done with vehicles belonging to the factories.

2. Workers in two unions, one of which is in the Monserrat supermarket (which is in the hands of the workers), have formed a committee to organize a people's store for the *cordón*. It will operate out of one of the factories.

The following was projected: a) that industries that produce food or other consumer goods will supply the store with them; b) that industries that produce something needed by the consumer-goods-producing industries will supply them; c) that factories that have been taken over by the workers and that possess vehicles will make them available for transporting the above; d) that the *cordón* demands that the Distribuidora Nacional (DINAC — National Distribution Agency), which is owned by the state, supply goods; e) that the private distribution agency, CODINA, will also be pressured to do the same; f) that a meeting will be held of all the popular and peasant groups in the area in order to organize the distribution of goods to them via the people's store in the *cordón*.

3. To reactivate the Vigilance Committees for the Protection of Enterprises in places where they existed last October, and create them where they did not. These are pickets that are more or less equipped to defend industries, since there is a danger that the reactionary forces will attempt to take them over. In addition, these committees and all the workers in general are to remain on the alert for any seditious activity by the right wing.

4. Agitation and propaganda are to be stepped up. Since only a small number of the factories in the zone are affiliated with the *cordón*, the work of the *cordón* must be made known to the broadest layers of the rank and file. It is felt that the people's store, which is taking charge of a vital problem for Chile, will enhance both the prestige of the *cordón* and the need for it.

5. Not to return to private ownership the Andina Spinning Mill, which was taken over by the workers and is operating better than ever since it lost its boss. The Supreme Court has ruled in favor of returning it.

Problems like the distribution of goods are not mere conjunctural problems. As a result, they can serve as a permanent axis for developing the dynamism of the *cordón*. Thus the working class is offering a challenge not only to the right wing and its escalation, but also to the retreat of the forces of reformism in the face of this escalation.

The producing class is beginning to take up the problem of organizing the distribution of the goods that it produces. In itself this is a very serious matter. But it is all the more so in a context in which the bourgeoisie has been making statements such as the one made in the May 12 editorial of *El Mercurio*: "Civil war, or at least confrontation, appears inevitable."

It is in view of all these factors that the great proposal of the CP for the present situation takes on its full flavor: "Collect signatures against civil war."

The Workers' Cordones Challenge the Reformists

By Hugo Blanco

Santiago

The *cordones industriales* have emerged from the rise in combativity of the Chilean workers. The reformists, especially the Communist Party, have taken a hostile attitude toward these bodies from the very start. The reason is clear: they are dynamic bodies that elude the control of the CUT, whose leadership is reformist—for the most part Communist. The reformists accuse the *cordones* of being "illegal," "unconstitutional," etc.

Nevertheless, the reformists have had to change their tactics as the workers have ignored their evaluation and have begun to regard the *cordones* as their own vanguard organization, around which they unite during critical moments. In recent months, the reformists have been talking about the *cordones*, but by referring to them as bodies that ought to be under the authority of the CUT.

Now that the Chilean process initiated by the Popular Unity is in a state of retreat, the *cordones* are standing out as the main focus of resistance. In view of the seriousness of the situation Chile is going through, preparations are being made for a meeting of all the *cordones industriales* and the *comandos comunales* (community commands—bodies that involve squatters and peasants as well as workers) in Santiago Province.

The Cordón Cerrillos is planning to hold a community meeting prior to the provincial meeting. It was during a meeting called to help organize this community meeting that the new tactic of the CP toward the *cordones* could be seen in action.

The report by the president of the *cordón* went more or less as follows: "The *cordones* are nuclei of popular power and must be developed because the government is locked into the framework of bourgeois institutions, which prevents it from thoroughly confronting the bourgeoisie; as for the state bureaucracy, it leaves much to be desired, and we can state that it is in the service of the bourgeoisie.

"Beginning September 4, 1970, there has been an intensification of the class struggle, but in spite of this the government has made concessions to the bourgeoisie. The *cordones* must be restructured and reorganized and must extend their activities and their propaganda and struggle to take control of the economy out of the hands of the bourgeoisie by nationalizing the monopolies and introducing the direct distribution of goods.

"The perspective of civil war is being constantly posed, and the only way to avoid it is to prepare for it, not to go around collecting signatures [a direct reference to the approach of the CP]. Preparations for civil war must be made."

The position of the CP, expressed by CUT delegates and certain union leaders, hinged around the following points: "We have major organizations that cannot be ignored. The CUT is the body of all the workers, and it must be represented in the *cordones*. . . . Parallel organizations are being created out of a desire not to be under the jurisdiction of the CUT. . . . We agree that the meeting should take place, but the statutes and norms of the CUT must be respected. Let the CUT issue the call for the meeting and we will put out the publicity for it. . . ."

"Attendance should be restricted to union representatives. The *comandos comunales*, the JAPs, students, etc., should be excluded. . . . It is true that the community CUT is not functioning, but it is not necessary to create parallel bodies. . . . The community CUT should be reorganized and the representatives of other groups should join in discussions with the CUT."

Workers' representatives who were not from the CP responded: "The *cordones* are not trying to be parallel bodies. The *cordones industriales* and the *comandos comunales* sprang up in the face of the inactivity of the CUT. . . . What did the leaders of the CUT do in October? . . . Without consulting anybody the CUT approved the plan for the social sector of the economy [the Millas bill, which called for returning many intervened factories to the capitalists]. . . .

"All the mass organizations must take part in the meeting. There must be an effort to achieve unity among all the squatters, peasants, and workers, because there are even workers who are not in the CUT. . . . We must struggle for the solid unity of all the workers against the bosses. We must struggle together with all the exploited to build real power of the people. . . .

"It is true that the bosses are preparing for civil war, but the only way to prevent it is for us to prepare for it. . . . Extremism is bad, but there will be extremism as long as there is reformism. . . . There is no reason to get alarmed over talk about a bureaucracy since we all know that there is one. . . ."

Then representatives of political parties took the floor. Basically, there was agreement among the MIR, the MAPU, the Revolutionary Socialist Party, the Christian Left, and the Revolutionary Communist Party on the following: "Workers' control and popular power must be developed. Confronted with a vacuum of leadership, the working class filled it by creating the *cordones*. All organizations of the people must take part in the meeting because the problems that are going to be taken up affect everyone. Signatures alone will not be enough to deal with the preparation by the bosses for civil war; the workers must be prepared to meet this eventuality."

The Socialist Party (whose positions depend largely upon which delegate happens to be representing it at any given time) defended the "government of the workers," although it admitted that it had shown a lack of decisiveness. It agreed that all popular organizations should take part in the meeting "because there must be a deepening of the mobilizations and of the revolution."

In general, the CP put forward the following line: "Only union leaders should be invited to the meeting. The CUT is the only body representing the workers. The *cordones* must not hamper the work of the CUT. Civil war must be avoided because it can be avoided. More must be produced in order to solve the problem of the supply of goods. There must be more voluntary labor."

The president of the *cordón* then spoke again: "The battle for production can only be won if workers' control is extended to all factories—for example, to those that supply raw materials to many of the factories that have been taken over. Take for example the FENSA and FANTUSI factories: one is closed down and the other on the verge of being closed because of a shortage of raw materials due to the bosses' boycott.

"The *cordones* came into being as an expression of the will of the class. All popular organizations must be invited to the meeting because production and distribution concern peasants and squatters just as much as industrial workers. . . . In Maipú there is a shortage of agricultural products because, of the sixty existing ranches, only five have been expropriated. . . . The aims of the *cordón* are not limited, and for this reason all the workers and the exploited in general must take part in the meeting."

The maneuvers of the CUT and CP representatives came to naught. The gathering decided by acclamation to organize the meeting along the lines proposed by the executive board.

In spite of this, there is not much reason for optimism. The statements of the *cordones* have, generally speaking, always been correct, but unfortunately they now only involve vanguard sectors which will increasingly tend to grow smaller unless a thoroughgoing campaign is undertaken to involve all the rank and file. The problem is not one of making fine statements; it is one of organization and propaganda. It is to be hoped that the next meeting of the *cordones* will be an important step toward overcoming this weakness.

The Miners' Strike Poses a Dilemma for Allende

By David Thorstad

"Leaders and backers of Dr. Allende's Popular Unity Government rail incessantly against 'fascists and traitors' but they cannot obscure the cardinal fact about the present crisis: it was precipitated by a bitter strike against the state-owned Copper Corporation by workers at El Teniente mine, many of whom voted for Dr. Allende in 1970 and hailed his nationalization of copper.

"It was Marxist managers, not Yankee oppressors, who fired men for striking and brought strikebreakers to El Teniente. And it was a Marxist-led Government that ordered police to use tear gas and water cannon to break up a march on Santiago by 4,000 miners determined to press their case for a wage boost. To add to the irony, the 'bourgeois' opposition has impeached the Marxist Ministers of Mining and of Labor for violating the constitutional rights of the miners to strike."

As this editorial in the *New York Times* June 25 indicates, the imperialists can scarcely conceal their delight over the present crisis confronting the Popular Unity coalition in Chile.

The crisis developed out of a strike by workers at El Teniente mine, which accounts for a third of Chile's copper sales abroad. The strike, which began April 19, is costing Chile about $1 million a day and has resulted in an estimated loss in foreign exchange of more than $50 million.

The issue that set off the strike by the mine's 13,500 workers was the demand for a 41 percent wage increase to offset rampant inflation, in addition to the escalator clause already included in their old contract. The government gave the workers a choice of a blanket readjustment or sticking to the escalator clause. The miners say they are entitled to both.

"After several weeks of virtual shutdown at El Teniente," wrote Lewis Diuguid in the June 16 *Washington Post*, "the government offered productivity bonuses and a lump payment that it said would cost the state copper company more than the strikers' original demands.

"This offer split the copper workers into two factions: The majority of the unskilled workers and virtually all card-carrying members of the parties in Allende's ruling coalition voted to accept the offer and went back to work. Virtually all of the skilled workers backed up their leaders, who refused to vote on the government's offer. They have not worked since."

Production at the mine is now reportedly maintained on only one of the three daily shifts.

"Rancagua, where most of the miners live," Diuguid wrote, "clearly was in the hands of the strikers. Support for the strikers was impressive, and indicative of how anti-Allende forces have taken advantage of the workers' conflict to embarrass the government.

"Each morning, armed convoys of buses carrying strikebreakers go up to the mine. During the day, large numbers of strikers meet to argue about tactics and to receive food driven by truck convoy from sympathetic farmers to the south. The trucks are provided by the same owners who played a critical role in the nationwide strike last October."

The government has branded the strikers "fascists" and "traitors" and warned of the need to "avoid civil war."

In mid-June, the strikers voted to stage a march to Santiago in order to bring new attention to their cause. On June 14, as the column of 4,000 to 5,000 marchers, led by a number of legislators from the opposition Christian Democratic and National parties, reached the border of Santiago Province, they were stopped by a battalion of national police. "The government said they had no permission to march," Diuguid reported, "and when they attempted to proceed they were cut down by tear gas and water cannon."

Although most of the marchers turned back, some 2,000 were said to have been smuggled into Santiago in private vehicles. Two days of bitter street fighting followed involving police, miners, opposition supporters, and supporters of the Allende regime. The clashes left one leftist student shot dead and seventy-six others wounded, according to Associated Press.

On June 15, Allende held a meeting with representatives of the strikers in an effort to reach agreement on ending the strike. Previously, he had refused any such meeting. He was immediately and publicly denounced by both of the main parties in the Popular Unity coalition—the Communist and Socialist parties. The joint statement denounced the "artificial nature" of the miners' dispute and warned that "this false union movement, planned and sustained by all the forces of reaction," represented an "openly fascist and seditious approach." The meeting with the strikers, it said, was a sign of "vacillations and weaknesses" that must be avoided.

On June 20, tens of thousands of physicians, teachers, and students went on a twenty-four-hour strike in support of the miners. The same day, a peasants' organization led by the Christian Democrats declared a forty-eight-hour strike in support of their own demands as well as the strikers'. The following day, about half the country's 10 million inhabitants were affected by a series of strikes—including a general strike called by the CP-led CUT as a show of support to the government.

According to Associated Press, Allende told a crowd of 1,000 progovernment demonstrators that he would attempt to quash the opposition National Party and outlaw the right-wing Patria y Libertad. The way he would fight them, he said, would be to take their leaders to court.

The opposition has succeeded in turning the miners' strike into a serious challenge to the Allende regime. Allende's handling of the strike, moreover, has given the opposition a handle in its effort to divide and confuse the working class. The presence of the miners in Santiago, noted Pierre Kalfon in the June 19 issue of the Paris *Le Monde*, makes it possible for the opposition "to use the theme of 'solidarity with the strikers' to mobilize a section of the population that usually shows little inclination to do anything about the misery of the workers." In the city's well-to-do neighborhoods, "ladies in fur and young women in miniskirts are out collecting money for the strikers."

While the long-range strategy of the opposition is to bring down the Allende regime, the tactics it is following are not as unified as the government's high-pitched warnings about "civil war" might imply. While it is true that the far-right National Party is openly calling for civil disobedience ("The price to pay for overthrowing a dictatorship is civil war," said its president, Onofre Jarpa), the approach of the Christian Democrats is less straightforward. Its tactic—which it is implementing in the miners' strike—is to undermine and discredit the government, and cut it off from its base of support by spreading economic chaos.

The current wave of unrest has now reached the point that it is thought likely that Allende may again bring representatives of the military into his cabinet.

The Struggle Revives
By Hugo Blanco

Santiago, June 22

With the paradoxical strike by the copper miners of El Teniente serving as the starting point, the past week has seen an increasing unfolding of mobilizations by the left and the right.

The paradox of the Teniente strike lies in the fact that although it is a strike in which the workers are struggling for demands that defend their standard of living in the face of the runaway inflation that is plaguing Chile, from an early stage it was branded a "fascist approach" by practically the entire left (mainly the Unidad Popular, and to a lesser extent the MIR). This was a godsend for the right, which in October had already experienced how dangerous it was to confront the working class as a whole, but which now has an opportunity to divide the workers by supporting this and other conflicts condemned by the UP. There is no doubt that this right-wing maneuver is facilitated by the lack of sufficient political clarity among certain sectors of the working class, such as the miners, who, by not vigorously exposing the rightist ploy, are isolating themselves from their class brothers.

Within this confused context stands out the clear position of the Revolutionary Socialist Party, Chilean section of the Fourth International, which is denouncing the ploy by the right and showing how reformism is aiding it by calling the struggles of the workers for their demands "fascist." Unfortunately, the smallness of the PSR's forces makes it impossible for it to bring its position to large sectors of the working class.

It was in this atmosphere of confusion that the march of the striking miners to Santiago last week took place. This was used as a pretext for the right, including fascist bands, to mobilize, claiming that they were taking to the streets "in support of the miners." The UP played into their hands by attempting to halt the advance of the miners and by calling on the people to prevent these workers from "taking over the government house." Fortunately, there were few clashes between workers because the miners acted only in a defensive fashion. Those who were really very active were the fascist bands.

Confrontations occurred throughout the entire downtown area of Santiago, where tear gas hung in the air. In one of these confrontations, Nilton da Silva, a Brazilian revolutionist, was murdered. Da Silva had been forced to leave his own country by the monstrous repression with which the military dictatorship defends its existence. Nilton da Silva was a member of the MIR in Chile, and fell as a new Che Guevara, a symbol of proletarian internationalism.

His death stirred the masses of the left with indignation, and his funeral was a vigorous demonstration of a determination to struggle. The right called attention to the fact that he was a foreigner as proof that "there are foreign agitators." The UP tried to obscure this fact. The MIR, fortunately, singled it out through one of its speakers, who spoke "in the name of the foreign members of the MIR."

Street incidents continued in Santiago and other cities during the following days, one of their prominent features being attacks by fascist groups, which assaulted the headquarters of left-wing political groups and carried out other armed attacks. The show of strength by the right reached its high point with a demonstration "in support of the miners" that attracted around 80,000 persons.

Along with this, in the parliament the right moved to censure three ministers, and the National Party declared in the pages of *El Mercurio* that "in the light of justice and morality, no one is obliged to respect or obey a government that has ceased to be legitimate." Its next move was to call on Congress to "consider the illegitimacy of the activity" of the government.

In response to this rightist escalation, the CUT found itself forced to call a strike and a demonstration for June 21. Anticipating that the mobilization would be a success, the right had the foolishness to call for a "strike of Chile" against the government for the same day, urging people "not to leave their houses," and "to present the picture of a lifeless city."

There was unquestionably nothing lifeless about Santiago June 21, with hundreds of thousands of demonstrators winding through its streets. Huge columns from the Cordón Vicuña Mackenna and other sectors gathered in the hotbed of reaction — Providencia. One could not tell whether the rattling of windows was the result of the deafening voices of the demonstrators or the trembling of the terrorized parasites inside their homes. Thus the working class defended its gains, among which it included the government that it had put into office.

Together with unenthusiastic chants like "*No* to civil war," and "I stand in line but, no matter what, I am sticking with the UP," could be heard other, more vigorous chants, like "If the parasites want war, that's what they'll get," "How do you prevent or win a civil war? By struggling and creating people's power," and "Create, create, a popular militia."

About one million persons gathered in Constitution Square and the adjacent streets in the biggest demonstration in recent years. In spite of the transport strike, there were many people who came from outlying suburban shantytowns. Unlike earlier demonstrations, this time workers came with their work vehicles — tractors, trucks, garbage trucks, etc. Large crowds also took to the streets in other cities.

Allende and Godoy, president of the CUT, spoke in a much less lukewarm tone than at the May Day demonstration. Among other things, Allende had to pick up on the chants for "creating people's power," but he did so by explaining that this should not be done in contradiction to the government. Godoy spoke of the need to centralize the distribution and supply of food.

The Popular Unity press is reprinting Godoy's speech, but not Allende's. It could be that he said something that was not in the script in response to the gigantic chorus with which the entire crowd greeted his speech. "Firm Hand! Firm Hand!" they roared. The criticism appeared to strike home, because he began by stating that he had never used a gentle hand, and later on he said that his was not a reformist government — yet he mixed this up with charges that the right had "branded [!] his government as Marxist without respect to the military ministers."

Repeated appeals for people to remain calm did not stop the masses from stoning the headquarters of Patria y Libertad and the Catholic University. A large number of the demonstrators carried clubs or "spears" without attempting to conceal them.

The reviving of the masses of the left can also be seen in the occupation of various ranches by peasants in Maipú, near the Cordón Cerrillos; the take-overs were supported by the workers in the zone. It is also worth noting that the Cordón Vicuña Mackenna is becoming more active.

In addition, *El Mercurio* was suspended from publishing for six days. [An appeals court invalidated the closure, enabling the newspaper to resume publication on June 23, after not coming out for one day.]

V

THE APPROACHING SHOWDOWN

An Attempted Coup is Foiled
By David Thorstad

As office workers in the downtown section of Santiago were heading for work on the morning of June 29, they got caught in traffic jams created by heavy fighting going on around the presidential palace. Rebel troops from the Second Armored Regiment stationed on the outskirts of Santiago had chosen that morning to attempt a coup against the Popular Unity government of President Allende.

Fewer than 150 of the 900 troops in the regiment took part in the coup, which was headed by Colonel Roberto Souper. There was no sign of support from either the navy, the air force, or the rest of the army. It was all over three hours after it began.

The Buenos Aires daily *La Razon* carried the following early report from United Press International in its June 29 edition: "An intense shoot-out began when the armored cars and the soldiers reached the Moneda presidential palace, and the cracking of gunfire could be heard throughout the entire center of town, while the civilian population fled the area.

"The armored cars and tanks reached Bulnes Square, in front of the Moneda Palace, just after 9:00 a.m. and immediately began their martial activity. Buses and other means of collective transportation quickly got out of the area of fighting, as did the civilians who were in the vicinity. Other armored cars were posted at the Ministry of Defense, located on the other side of La Alameda, which runs in front of the presidential palace; one of the tanks was placed in the door of the ministry itself, thereby blocking the entrance.

"The . . . police guarding the presidential palace responded to the shooting as the armored cars circled the building. Various projectiles hit the residences that face onto Bulnes Square; one of these contains the offices of United Press."

The government said that twenty-two persons were killed, most of them civilians, and at least thirty-two wounded. The civilian victims appear to have been caught in crossfire. UPI described the scene inside the presidential palace in a dispatch published in the July 1 issue of the New York daily *El Diario*: "Bullets bounced off the marble walls. Various persons who were in the vestibule were hit by these bullets. One man, wounded in the neck, cried: 'My god! My god!'"

At 10:00 a.m., Allende went on radio to appeal for people to remain calm and stay out of the area. He called on the workers to take control of their factories and to await further instructions. "People must remain calm," he said, "for I have complete confidence that loyal forces will normalize the situation."

Left wing broadcasts urged workers at communications centers and hospitals to keep the buildings under their control.

New York Times correspondent Jonathan Kandell reported from Santiago June 29 that spokesmen for the main opposition party, the Christian Democrats, called for support of the government and constitutional order. "We Christian Democrats have a long tradition of fighting for democracy," said Claudio Huepe, a Christian Democratic member of the Chamber of Deputies, in a broadcast during the revolt. He called for support to "the constitutional government" and urged his party's followers, "Stay in your houses."

Shortly after noon, Allende arrived at the presidential palace. By 1:00 p.m., he was able to announce that the revolt had been put down. The government, he said, would use "all means to reach the real culprits and as always they will try to disguise their responsibility."

"Shortly after the revolt had been quelled," reported Kandell, "pro-Government supporters marched through the streets on the periphery of a heavy cordon of loyal troops surrounding the Presidential palace. 'A united left will never be defeated,' the demonstrators chanted. 'Allende, Allende, the people are defending you.'"

Later that evening, Allende spoke to thousands of cheering supporters. He accused members of the fascistlike Patria y Libertad of having participated in the revolt. Some of them, he said, had taken refuge in foreign embassies when it failed.

Reuters reported July 1 that five members of the organization had sought political asylum in the Ecuadorian embassy.

According to a report in the June 29 *La Razón*, Communist Senator Luis Valente Rossi charged that there had been an "invasion of mercenary troops" in the northern part of the country and that Patria y Libertad had helped to organize it. "The legislator claimed that it was an attempt to create border problems and that persons from Patria y Libertad were traveling by plane to the northern zone and preparing an option for an incursion of troops through this sector; they were said to be doing this with Arturo Marshall, former Chilean army major who headed various subversive movements and who is living in voluntary exile in Bolivia. Orders for his arrest are out for having violated the law on state internal security."

Following the attempted coup, a state of emergency, already in effect in O'Higgins and Santiago provinces, was extended to the rest of the country's twenty-five provinces.

The revolt came some twenty-four hours after General Mario Sepúlveda, commander of the emergency zone in the Santiago region, announced that a "barracks revolt" had been crushed in the egg. The aim of the thwarted revolt, he said, had been to "break the institutional processes" of the military. Arrests of its leaders, he said, "have totally aborted this barracks uprising." On June 28, Minister of Defense José Tohá told the parliament that nine officers and sergeants had been arrested for taking part in a plot to overthrow the government.

Government spokesmen provided few details of the thwarted conspiracy, not even revealing the regiment involved. According to a report by Kandell in the July 1 *New York Times*, however, it was the same regiment that attempted the coup the following day. Indeed, he reported, Colonel Souper "was about to be arrested as the head of a barracks plot uncovered by army officials earlier in the week" when he went ahead and led the abortive coup attempt.

The announcement that the barracks revolt had been crushed followed what the government described as an attempted assassination June 27 of the army commander in chief, General Carlos Prats. "Government dailies," reported the Buenos Aires *Clarín* June 29, "label the incident a plot to kidnap or — according to some — to assassinate the former minister of the interior. The opposition press says that it was a simple incident between a woman and General Prats."

Kandell gave the following account of the incident in the

June 28 *New York Times*: "Prats . . . was riding in his chauf-
fer-driven Ford when a middle-aged woman in a small red Re-
nault passed his vehicle on a main avenue. Recognizing General
Prats—who has been increasingly accused by conservatives
as a supporter of the Marxist Government—the woman stuck
out her tongue.

"During a brief chase, General Prats allegedly fired twice—
once into the air and once at the vehicle—before the woman
stopped her car. According to witnesses living in houses over-
looking the scene of the incident, General Prats descended from
his car and approached the woman, brandishing a pistol and
demanding that she apologize."

A near riot ensued, during which the tires on Prats's car
were deflated. The woman, Alejandrina Cox Palma de Val-
divieso, when asked why she stuck her tongue out at the general, replied that she did it "because I enjoyed doing so."

The government took a dimmer view of the incident; it declared a state of emergency throughout the capital region.
It said that the housewife's car had hemmed in the general's,
leading him to think that he was about to become the victim
of a terrorist attack. The general secretary of the government,
Aníbal Palma, called it "a strange siege" and said it "bore
all the characteristics of an ambush."

In the wake of the attempted coup, Allende's position appears to have been strengthened. So does the likelihood that
he will again try to name military officers to posts in his government.

Allende singled out General Prats as the man most responsible for putting down the army revolt. Prats personally super-
vised the military operations around the presidential palace.
Photographs of him carrying a machine gun and leading loyal
troops will no doubt help refurbish his image, tarnished somewhat by the Cox incident.

Allende himself, who had been warning for weeks of "fascist
plots" against his government, will use the abortive coup to
strengthen his image as an upholder of the bourgeois constitution and to cast his bourgeois opponents as the subversives.
"Even some of the more moderate members of the Opposition
today compared the effects of the revolt to the Bay of Pigs
invasion of Cuba [in] 1961, which followed repeated warnings by Fidel Castro that his Government was being threatened
and which strengthened his popular support," observed Kandell in a June 30 dispatch from Santiago. "In a congratulatory
message to Dr. Allende last night, the Cuban Premier was
quick to liken the episodes."

The Workers Respond
to the Threat of a Coup

*The following two statements were responses by vanguard
workers to the rightist threat that was clearly mounting in
mid-1973. Both were printed in the July 30, 1973, Intercontinental Press.*

*The first was issued on June 29, while tanks were deploy-
ing in downtown Santiago, by representatives of leftist parties
in the Elecmetal factory, headquarters of the Cordón Industrial
Vicuña Mackenna. Members of the Communist and Radical
parties were among the signers, although the line of these
two parties differed sharply from the demands in the statement.*

*The second statement was adopted July 9 by the council of
the Cordón Vicuña Mackenna. Aside from a reference to the
"armed forces, loyal to the people," it charts a course of independent struggle to head off "the next coup."*

Statement Signed by Representatives of the Left

We representatives of the undersigned left-wing parties express our total support to the measures taken by the Command
of the Cordón Industrial Vicuña Mackenna in its Instructions
Numbers 1, 2, and 3 [a reference to factory take-overs and
preparations to defend the *cordón* with all means available
at a time when the attempted coup had not yet been put down].

The workers will not allow the government, installed by
us, to be overthrown by the bourgeoisie. We will not permit
the gains we have achieved over long years of struggle to be
swept aside by a fascist mob. The workers will crush sedition;
we will make no truce with the bourgeoisie, but will crush
it once and for all.

1. All plants will become part of the social sector of the
economy; not one plant that is important for the workers will
remain in the hands of the bourgeoisie.

2. *Workers' Leadership.* Production and distribution will
remain in the hands of the workers, and the people will exercise
complete control over community territory.

3. *Popular Militia.* The organized people must protect their
gains. Create a Defense Committee and arm it in every industry and neighborhood.

4. The leadership of the defense and the advance of the

people will be assured only if they rest in the hands of the organized working class.

Eloy Bustamante, Socialist Party
José Urrutia, Communist Party
Augusto Alcayaga A., Radical Party
Sergion Sotomayor, Christian Left
Enrique Fernández, Revolutionary Socialist Party

Statement by Cordon Vicuna Mackenna

The events of Friday, [June] 29, as a culmination of all the provocative activities of the right, clearly showed that democracy and defense of the Constitution, loudly proclaimed by the right, become nothing but empty words when it sees that the people are extending their rights and conquests.

Imperialism and the bourgeoisie and its parties understood that their parliament and their courts were not adequate instruments for crushing the people. Thus they turned to a military coup. After this, they no longer have the right to talk about democracy or constitutions.

The coup was prevented from succeeding by the quick and vigorous response of the workers and the other exploited sectors of the people together with the armed forces, loyal to the people and the government they elected. Faced with the response of the workers and the people, the sectors that are bent on a coup have for the moment delayed their action. We must be clear about one thing: the people stopped the coup by crushing the political offensive that provided the framework for the military offensive.

Nevertheless, the danger persists. The plotters who did not surface during the June 29 coup are preparing for a decisive blow. The workers and the people must not lose a minute. Let us prepare to repel the next coup, taking into account the fact that the June 29 coup was only a small test in which just a few of the plotters became visible.

We must hold assemblies in workplaces, shantytowns, and in the countryside to discuss the measures and forms of organization and struggle that we will have to adopt in the face of the attacks of the right wing and of the next coup.

We must devote this period to gathering forces and organizing organs of popular power.

In view of the seriousness of the present situation, the council of the Cordón Industrial Vicuña Mackenna has passed the following resolutions:

● The only way to overcome the crisis that the country is experiencing as a result of the sabotage by the bosses is to see to it that all of production and all essential distribution of goods is transferred to the social sector of the economy (as is the case with other work centers, where the workers are deciding this), and that they be placed under the guidance and control of the workers.

● Imperialism, the capitalists, the fascist bands, and the coup-bent military are demonstrating day after day that the bourgeoisie will not allow the process to move forward peacefully, but that as long as it has the strength to do so, it will use violence against the people.

To every blow from the right, we will respond with a blow where it will hurt them the most.

● Let us advance the right of the people to defend themselves and defend their gains, and to move forward, without compromise, toward socialism.

Only the leadership of the working class will guarantee that the process will move forward.

The specific measures that must be taken in this respect are:

● The workers in every plant will name an administrative committee to run the plant. The committee can be replaced at any moment by an assembly of the workers.

● Production in the social sector will give priority to products for popular consumption.

● Factory and farm goods will go essentially to people's stores in communities where they exist; they will be administered by the workers and squatters, who will distribute the goods through their own groups. Small merchants who are part of the exploited will be allowed to take part in the distribution if they observe the norms laid down by the squatters: either they place themselves at the service of the people or they will find themselves squeezed out of the distribution process.

● Certain areas will be specified as having preferential status with regard to distribution, such as shantytowns, industries, governmental bodies, hospitals.

● Only through these measures — such as the transfer of Loncoleche and Luchetti into the hands of the workers and their direct entry into distribution at the hands of the people — will it be possible to guarantee that goods find their way into the hands of the workers.

● Creation by the workers and the peasant communities of a Committee for the Defense and Protection of Industries, in line with the call issued by the CUT.

● Prohibit the sale of newspapers used by the capitalists to slander and denigrate the workers.

This program must be discussed in the assemblies of all factories and other workplaces, and in every shantytown and peasant community.

The *cordones industriales* must assume their responsibility of linking up with the other mass bodies in order to organize community councils.

The Cordón Industrial Vicuña Mackenna calls on the other *cordones,* the community councils, all the mass organizations, the left-wing political parties, and the union rank and file to support and struggle for these tasks.

At this time we must put aside harmful sectarianism. All those who take upon themselves these tasks will constitute *a single force.* Our *cordón* cannot be divided by sectarian attitudes, which constitute suicide and irresponsibility, such as the attempts to bring into existence a parallel and last-minute *cordón* in Progreso.

A unified leadership for the *cordones industriales* and other mass bodies is necessary and urgent; for this reason we propose the opening of discussions between the leading bodies of the *cordones industriales* and other organs of popular power.

Finally, we must point out that *the members of the military who fell were ordinary soldiers. Those who have now been soldiers for a few months were workers and peasants, and within a few months they will return to that status. They must struggle alongside the people, of whom they are a part. They must struggle for the people's cause, which is their cause. They must not let themselves be won over to fascism. If they must die fighting, let it be for the interests of the workers, who are the people.*

In the Aftermath of the Coup Attempt
By Hugo Blanco

Santiago

On June 29 desperate sectors of the right attempted a coup d'état here.

In view of the gravity of the situation, the CUT found itself forced to call for seizing the factories as a preventive measure. The working class carried this out. In the face of the rapid response by the workers, many of the plotters stayed under cover and the putsch was quickly put down.

Many workers took advantage of the occasion to demand that their places of work be added to the nationalized sector.

Another important consequence of this attitude on the part of the workers was the strengthening and partial arming of their defense committees. The workers guarded their places of work day and night. Some factories have already been intervened, and not a day passes without at least another one being taken over.

There are very interesting cases such as the Luchetti noodle factory and the Loncoleche powdered milk plant in the Cordón Vicuña Mackenna. They were seized while the tanks were at the gates of La Moneda. The *cordón* strongly supported these take-overs, considering that these plants were essential to popular consumption. Now the distribution of their products is controlled by the workers, fundamentally by the *cordón's* distribution body as well as that of the homeless people's association. Thus the *cordón* has won its demand that the interventors of both factories be persons in whom it has confidence.

The case of the Vinex factory is also very important, but for another reason. The workers had already taken it over before June 29. They demanded that the manager of this state-owned factory be fired. The majority of the workers as well as the trade-union leaders belong to the same party as the manager — the Socialist Party.

Faced with government procrastination in solving the problem of the Vinex factory, the *cordón* decided to appoint the interventor itself, naming one of the employees of the plant. He was nominated by the union and approved by the rank and file. This is the first case in which the *cordón* has assumed this kind of responsibility, and with the help of the *cordón* the Vinex factory has started to sell the wine it produces.

In the Cordón Cerrillos many take-overs are also being carried out and the organization of defense committees is moving ahead steadily. The factories in the vanguard of this *cordón* are Textil Artela and Cristalerias Toro. Because of the scarcity of glassware, the latter is considered strategic. And Textil Artela, which is on strike, wants the factory confiscated by the state and put under the direct administration of the workers. The *comando revolucionario de huelga* (revolutionary strike committee), which was formed to lead the union in the conflicts, is in agreement with this.

By comparison with the other *cordones,* the Cordón Cerrillos has the advantage of being closely linked to the peasant organization in the area.

In the other *cordones* in Santiago we have also seen the same agitation, as in Panamericana Norte and Macul, where factory seizures have become the order of the day recently. Another combative sector is the hospital workers, who during the days when the curfew was in force held all the hospitals and were ready to treat the *compañeros* who fell wounded.

I should also note the seizure of ENDESA (Empresa Nacional de Electricidad — National Electricity Company), which controls the distribution of electricity to Santiago and Valparaíso. In the rest of the country, similar things are happening, although to a lesser degree, as in Concepción and Valparaíso, for example.

The right began to send up a cry of alarm over the first seizures and the setting up of the first defense committees, and, although they are continuing to do so, their tone of protest has begun to drop to a lower register.

The armed forces, especially the navy and the air force, have begun to carry out raids, looking for alleged arsenals. Sometimes they find arms; other times not.

The parties of the revolutionary left, including the left wing of the SP, have stepped up their campaign aimed at the ranks of the armed forces and are trying to strengthen popular power.

The tension has dropped in Chile but the present "calm" is very relative. It is expected that the right will attempt another coup. The sectors of the right that favor a "constitutional" solution are constantly shrinking.

On the other hand, the situation of the UP leadership becomes more difficult every day. Because of the coup, it had to appeal to the masses. Allende called on the workers to come with "what they had," just as CUT called for taking over factories as a preventive measure and alerted the defense committees.

Although, in his speech on the afternoon of the coup, the president gave credit for crushing the uprising to the armed forces, the generals did not want to enter the cabinet again unless Allende promised first to clear out the factories and other things like that. In these conditions, an acceptance by Allende would have meant a complete surrender to the right and a break with the masses, who are far from being beaten and are more than ever demanding new advances. The new cabinet is almost the same as the last. This doesn't mean that the government isn't still looking for a deal, but this is becoming more and more difficult.

Popular power is growing and the confrontation is coming ever closer.

Allende Names an All-Civilian Cabinet

By David Thorstad

"What we fear most is that some right-wing group will go off half-cocked against Allende. That would be just what he wants. He could put on emergency powers, suspend the constitution and rule by decree. We'd be finished as an opposition." These fears, expressed in June by a member of the Christian Democratic Party, have proved to be a bit exaggerated. While President Allende has emerged strengthened from the June 29 crisis, such extreme measures were not used.

Following the failure of the coup, five top leaders of Patria y Libertad sought asylum in the Ecuadorian Embassy in Santiago. They were Pablo Rodríguez Grez, John Schaffer, Benjamín Matte, Manuel Fuentes, and Juan Hurtado Larrain. Rodríguez Grez is president of the organization, and Matte was, until recently, head of the National Agricultural Association. He resigned when it was discovered that he belonged to Patria y Libertad.

With the crushing of the revolt, Allende moved to consolidate the position of his Popular Unity government.

On June 30, amid booing from the opposition, his government requested Congress to extend the state of emergency into a state of siege. Such a measure would have set aside many constitutional guarantees for a period of ninety days and given the president the power to order house arrests and search and seizure without warrant. On July 2 the Chamber of Deputies rejected the petition by a vote of 81 to 52. In response, Allende issued a statement in which he warned that "every citizen should be aware that the nation is on the border of a new civil war, which the Government is pledged to avoid."

From *Intercontinental Press*, July 16, 1973

On July 1, a government offer was accepted by striking workers at Chile's giant Teniente copper mine, bringing to an end their two-and-a-half-month strike. "The strikers last night agreed to return to their jobs tomorrow after accepting a Government offer of a bonus payment of $225 and a wage increase of $15 a month," reported Reuters July 2. "But they are demanding that sanctions against 60 miners dismissed for occupying a radio station in Rancagua, near the mine 50 miles south of Santiago, be called off. The Government has insisted that a commission be set up to try the 60." The strike cost Chile an estimated $70 million to $100 million in lost production.

By July 5, five days after the attempted coup, Allende felt that the situation had stabilized to the point that he could call off the state of emergency imposed throughout the entire country, as well as the 11:00 p.m. to 6:30 a.m. curfew in the capital. Almost 2,000 people had been arrested in Santiago for curfew violations, but most were released after spending one night in jail.

During the state of emergency, police powers were turned over to the military. The military also had authority to censor newspaper stories. Associated Press reported July 2 that "Santiago newspapers appeared on newsstands today with numerous blank spaces caused by military censorship. Both pro-Government and opposition newspapers were affected."

The government called off the emergency decrees, according to Interior Under Secretary Daniel Vergara, "because the causes that forced imposition of the measures have disappeared."

The growing prominence of the military in the increasingly tense situation in Chile had led to mounting speculation that some military officers would again be named to the cabinet. General Carlos Prats, commander in chief of the armed forces and former interior minister, was frequently mentioned as a likely candidate. His prominent role in personally leading the crushing of the June 29 coup attempt seemed to make his appointment all the more likely. It was known, according to an AP report July 3, that the military "had repeatedly demanded not only wider participation in the Cabinet, but jobs as ministry undersecretaries and provincial governors as well."

In addition, not long before the coup attempt, Allende's own Socialist Party issued an unusual statement praising the military and urging it to collaborate with the government. "We have never conceived of the armed forces as henchmen for oligarchic interests and foreign monopolies, nor as being subject to the game of petty partisan interests," stated the document, according to a report in the July 4 issue of the Buenos Aires daily *La Opinión.* "As we have already said, their role is to be part of, and to press forward, an irreversible historical process for all Chileans, which is not the personal possession of select groups of politicians."

Nevertheless, when the fifteen-member cabinet resigned July 3 in order to give Allende a free hand in choosing new ministers, the president announced that he had decided not to appoint any military figures to the body. Two days later, the new cabinet was named. While it represents one of the most extensive cabinet reshuffles since Allende took office in 1970 (seven new ministers), the new cabinet retains the political balance of the preceding one. Four portfolios went to Socialists, four to Radicals, three to Communists, and the rest to independents or members of smaller parties.

The first task of the new cabinet, Allende announced July 6, will be to implement, within a month, a new "emergency plan" that "will require great sacrifice and effort, which we all have an obligation to make."

According to the United Press International dispatch published in the July 8 issue of the New York daily *El Diario,* the new plan will include, among other things, the following measures: "Strengthening of the authority of the executive branch in economic, political, and administrative matters; economic austerity in order to confront the inflationary spiral, which reached 163 percent last year; better distribution of consumer items, with state control over the market for essential goods."

Allende added that "in this difficult time, it is urgent that those who do not wish to understand should realize that the destiny of our country obliges us to act generously."

The same day that he made his appeal for "generosity," the Frente de Trabajadores Revolucionarios, which is connected with the MIR, issued a call for a nationwide strike. The FTR statement noted that "the only way that we workers can hold back the offensive that is aiming at a coup or capitulation is by taking a big step forward. . . ." This step, it said, would be "a big, national work stoppage." The response to the FTR appeal is not yet known.

The Counterrevolutionaries
Step Up the Pressure

By Gerry Foley

The rightist offensive that began with the attempted military uprising of June 29 was escalated July 25 with a new bosses' and professionals' strike. It was spearheaded, as in October, by the truck owners. The far right tried to give the maximum intensity to the campaign against Allende by launching a wave of terrorist acts, beginning with the assassination of the president's aide, Captain Araya, on July 27.

The prolonged crisis of the Allende regime—regarded not so long ago by the pro-Moscow Communist Parties as a showcase of the peaceful and electoral road to socialism—has reached a new peak. An inexorable process of polarization between the capitalists on one side and the workers and poor farmers on the other has drastically reduced the room for class-collaborationist maneuvers.

From the moment the popular front government was brought to power by the rise of the workers' movement, the bourgeois parties have been steadily stepping up the pressure on Allende to force the Unidad Popular to retreat and to demobilize and disappoint the masses. The objective of the main bourgeois political strategists has been to wear away the popular hopes inspired by the UP victory, while at the same time keeping Allende in power as the best means of holding a rein on the popular strata supporting his reformist government.

Despite the capitulationism of Allende and the Communist Party, which forms the real leadership of the UP, the bourgeoisie's war of attrition has involved escalating risks.

In the first place, sectors of the ruling class and the right have shown a tendency, in view of the rise of mass mobilizations, to become panicky and to go too far. The assassination of the commander of the armed forces, General Schneider, on the eve of Allende's inauguration reflected these dangers. The murderers represented a rightist faction in the army. As the tensions have grown, it has apparently become more and more difficult to make sure that only the right amount of pressure is brought to bear against Allende.

On the other hand, the assaults of the right against the UP

regime have provoked responses from the workers that Allende could not control and that went further and further toward irrevocably undermining the bases of the capitalist system.

The abortive uprising of June 29 may have represented simply an outburst by panicky rightist officers like the assassination of Schneider, or, as *Chile Hoy* suggested, possibly the first in a series of limited military rebellions designed to slowly tighten a noose around the neck of the government. In any case, the tank assault on the presidential palace touched off a working-class mobilization similar to the one that responded to the rightist offensive in October 1972. Workers staged a new series of plant seizures, and the *cordones industriales* were strengthened.

Following the June 29 putsch, *Chile Hoy* noted an increasingly bloodthirsty tone in the conservative press. The magazine's July 27 issue quoted an article in *El Mercurio* by Héctor Precht Bañados entitled "Anti-Communist Satisfactions," in which he said: "Traveling through anti-Communist countries like Brazil offers profound satisfactions for those of us who have had to put up with the Communists for almost three years. In the first place, you find the Communists in their proper place, in hiding."

In the same issue of *El Mercurio*, an editorial seemed to advocate an "Indonesian" solution, as *Chile Hoy* saw it: "The editorial was entitled 'The Communists Set Jakarta Plan in Motion.' The historical truth was nothing less than this: 'The Reds, instigated and equipped from Peking, tried in September 1965 to take over the country by liquidating the military high command, which they considered their main enemy.' But the plan failed, *El Mercurio* explained, and 'then the anger of the people was aroused, and a general crackdown on the Communists started up, which was all-embracing and spontaneous and horrible.' But it really wasn't so horrible because, thanks to this opportune repression, Indonesia 'is one of the leading nations in southern Asia. . . .' Its population is so large that no one even notices that in 1965 the 'spontaneous' repression caused the 'death of hundreds of thousands of leftists.' Thanks to this purge, 'the economy has been stabilized and order prevails.' The message is quite clear."

But not just the classical right (to say nothing of the growing fascist element) seem to be thinking in stark terms. *Chile Hoy* also quotes former "center-left" President Eduardo Frei, now president of the Senate, in a speech two days after the

June 29 coup attempt: "After denying any participation by the 'democratic sectors' in the rebellion of the Second Armored Regiment, he noted that as a result of this event 'the occupation of factories and ranches was ordered. The *cordones industriales*, with which they are trying to surround the city, were strengthened. And what is graver still, the certainty exists that arms were distributed. Strategic deployments were made and orders were issued as if Chile were on the brink of a civil war.'"

The former Christian Democratic president warned, according to *Chile Hoy*: "'The constitution of a popular power means in fact creating a parallel army,' which has to be crushed, 'before it is too late.' This was the response of the noted 'democrat'—who waited in silence to see how the June 29 attempted coup would turn out—to the dialogue that President Allende offered to his 'opponents.'"

Despite the rightist attempt to overthrow the government by armed force on June 29, and despite the multiplying acts of terrorism by the fascist Patria y Libertad, Chile's "democratic armed forces" turned their main attention toward crushing in the egg the "parallel army" of the workers. The "arms control" law that was passed with relatively little protest by the opposition-controlled parliament at the height of the October crisis suddenly seemed to emerge as the most important statute in the code.

Even *Chile Hoy*, which in October and November had praised the "people's army" as "patriotic," was shocked by what seemed to be at least overzealousness on the part of the military in enforcing this law. The July 13 issue offered some mild criticism in a civic spirit:

"A year ago . . . the left members of parliament warned that the rightist opposition was trying to assign to the armed forces a role for which they were unsuited and unprepared. These warnings were confirmed dramatically early Sunday morning when about two hundred airborne troops, supported by three helicopters, four trucks, two buses, and two vans and aided by the light of flares, raided the Cementerio Metropolitano [Metropolitan Cemetery] just hours before army troops carried out an equally spectacular raid of the offices of DINAC [Distribuidora Nacional— National Distribution System] in Valparaíso. On Friday, also in Valparaíso, marines stormed into a boys' school so violently that the high command later apologized to the principal."

The airborne troops that raided the cemetery were ruthless in their "counterinsurgency" mission, as indicated by the account the groundskeeper's wife gave to *Chile Hoy*:

"My husband was going out to the privy when he was arrested by the military. They also took me out of the house, and we barely had time to dress. Then they took out the children (they had seven) who had not had time to put their shoes on. There were twenty of us lying for some time in the mud and rain. They were not people that the military found when they arrived inside the cemetery but neighbors who came to see what was happening. From the noise, you would have thought an airplane had crashed. But afterwards we realized that it was helicopters landing in the cemetery. All those who approached were forced to lie down in the mud with their hands behind their heads. We were there for a very long time, and when we complained of the cold, they kicked us."

Chile Hoy noted reprovingly: "After six hours of this intensive operation, the men of the Chilean armed forces withdrew. In this space of time they had done almost as much damage to the image of their institution (the same thing happened in Valparaíso) in the eyes of the people as the soldiers did to the army's image in the previous unfortunate incidents in El Salvador (1966) against the miners and in José María Caro (1963) against the homeless people."

Using the army for such repressive tasks, *Chile Hoy* warned, would "only separate the soldiers—who are trained to operate on the basis of brute force—from the people. Of course this is precisely what the right wants today."

The armed forces command very quickly showed its readiness to use brute force not only against civilians but also against their own enlisted men in order to prevent anyone from taking too seriously the talk about the "democratic traditions" of the Chilean military.

The use of brute force was especially salient in the navy, where, according to the August 24 *Chile Hoy*, rightist officers had been preparing for months to play a key role in toppling the Allende government. The plan reportedly consisted of two parts. The first was to use the navy to block the shipment of provisions and supplies over water and thus complete the blockade imposed by the transport industry. The second was to support a series of small risings such as the June 29 mutiny.

"These plans were jeopardized, however," the pro-UP maga-

zine noted, "by the situation among the sailors and petty officers. For months it had been clear that the majority sentiment
was running against a coup and in favor of loyalty to the
government. In practically all units of the three zones into
which the navy has divided the Chilean coast—Valparaíso,
Talcahuano, and Punto Arenas—events have been taking place
that are peculiar for a country where both the left and right
have cultivated the idea that the armed forces should be 'apoli-
tical' and strictly 'professional.'

"Rightist officers have been delivering harangues, especially
to the petty officers, using exactly the same language as politicians like Onofre Jarpa [head of the National Party] and
Eduardo Frei. That is, the government does not intend to
rectify its policy. Not even the most energetic appeals have
any effect, and the only 'solution' is to overthrow it.

"In these same harangues, which were particularly frequent
in July, it was said that the essential first step was to destroy
the mass organizations of the left, especially the *cordones industriales* and the *comandos comunales* through using the
arms control law."

After the June 29 coup and the start of the popular mobilization it touched off, the naval officers made special efforts
to separate the sailors from civilians. They ordered that only
commissioned officers should carry weapons. Supplies of arms
were hidden. At the end of the first week in August, a large-
scale repression was launched to eliminate "sedition," that is,
opposition to the rightist plotting.

The arrests of "extremist" sailors and navy yard workers
were described in the August 24 *Chile Hoy* by Pedro Enríquez, their lawyer. Enríquez, a member of the MIR, said: "The
charge of subversion and extremism raised against these sailors
and workers by the naval authorities will not stand the least
examination. Let us just note that, starting August 5, 1973,
about one hundred sailors and workers were arrested and
savagely tortured. On August 14, the head of the naval tribunal in Talcahuano, Don Fernando Jiménez Larraín, found
them guilty of 'dereliction of military duty' according to Para-
graph 3, Article 299, of the Military Code of Justice, a clause
that is used when no other definite infraction can be lodged.
To make myself clear: When you can't charge them with anything else, you can find them guilty of dereliction of military
duty, which covers infractions from not getting a haircut up
to and including violating a regulation.

"The truth is quite different from these claims. From the

time that they learned Allende had won the presidential elections, the reactionary sectors of the armed forces began to prepare to stage a coup at the opportune moment against the constitutional government. These putschist preparations were widely noted by the sailors and workers, both on large ships like the *Blanco Encalado*, the *O'Higgins*, and the *Prat*, and in the various navy yards.

"This prompted some petty officers and sailors, as well as some workers, to talk about refusing to let themselves be used for a coup against the legal government and — if one occurred — to oppose it. These conversations reached the ears of those involved in the putschist maneuvers, and they used their influence in the commands and among the reactionary officers to cook up a monstrous farce about 'subversion' and 'extremism' in the ranks of the armed forces.

"The only offense committed by the sailors and workers who were beaten up and put on trial was that they professed leftist ideas and were ready to oppose a coup against the constitutional government. This is what they said to the tribunal, and that is why the authorities haven't been able to charge them so far with anything less vague than 'dereliction of military duty.'"

In its physical intimidation of the imprisoned sailors and navy yard workers, the Chilean military did not seem notably inhibited by its much touted "democratic traditions." Essentially the same methods were used as those made familiar by the Brazilian military dictatorship in particular. This is the account that eight of these prisoners gave Enríquez:

"They took us one by one to the so-called Cuartel Borgoño, where they violently forced us at gun point to strip completely. Since we weren't quick enough in their opinion, they kicked us and beat us with their rifle butts. Then they took us to a place where there was a drainage pit or, as they called it, a 'swimming pool.' It was filled with mud, excrement, gravel, and slime. They forced us to splash around in it.

"Then after a long period of this kind of softening up, they took some of the men, bound hand and foot, and propped them up against a wall, while one beat them with his fists, concentrating on the stomach. Others were forced to prop themselves up against a wall or on the ground with their arms and legs far apart. Then we were in just the right position for them to kick us in the mouth and stomach until we could not hold ourselves up any more. When we fell, they kicked us all over.

"Finally we were submerged in an oil drum filled with muddy water and excrement. They threw us in head down and held us by the legs. When they thought we might die if they kept on with such treatment, they took us out. At last, when they thought that our physical and moral resistance was broken, they asked us questions. If anything in the answer didn't suit them or fit in with the models offered by some officers, we were thrown into the drums again to 'soften us up' once more."

Reports of "subversion" in the Chilean navy were mentioned in the international press, but an informant in Valparaíso told *New York Times* correspondent Marvine Howe that there was no need to worry about the leftist influence in the fleet: "'The Miristas' — radicals from the Movement of the Revolutionary Left — 'were trying to infiltrate the enlisted men but it isn't a real problem because the navy has American instructors and is solidly anti-Communist,' the agent for a steamship line said."

Furthermore, the popular front government was clearly incapable of combating the conspiracies of the rightist officers in the only effective way, by organizing the enlisted men to defend their democratic rights and involving them in the process of class struggle going on in the country. In fact, instead of going to the aid of the sailors and workers persecuted by the rightist plotters against his regime, Allende echoed the false charges against them. Enríquez complained:

"In my opinion, the relationship of forces among the officers in the armed services, especially the navy, is unfavorable to the left at the present time. Clearly, the great majority of the officers in this branch are against the government and the left. I think that the policy officially promoted by the government toward the armed forces bears some responsibility for this. The regime has tried to quarantine the officers from the class struggle in conditions where this has only favored the advance of reactionary sectors, which have been able to carry out their plans undisturbed, almost without opposition.

"It has become a virtual taboo in the traditional left parties to do any work with a correct orientation aimed at the armed forces, especially that portion of them that is the people in uniform. One example will suffice. While the workers in the navy yards and the sailors suffered and continue to suffer the most bestial repression in memory for identifying with the left, when Dr. Allende swore in his so-called 'National Security Cabinet,' he disavowed these workers, saying that they were ultraleftists linking up with the ultraright. Saying such things about workers and sailors who are ready to oppose a coup against the government seems, to say the least, gravely mistaken."

Not only Allende was determined to keep the armed forces quarantined from the class struggle. The best-organized, most homogeneous, and politically most consistent party in the UP government, the Communist Party, on which the president has come more and more to lean, was, if anything, even more outspokenly in favor of such a policy. CP General Secretary Luis Corvalán put it this way in a speech quoted extensively in the July 31 issue of *Chile Hoy:*

"Because the workers took some immediate security measures against the recent attempted coup and maintained these precautionary measures, some reactionaries have begun to send up a howl, thinking that they have found a new issue to use to drive a wedge between the people and the armed forces. They are claiming that we have an orientation of replacing the professional army.

"No sir, we continue and will continue to support keeping our armed institutions strictly professional."

Despite the efforts of Allende and the Communist Party, however, the mass mobilizations provoked by rightist attempts to undermine the UP's social reforms have inevitably had an impact in the armed forces. A soldier interviewed in the July 20 issue of *Chile Hoy* indicated one avenue by which the class struggle has penetrated into the army. "Take my case, for example. Since I am a bachelor, the army doesn't give me enough to live on to make it through the month. If we in our neighborhood had not organized a JAP we would perish from hunger. There is an order that says we can't take part in the JAPs, but what would we get out of obeying such an order? Many have disregarded it."

Thus, the reasons for the nervous and violent mood of the officer corps and the bourgeois politicians are clear, and with them the reasons for the lengthening shadow of the gun over Chilean political life.

Under the threat of the June 29 coup, the workers carried their mobilizations and independent initiatives another long step forward. The tendency to create a "parallel army" is inherent in the situation; it is the logical and essential next step for the Chilean workers, and it goes hand in hand with splitting the ranks of the military. Unless an effective popular force is created quickly, the bourgeoisie is likely to lash out suddenly and desperately to crush the workers' movement and impose a Brazilian or even an Indonesian solution. The workers seem already to have advanced further than the bourgeoisie can tolerate.

It is the situation itself that inspires the fears of the bourgeoisie. There is still no real revolutionary party in Chile that can initiate the process of organizing a workers' army or splitting the ranks of the armed forces. The MIR's defense of the political rights of enlisted men could have an important impact and lead to serious work within the armed forces. But so far this organization has conspicuously failed to raise slogans to prepare the way for arming the masses and creating a popular army. Its demands for giving the right to vote and better treatment to soldiers are not a sufficient program for work in the army, and time is rapidly running out.

Under the pressure of events, the need for a revolutionary offensive seems to be becoming more widely understood. In the Cordón Industrial Vicuña Mackenna, where a group of Chilean Trotskyists is active, statements pointing in the right direction were issued around the time of the June 29 coup attempt by representatives of several left parties. The council of the *cordón* itself issued a program for a counteroffensive. But there is still no party that can take up this example and spread it throughout the *cordones* and throughout the country.

Nonetheless, the process of polarization has advanced so far that it does not seem that the bourgeoisie and the reformists can maintain the formulas for class collaboration that they adopted during the rise of the UP government and in the October crisis. The first condition set by the Christian Democrats for accepting a "dialogue" with Allende was that representatives of the military be brought back into the cabinet so as to guarantee "observance of the constitution."

On August 10, Allende complied and installed a "cabinet of national security" including General Prats, the commander of the armed forces. But the entry of the military into the government and the threat of martial-law measures against the truck owners did not resolve the situation as it did in October 1972, not even temporarily. The military were not accepted as impartial arbiters by important sections of the UP, especially the SP left wing, which is most susceptible to pressure from the masses, or by important sections of the right. The military cabinet was seen much more clearly as a betrayal by the workers. On the other hand the right, emboldened by Allende's repeated capitulations, would accept nothing less than complete surrender, which Allende could not grant. Under these pressures, the military cabinet collapsed. On August 18, the holder of the most sensitive post, General César Ruíz Danyau of the air force, resigned as minister of transport.

He had not moved very energetically against the truck owners. "The military has taken a very placid, almost courteous attitude toward the truckers," *Le Monde's* correspondent noted in the August 18 issue. The military carried out one arms search near Santiago. "In the rest of the country it has not yet intervened."

Despite the entry of the armed services commanders into the cabinet, the Christian Democrats had continued to support the new "bosses' strike." *Le Monde's* correspondent wrote: "The truck owners' association feels that it has the support not only of the rightist political organizations (the National Party) and the extreme right but also the Christian Democratic Party, which has declared that it supports the action without any reservations.'"

Allende depended entirely on the army to restore order: "The president of the Chilean trade-union federation, Figueroa (CP), and the general secretary, Calderón (SP), have offered Allende the support of the workers both in organizing surveillance of key points in cooperation with the army and in taking over and putting back into operation the trucks that have been stopped and sabotaged by their owners. So far Allende has preferred to rely exclusively on the military apparatus," *Le Monde* reported.

At the same time, Allende could not accept his gold-braided transport minister's demands for complete surrender to the truckers, so Ruíz resigned both his ministerial and military positions. At the same time, Allende fired his undersecretary of transport, Jaime Faivovich of the SP, as the truckers had demanded. But Frei suddenly took a new attitude toward the presence of the military in the cabinet, accusing the UP of "skillfully and impudently using the armed forces so as to make them take the responsibility for the economic, political, and social disaster facing Chile."

Ruíz's resignation sparked discontent in the air force that threatened to lead to a new coup. "It is evident that the deep division of Chilean society is being increasingly clearly reflected in the military institution," wrote Enrique Alonso, a correspondent of *La Opinión*, in the August 21 issue of the Buenos Aires daily.

Alonso also pointed out why Allende could not accept Ruíz's demands for a "friendly settlement" with the truckers. "For the leaders of the CUT it was getting harder and harder to hold back their rank and file who wanted to 'leave the factories to restore order in the country.'"

On August 25, Prats himself was forced to resign to "preserve the unity of the army," as he put it.

Speaking to a group of progovernment students on the night of August 25, Allende explained that Prats had resigned after recognizing the wives of several high officers in a protest demonstration in front of his house.

Although Allende was able to put together a new national unity cabinet in the last days of August by bringing in lower-ranking officers, the formula did not seem very promising, as the *New York Times* noted in an editorial August 31: "It is by no means clear, however, that these men will be able to succeed — where their commanders in chief in the previous Cabinet failed — in ending the strikes and violence, restoring public order and confidence and shoring up Chile's battered democratic institutions."

In face of such deep divisions, the traditional answer of the Latin American bourgeoisie is to put a demagogic Bonaparte in power. The UP and the CUT bureaucrats have obligingly built up the image of General Prats as a likely candidate for "savior of the nation" — if, by their failure to organize the masses effectively against the rightist plotters in the army, they have not prepared the way for an Indonesian or Brazilian outcome to the present crisis.

VI

THE DOWNFALL OF
POPULAR FRONTISM

The Coup

By Gerry Foley

By the beginning of September the shortages caused by the economic sabotage of the native bourgeoisie and the imperialists, as well as the government's indecisiveness and bureaucratism, were reaching catastrophic proportions. Supply was hampered by the prolonged strike of truck owners determined to bring the government down. Finally the delivery of wheat to Santiago was cut off altogether by rightist terrorist attacks. Allende was forced to admit September 7 that only three or four days' supply of flour remained.

Large sections of the petty bourgeoisie, driven into a frenzy by the malfunctioning of an economy torn by a class struggle that Allende would not lead but was increasingly unable to contain, were mobilized by the right in wave after wave of attacks on the regime.

On September 5, about 150,000 middle-class women gathered in front of the Catholic University and called on Allende to resign or commit suicide. This was the only way, they chanted, to avoid civil war. Fascist commandos participated in the demonstration.

Another sign that the class polarization was reaching a critical point was that, for some time, the advocates of patience on the bourgeois side had been withdrawing from the scene. As in the period of civil war in Russia, the most ruthless leaders of the reaction were coming to the fore.

Allende's last bridge to the military was cut August 27 when Admiral Montero resigned as head of the navy. The naval officer corps would accept no replacement but Admiral José Toribio Merino, a well-known rightist.

Condensed from the September 24 and October 1, 1973, issues of *Intercontinental Press*

Allende continued to court the military as a prop for his regime against the mounting attacks from the right. But they were already beginning to move against the Unidad Popular's real supporters and defenders, the workers in the occupied plants.

To whatever extent the workers had armed themselves, they had done so essentially in response to the escalating violent attacks by the bourgeoisie on the key points of the economy and on the most militant sectors of the workers' movement. The left-wing parties had not organized a workers' militia. The MIR had raised a number of correct demands for mobilizing the workers to take direct control of the economy and — unlike the UP parties — had warned about the putschist intentions of the military, but it never concentrated on the need for arming the workers. Its formulations in this regard were vague and timid at best.

On September 7 air force troops surrounded the Sumar textile plant and shooting broke out. Finding themselves in turn surrounded by people from the neighborhood, the troops withdrew. This was only a probe, but it gave a foretaste of the coming confrontation.

Pierre Kalfon reported in the September 11 *Le Monde:* "As the armed forces — essentially the air and naval arms — have proceeded to carry out the searches authorized by the 'arms control law' [passed in October by the votes of the bourgeois opposition in parliament; the UP deputies abstained and Allende did not veto it], many supporters of the Unidad Popular are coming to wonder if the June 29 coup was as much of a failure as believed. Since that day, in fact, the army seems to have been progressively dropping the neutrality that was its pride and has been choosing to launch its 'mop up' operations against worker and peasant areas rather than among the bourgeoisie, which, nonetheless, does not make any bones about the fact that it is ready to 'go the limit' to overthrow President Allende."

"Could Salvador Allende have been unaware," Marcel Niedergang asked in the September 13 *Le Monde*, "that the real leader of the opposition, Eduardo Frei, the former chief of state and now president of the Senate, was no longer bothering to conceal that he saw as the only recourse a resort to arms?"

But Allende continued to proclaim: "There will be no coup d'état and we will avoid civil war." As a solution to the conflict, he offered a plebiscite to determine the will of the majority of the Chilean people, a proposal reminiscent of the Communist Party's petition against civil war.

A bitter early morning awakening

Very rapidly, the time came when the reality of class society could no longer be denied.

On September 11, in the early morning hours, the navy seized the port of Valparaíso. At 7:00 a.m., according to the September 13 *Le Monde,* Argentine radio monitored a broadcast proclaiming that a military junta had replaced the Allende government. The new regime was headed by General Augusto Pinochet of the army, whom Allende had appointed commander in chief only a few weeks before; General Gustavo Leigh, commander of the air force; Admiral José Toribio Merino, the commander of the navy; and General César Mendoza, head of the Carabineros. In short, all those forces that Allende had praised at his inauguration for allowing him to take power had now risen up to take it from him.

Some 3,000 persons were arrested in Valparaíso alone, according to the September 13 issue of the Buenos Aires daily *La Razón.* They were imprisoned on warships in the harbor. That is, according to this report, the navy seized one prisoner for every five of its total personnel, or almost 1 percent of the entire population of the port city.

Thus it seems, if the report is not exaggerated, that the commanders of the fleet must have moved with a ruthlessness unprecedented in Chilean history to restore "discipline" among the ranks of pro-UP sailors and navy yard workers who had already been abandoned to reactionary persecution by the government they sought to defend.

At 7:15 a.m., the military gave the Carabineros guarding the presidential palace a few minutes to evacuate the area. Meanwhile, Allende, who had apparently just been informed of the coup, rushed to the palace from his home. According to the September 12 issue of the Buenos Aires daily *Clarín,* the UP government had been expecting a coup for ten days, that is approximately since the resignation of Admiral Montero. So even when it knew that a coup was coming, it allowed the putschist officers in the navy to crucify its supporters.

Furthermore, the MIR had issued a statement giving the general scenario of the coup, as a report in the September 8 *La Opinión* showed. The uprising was decided on in late August. All that was left to be determined was whether it would install a new civilian government or an open military dictatorship. The Christian Democrats generally favored the former, the extreme right-wing Nationalists the latter. Probably the actual events would have to show which alternative was most realistic for the bourgeoisie.

It is still not clear how much of the shooting and bombing in Santiago actually had a military objective and how much was intended to intimidate the population. According to *Clarín*, Allende was left without any support from the official armed forces. "Allende found that the only ones who obeyed his orders were a small parapolice group, the GAP [Grupo de Amigos Personales — Group of Personal Friends, ex-guerrillas who, after opposing participation in the elections that brought Allende to power, pledged to defend him]. They went out in the street carrying machine guns and small arms but were rapidly cut down after a brief burst of fire."

The shooting continued on into the night and became even more violent in the industrial suburbs and poor neighborhoods. "No official version of these confrontations has been issued," *La Razón* reported. "But persons connected with the UP have described these armed clashes as being in fact 'massacres.'"

Following the surrender of La Moneda (the presidential palace), the military-controlled radio announced that President Allende had committed suicide. The junta refused the request for an investigation of Allende's death or for an autopsy. The most prominent practitioner of the "peaceful road to socialism" in recent years was buried September 12 in a secret ceremony in a cemetery outside Santiago as the sound of tank cannon and bombs in the industrial suburbs signaled a massive terror against the workers' movement, which he could not lead to victory.

The price of the defeat

Reports filtering out of Chile pointed to a slaughter of historic proportions, comparable to the massacres in Indonesia in 1965 or the atrocities of the Nazis.

"An American doctor who was in Santiago during the coup that overthrew Marxist President Salvador Allende said yesterday in this city that anywhere from 5,000 to 25,000 Chileans were executed," the New York daily *El Diario* reported September 24. "Dr. Phillip L. Polakoff said that there was 'widespread massacring of civilians and torturing of prisoners by the junta.'"

The main targets of this massacre were the thousands of foreigners living in Chile, workers who had occupied their plants, left-wing students, and inhabitants of working-class neighborhoods. Mark Cooper, a correspondent in Chile for

Pacifica Radio and one of Allende's translators, gave the following account—based on his own observations and reports from friends—to the New York Trotskyist weekly *The Militant.*

"Within three or four hours of the uprising by the military there began what could only be described as massacres. By about 12 noon, the state technical university in the western part of the city was invaded by the army.

"Of the three universities in Santiago, this is the one that is considered predominantly leftist.

"There were several thousand students on the campus at the time, and the army moved in to make sure that these students had no time to organize anything. First the university was strafed by British Hawker-Hunter jets of the Chilean air force. It was then surrounded by troops, who used mortars against it and moved in with machine guns.

"Firsthand accounts, from people I can guarantee are very responsible, estimate that between 600 and 700 students were killed on this one campus, within a matter of an hour.

"At about 6:30 that evening, army supply trucks came to cart away the bodies.

"One of the first statements of the military junta was that the coup had to take place because Chile had become dominated by 'foreign extremists,' specifically by Cubans and by Latin America and other exiles. The junta claimed there were 14,000 'illegal foreigners' in the country.

"About 10:30 in the morning, the armed forces began reading a list over the radio of foreigners of all nationalities, but primarily Bolivians, Brazilians, and Uruguayans. They said that these people had five hours to turn themselves in.

"This campaign against foreigners intensified throughout the morning, with statements that the intention of the coup was not only to overthrow Allende but to drive all foreigners out of the country. . . .

"At the same time, on the first day, the army moved against factories in the areas of industrial concentrations, the industrial belts, especially the Vicuña Mackenna area and the Cerrillos area. Claiming that the workers inside the plants were resisting, they began to attack with machine guns and mortars.

"I think we should get the picture straight here—in Vicuña Mackenna, for example, we're not talking about workers coming out in armed militias and resisting the army, because that's not what occurred. What happened is that the workers were caught in the factories. They were trapped. And they were fighting for their lives with whatever they had, in a more or less disorganized manner. They had no choice except to fight.

"But they were greatly outnumbered in terms of armaments. And in the areas where they couldn't make the workers surrender with machine gun and mortar attacks, they would bomb from the air."

In its September 18 issue, the Italian leftist daily *Il Manifesto* described a savage onslaught on one of the major plants in the industrial suburbs of Santiago:

"The Sumar textile plant was one of the last to surrender after the coup d'état. Although it was attacked by heavy artillery and bombed from the air, the workers held out until Friday [September 14], for almost five days. When the putschist troops finally entered the shops, bodies were lying all over the floor. (Even the correspondents of the Western press spoke of 500 dead.) Then there was a hand-to-hand struggle inside, a last desperate attempt to hold the factory. Then the survivors were flushed out and taken with their hands in the air to the stadium, together with other workers, teachers, and students who were caught with arms."

Il Manifesto reported a telephone call with a correspondent in Santiago who said: "Now it's practically nothing but a massacre. Thousands of Communists, comrades, workers, have been killed."

Two American graduate students released from an improvised prison in Santiago, Adam and Patricia Schesch, reported, according to a September 23 AP dispatch: "We personally saw the shooting of 400 to 500 prisoners in groups of 30 to 40, at the National Stadium, where we were being held."

It was evident from every source that the antiforeign pogrom was reaching demented extremes. The fact that the generals were apparently prepared to pay the political and diplomatic cost of the excesses against hundreds if not thousands of foreign nationals indicated that (1) they were ready to resort to the most savage slaughter, in the Indonesian pattern; (2) they needed a scapegoat for large-scale terror.

No foreigners were safe. *New York Times* correspondent Marvine Howe reported that an American film-maker suddenly disappeared, apparently taken by the military:

"'I don't know why they came,' Mrs. Hormon said in tears. 'Maybe some neighbors denounced us, although we have only been here six days.'

"Mrs. Hormon showed pamphlets that had been distributed in her neighborhood saying 'Chileans, do not be afraid to denounce your foreign neighbors, who have come here to kill Chileans.'"

The fate of many other foreign residents has already created a scandal in Latin America, although it has been barely mentioned in the U.S. press.

The embassies in Santiago were packed with foreign political exiles seeking shelter from the xenophobic terror, as well as with Chileans now forced to seek refuge from a military dictatorship in their own country.

"In Santiago as well as the rest of the country, they are shooting down people indiscriminately," Manual Meijido reported. The correspondent for the prestigious Mexican paper *Excelsior* fled Chile September 19 and gave this description of the reactionary terror going on in the country to *La Razón:*

"I have the most direct and reliable information that there is a perfectly well-prepared list of 13,115 foreigners and all the members of the GAP and the MIR. . . . All are in effect condemned to death.

"Now the worry of many diplomats and many foreigners in Santiago is how far the extremism of the Junta Militar will go. . . . It is reaching unheard-of lengths. On Monday [September 17] the Argentine consulate was raided. . . . On Friday [September 14] they sent two Carabineros into the home of the Mexican ambassador. . . . There is no telling how far things will go."

From one report, in particular, it seemed that the military commanders were determined to stage a deliberate slaughter of foreigners, perhaps with the idea that their corpses would support their story about exiled leftists forming a secret guerrilla army to impose "red terror" on Chile.

This is the way a business correspondent from the Caracas daily *El Nacional* described the death of a young compatriot in Santiago, according to an Agence France-Presse dispatch in the September 20 *Le Monde:* "Without giving the reasons for the arrest of Maza Carvajal [a twenty-two-year-old electronics student], the reporter . . . told how the young man was taken to an industrial district to be shot on the spot, in front of workers and students. The commander of the firing squad ordered him to flee: 'You are a foreigner, you are a Venezuelan. You can save yourself.' . . . When he refused, the soldiers dragged him up against a wall and shot him, telling the witnesses that he was an 'example.'"

Reports from escaped exiles indicated that Allende himself fell victim to the indiscriminate terror unleashed by the military. A government press officer, Jorge Uribe, who was in La Moneda when the military attacked, told *Siempre* reporters in Mexico City: "Allende ran toward a window and fell wounded." Apparently he was cut down by the withering barrage the military directed at the historic building. A member of the GAP who managed to escape with Uribe (he was called just "Ramón") said: *"El compañero presidente* was in bad shape when the soldiers came in shooting. They finished him off. They kicked *el Negro* Jorguera, who was wounded, in the face, and stomped him to death."

In the same issue of *Siempre,* León Garcia wrote that troops machine-gunned the entire staff of the MIR magazine *Punto Final* in their offices, as well as the journalists of the Cuban press agency, Prensa Latina.

Furthermore, even the *New York Times* report on the 7,000 prisoners the junta admits it is holding in the National Stadium in Santiago shows that the repression has extended to relatively broad layers of the population.

"About 150 Chilean and foreign newsmen were taken on a tour of the National Stadium today and shown some 800 of the prisoners at a distance," Howe reported from Santiago September 22. "The newsmen were allowed to shout questions at the prisoners sunning themselves in the bleachers behind an iron barricade but could not converse with them. The prisoners appeared to come mostly from the working class.

"Asked if they were Communists or Socialists, several answered simply, 'We are workers.'"

In this context, the junta's moves to block all paths of escape for the bulk of the estimated 14,000 political refugees in the country are an ominous sign of its intentions, not only toward the exiles but toward the Chilean people. On September 23, the dictatorship announced that it would no longer honor safe-conduct passes out of the country granted by foreign embassies.

Other Latin American regimes and, most importantly, the United States have undoubtedly given behind-the-scenes encouragement to the junta's determination to eliminate the left-wing exiles gathered in Chile. The only objective can be to seize the occasion to deal a lasting blow to the entire Latin American left.

In this situation the campaigns launched in many countries to defend the victims of the terror, by publicizing the atrocities and mobilizing political pressure against the Chilean junta and the role of the U.S., assume special importance. In the U.S., rallies, teach-ins, and marches have taken place from coast to coast, as groups and individuals attempt to extend public awareness of the bloody repression in Chile and the collaboration of the U.S. government in these crimes. One of the centers of activity is the U.S. Committee for Justice to Latin American Political Prisoners (USLA).*

More time will have to pass before the full extent of the reactionary terror in Chile can be ascertained definitely. But there are already indications that the objectives of the generals and their backers in Washington may have been more ambitious than any observers at first suspected. The United States and Latin American capitalist regimes may have conspired to turn what the Stalinist and Social Democratic reformists believed could be the showcase of the "peaceful road to socialism" into the slaughterhouse of the Latin American left and an example of defeat and devastation that could intimidate the radicalizing masses not only in the countries of the "Southern Cone" but throughout the world.

U.S. imperialism responsible

"Satisfaction not unmixed with a certain embarrassment," was the way *Le Monde's* September 13 editorial described the mood of official circles in Washington when the Allende government fell. There is no doubt that, whatever the direct role of American governmental agencies in the actual coup, U.S. imperialism was responsible in the last analysis for bringing down the Allende government. Its economic blockade created the lion's share of the shortages that fueled the pettybourgeois revolt, in particular the shortage of spare parts for trucks. Its refusal to sell wheat to the Allende government when a desperate shortage developed just before the coup seems to have been the final step in this policy.

In 1964 Washington had spent millions getting Allende defeated and Eduardo Frei elected president. Some of the U.S. corporations—whose investments in Chile totaled $964 million in 1968—didn't feel their government was doing enough and decided to supplement its efforts, as evidenced by the 1970 offer by the president of ITT of $1 million to the CIA to help defeat Allende.

---

* For further information on this campaign contact USLA at 156 Fifth Avenue, Room 702, New York, New York 10010. Telephone: (212) 691-2880.

William R. Merriam, an ITT vice-president, later told a U.S. Senate subcommittee that in February 1971 he assembled a committee representing U.S. companies with major investments in Chile to work out a joint anti-Allende strategy. Included were representatives of the Anaconda and Kennecott copper corporations and the Bank of America. "We have these ad hoc committees all the time in Washington. It's just a form of life," Merriam testified, and there is no reason to doubt his word.

When the Chilean government took over foreign copper holdings in July 1971, the concerted strategy was already well under way. Although Allende promised "compensation" for the property seized, Anaconda and Kennecott pushed for immediate payment, and the Nixon administration used Chile's foreign debt ($3 billion — $1.7 billion of it owed to the United States) as a club to enforce the demand.

U.S. representatives on international credit agencies blocked loans to the UP government. World Bank officials admitted in September 1972, for example, that no new loans had been granted to Chile since Allende's election.

Even with the most generous of intentions, the UP government was simply unable to pay the full amount of the "compensation" demanded by the copper corporations. The inability was aggravated by a decline in the world market price of copper.

But at the same time the UP government refused to repudiate the national debt or take sweeping measures against U.S. corporate interests. Far from avoiding U.S. military intervention, this course gave Nixon time to build up the economic squeeze, isolate Allende, line up the generals, and equip them for their task.

While U.S. exports to Chile dropped 50 percent, according to U.S. Commerce Department figures released August 3, 1973, and while all other foreign aid to Chile was cut off, Nixon supplied the Chilean military with $10 million in weapons.

The officer corps that carried out the coup was trained and nurtured by U.S. imperialism. "In 1973," a study of the Chilean army in the September issue of *Le Monde Diplomatique* noted, "Chile remains, along with Venezuela, the main recipient in Latin America of U.S. aid for training officers. For this, it is to receive a million dollars. Finally, Chile has just been put on the list of countries that can buy F5E supersonic jet planes on credit. How can one fail to think that this cooperation can offer the opportunity for ideological penetration, whose fruits the United States doubtlessly hopes to gather one day?"

The Chilean armed forces are known to be among the most

pro-U.S. in Latin America. Here again the class-collaborationist president was not only unable to move against this proimperialist fifth column but encouraged it. One of his last official acts was to agree to joint maneuvers between the Chilean
fleet and the U.S. Navy in the hope that this gesture would
arouse more friendly feelings toward his regime in Washington.

The deepening radicalization in Chile, combined with the
revival of the workers' movement in Bolivia and the workers'
upsurge in Argentina, was obviously becoming a serious threat
to the interests of U.S. imperialism in Latin America. Among
other things, by recognizing Cuba the Allende government
set in motion the undermining of the U.S.-imposed diplomatic
blockade of the first workers' state in the Americas.

Appropriately, one of the junta's first acts was to break
diplomatic relations with Havana. This action was under-
scored by an attack on the Cuban Embassy during the coup
and on a Cuban merchant ship off the coast.

Was Allende too radical?

It could be hoped in some circles that the bloody overthrow
of the Allende regime will inhibit the workers' movement in
other countries from setting its sights too high. In particular,
Juan Domingo Perón, the bourgeois demagogue charged with
keeping the lid on the workers' upsurge in neighboring Argentina, was quick to hold up the fate of Allende to the radical
youth as an example of what happens when you try to go
too far too fast.

As far away as France, the Gaullist *La Nation* pointed to
the fall of Allende as a warning of the perils of voting for
the Union of the Left, which also promises a "peaceful road
to socialism."

Neither Perón nor *La Nation* seemed to realize that the workers and radicalized youth might draw some rather different
conclusions from the failure of the Allende experiment. The
coup in Chile was not, after all, the first overthrow of a government committed to "peaceful social change." In fact the scenario
was much the same in Guatemala in 1954, when a U.S.-spon-
sored plot overthrew the CP-backed Arbenz government. Che
Guevara, who was an adviser to that regime, drew some lessons from his experience that were put to good effect. In Cuba,
the revolutionary government destroyed the bourgeois army,
and a popular militia played a major role in defeating the
imperialist attempt to overthrow the Castro government in
the 1961 Bay of Pigs invasion.

Perón himself was overthrown by a coup in 1955. He escaped Allende's fate by making a quick getaway. The Argentine military is still run by officers who backed rightist governments for the two decades following Perón's fall. Might not the radical youth who rallied around the old *caudillo* as a symbol of thwarted anti-imperialism conclude from the failure of Allende that the Argentine military also will ultimately block any significant social reforms, and that Perón has already proved himself an even less effectual leader than Allende?

The CP's role in the disaster

Nor is Perón the only advocate of the "peaceful road" to social change that may be discredited by the failure of the Allende experiment. In the last three months, the two most powerful Communist Parties in Latin America have proved unable to mount any serious resistance to military coups. The Chilean CP, the largest in Latin America, has 100,000 members, almost twice the number of personnel in the armed forces of the country. It is the most disciplined political organization in Chile and deeply rooted in the working class. And yet it not only could not organize an effective defense against the coup, but it encouraged the capitulationist policy that led inevitably to grave defeats for the Chilean workers.

The Uruguayan CP, which completely controls the national trade-union federation, called a general strike that paralyzed the country when the military took over. But it could not lead a revolutionary struggle against the bourgeois state and thus allowed the strike to collapse, without projecting any political alternative to the Bordaberry government.

Furthermore, the fall of the Allende government shows the hollowness of the CPs' claim that a reformist policy is necessary to win over the petty bourgeoisie to the side of the workers. It was precisely the UP government's reluctance to move to reorganize the economy decisively on a socialist basis that enabled the right to rouse the petty bourgeoisie against the workers.

The failure of the government to move rapidly to take control of the big ranches and industrial establishments, as well as the big transportation and distribution combines, enabled the bourgeoisie and the imperialists to sabotage the economy and create the shortages and hardships that drove the poor but individualistic petty bourgeoisie into a frenzy against the government.

Trying to respect the essential property interests of the capitalists, the Allende regime could not base itself on a mobilization of the workers, which alone could have kept up and increased production in the transitional period and was the only force that could ultimately block the attempts of the bourgeoisie and imperialism to overthrow the government. At times, the Allende regime even came into sharp conflict with workers and peasants who, encouraged by the idea that at last they had a government of their own, carried their struggle against the exploiters to the point of seizing the means of production. The government's compromises did not reassure the industrialists and property owners, who were frightened and enraged by the militancy of the workers and the landless. The capitulations only encouraged the vested interests to arm openly in defense of their property and to plot with impunity against the regime.

At the same time, the government's refusal to repudiate the national debt to the imperialists and its agreement to pay what was in fact compensation to the expropriated imperialist companies deprived the country of capital desperately needed for development.

As a result of its "evolutionary" approach, the government was unable to unite the decisive masses of the population behind a clear program for reorganizing the economy. Because of its refusal to expropriate the big capitalists, it did not have sufficient control of economic life to offer any solution to the problems of the petty bourgeoisie. Furthermore, in the absence of a plan for transforming the capitalist system as a whole, the government's policies tended to conflict in important areas.

For example, Allende's agrarian reform, it turned out, did not fit in very well with his policy of appeasing the army, as a study in the September issue of *Le Monde Diplomatique* indicated: "The army is tending to become an outgrowth of the middle class. According to a study carried out seven years ago, 42% of the officers graduating from military school came from the big bourgeoisie, 39% from the rather comfortable middle class, and 19% from the straitened petty bourgeoisie. Some 65% of the higher officers came from the middle class; among them, however, a large number were linked to the upper class. In many cases, in fact, a young officer with no personal fortune takes the opportunity of an assignment in the south to marry the daughter of a landowner. One of the most unexpected results of the agrarian reform was to reduce the dowries of the brides of young officers." Such small examples could be multiplied many times, since in the context of imperialism most of the major economic interests interlock.

Need for a revolutionary party

But when the September 11 coup came, the forces were in existence that could defeat imperialism and its local supporters. The organized workers in control of the plants represented probably the most formidable revolutionary force yet seen in Latin America. They were not entirely unarmed, although their arms were almost certainly insufficient. The coup had been expected for some time and it had been necessary to defend the key economic installations from previous right-wing offensives.

What the workers lacked above all was a centralized political leadership that, understanding the realities of class struggle, could have marshaled their economic and physical power against the reactionary forces. A mass revolutionary party able to give leadership to the resistance could have completely changed the outcome. In the absence of this, the coordinated and carefully calculated strike of a relatively small military force threw the workers off balance. Resistance was heroic but scattered and without a perspective. The military was able to concentrate its strength at will against the most advanced sections of workers. Otherwise, 50,000 soldiers could never have defeated hundreds upon hundreds of thousands of determined workers in control of the vital centers of the economy.

Nixon Pleads Innocence

For three years the Nixon regime and the U.S. ruling class worked to strangle and undermine the Unidad Popular government. But after the military coup, Washington and Wall Street were forced to mute their obvious satisfaction with the fall of Allende.

The ambiguity stemmed from two factors. First, in light of the well-known history of North American interference in Chile, the Nixon administration had to spend the lion's share of its public-relations time in dampening charges that the coup was planned or assisted by Washington.

Second, the fact that the Chilean bourgeoisie had been unable to demoralize the working class into passivity and was forced

to engineer the coup was a reflection of the workers' high
level of militancy. And under these conditions, the U.S. ruling
class was simply not sure that the Santiago junta would be
able to stabilize the situation.

Both concerns were reflected in the editorials of leading capitalist newspapers. ". . . it is essential that Washington meticu-
lously keep hands off the present crisis, which only Chileans
can resolve," advised the *New York Times* on September 12.
"There must be no ground whatsoever for even a suspicion
of outside intervention."

And on September 16, in an editorial piously titled "The
Chilean Tragedy," the same board of directors wrote: "The traditionally non-political armed forces intervened not primarily
because of Dr. Allende's socialism but out of fear that a polarized Chile was lunging toward civil war. What cannot be
clear for some time is whether the violent destruction of an
elected Government, albeit a minority one, will make that ultimate catastrophe less likely or even more probable."

Official Washington clearly grasped the importance of keeping
a low profile in the days immediately following the coup.
Initially, the White House and the State Department declined
to make any comment on the situation. But Dan Morgan,
writing in the September 12 *Washington Post*, reported administration officials as saying privately that while the U.S. wel-
comed the departure of Allende, "this could be offset if the
country was plunged into a civil war. . . ." They also expressed
concern that "Chilean nationalists" would blame the United
States, particularly because of the earlier ITT affair.

At a September 12 news briefing in Washington, both Gerald
L. Warren, White House deputy press secretary, and Paul J.
Hare, a State Department spokesman, said it was "inappro-
priate" for the government to comment on the situation, viewing
it as an "internal Chilean affair." Hare went so far as to
say that the administration hoped for a resumption of "democracy" in Chile and that it was in no hurry to recognize
the new regime.

Apparently Washington is waiting for the situation to stabilize, and for other governments to recognize the junta, before
itself taking that step. "We will try to make taking up relations not significant in the timing, to glide in, so to speak — not
the first and not the last — so that no one can infer a special
meaning," said a high-ranking official, as reported by David
Binder in the September 15 *New York Times*. Another official,
masking Nixon's contempt for principle in the usual cloak of
"pragmatism," stated that "we will have to work with the gen-

erals and it makes no sense to issue some moral statement about democracy."

At a September 13 news conference—the second in as many days—Hare and Warren spent some time trying to explain away several incidents that suggested that Nixon had at least had prior knowledge of the coup. There had been reports that four U.S. Navy ships en route to Chile to participate in joint maneuvers with the Chilean navy had been suddenly ordered to veer away in order to avoid giving an impression of intervention. The problem was that the ships apparently changed course *before* the actual start of the coup.

Another strange incident was the two-day trip to Washington of Nathaniel Davis, U.S. ambassador to Chile. Davis was called to Washington on August 29, and was expected to stay a while. Instead, he returned to Santiago after just two days. "The purpose of the visit was not to report on any coup attempt," Hare said. "He returned to Chile immediately after seeing the secretary of state-designate [Henry Kissinger] because of the tense situation there and the desirability of having an ambassador in the country during this period."

In addition to explaining the incidents of the naval vessels and the capital-hopping ambassador, Hare and Warren had to account for a piece of information leaked by their loose-mouthed colleague Jack Kubisch, assistant secretary of state. The September 13 *Washington Post* had reported that at a September 12 briefing (closed to the public) of the Western Hemisphere Subcommittee of the Senate Foreign Relations Committee, Kubisch, while repeating denials of U.S. involvement, revealed that "the highest levels" knew of the impending coup the night before it occurred and decided on a "hands off" policy; that is, not to inform Allende.

Warren explained that the U.S. government had been receiving rumors of unrest in the Chilean military for more than one year and that "sometimes they mentioned specific dates and sometimes they did not. . . . Our embassy had instructions in the event that any elements came to them with plans for an uprising not to have anything to do with it, and these instructions were followed carefully."

Some specific dates mentioned were September 8, 10, and finally 11; "and this, as you know, turned out to be correct," Hare incisively observed. He added that there was no way of being sure that a coup attempt would be made on any of these dates, and that no efforts were made to warn the Allende government or to discourage the military from making the attempt. Not surprisingly, a spokesman for the Santiago junta came

232   *Disaster in Chile*

to Nixon's defense, asserting on September 13 that the generals had kept Washington in the dark.

The first reactions of the big U.S. corporations whose properties had been seized by Allende were equally as restrained as their government's. According to Michael Jensen in the September 12 *New York Times*, most of the companies concerned warned that it was too early to assess the prospects of resuming operations in Chile. But they are clearly watching developments closely. An ITT spokesman said his company's action would depend upon "what government emerges and what its position is going to be." Officials in the auto, chemical, and communications industries did not rule out the possibility of returning. The Ford Motor Company was particularly interested because of the favorable market for automobiles in Latin America. Its $7 million assembly plant was taken over in 1971.

Pools of Blood
on the Sidewalks of Santiago

By Gerry Foley

"It pains me to see everybody getting concerned about corpses that don't exist." This was the complaint of a junta official to *Le Monde*'s correspondent.

But John Barnes, a reporter for *Newsweek*, saw the corpses. He gave this description in the October 8 issue:

"Last week, I slipped through a side door into the Santiago city morgue, flashing my junta press pass with all the impatient authority of a high official. One hundred and fifty dead bodies were laid out on the ground floor, awaiting identification by family members. Upstairs, I passed through a swing door and there in a dimly lit corridor lay at least 50 bodies, squeezed one against another, their heads propped up against the wall. They were all naked.

"Most had been shot at close range under the chin. Some had been machine-gunned in the body. Their chests had been slit open and sewn together in what presumably had been a

From *Intercontinental Press*, October 15, 1973

pro forma autopsy. They were all young and, judging from the roughness of their hands, all from the working class. A couple of them were girls, distinguished among the massed bodies only by the curves of their breasts."

The daughter of a morgue staff member told Barnes that in the fourteen days following the coup, this one institution had processed 2,796 corpses.

The *Newsweek* correspondent added: "No one knows how many have been disposed of elsewhere; a gravedigger told me of reports that helicopters have been gathering bodies at the emergency first-aid center in central Santiago, then carrying them out to sea to be dumped."

The organization of the military take-over impressed some journalists. "The coup d'etat, staged with textbook precision, had been plotted for almost 11 months," Jonathan Kandell wrote in the September 30 *New York Times*, "by a military convinced that the late President's experiment in constitutional Marxism had 'succeeded in destroying the economic power of the middle class, which is the basis of our national institutions,' as one officer deeply involved in the planning put it last week."

If their military operations had been staged with textbook precision, the generals were much less precise in keeping their stories straight. "Admiral Toribio Merino himself admitted in an interview with the Dutch TV station Vara," the West German magazine *Der Spiegel* reported October 1, "that 3,500 civilians were killed." Officially, the junta claimed that only 95 had died in their "textbook" operation. "The lie is so cynical," the *Dagens Nyheter* correspondent Bobi Sourander wrote, "that it makes you boggle."

The Swedish correspondent wrote in the September 30 issue of the prestigious Stockholm daily: "There were reports of full-scale battles between military units in Santiago. Nothing like that happened. A few hundred snipers resisted for a few days in the cities. That was all. . . .

"When the military effectively cleared out the factories by shelling them with heavy weapons and sending helicopters over them, the resistance was sporadic and badly organized. It led to brutal retaliatory strikes that were rumored to be on the scale of extermination operations."

Whether the military intends to exterminate whole sections of the population will probably not be determined for some time. The population has been atomized by repression and censorship. In particular, the teeming shantytowns on the outskirts of the cities — where, from the bourgeoisie's point of view, the most dangerous and economically expendable elements are concentrated — are isolated from each other and from the rest of the country. In these conditions, the intimidating effect of the junta's savage terror is maximized.

Sourander's *Dagens Nyheter* report continued: "In Chile, people are still talking about tens of thousands dead, but no one can confirm or refute these rumors. And they need only be interlaced with a few horrifying facts to create a paralyzing terror.

"Dead bodies are being found in working-class areas. A refuse truck carrying a corpse drives by. Fresh bodies are found in large numbers. Fear spreads and generates treachery and cowardice.

"Everyone knows that the terror is continuing, but no one knows what its dimensions are. Already the political persecutions have gone down to the lowest levels. Leftists who cut their hair, took off their ties, and went meekly to work two weeks ago are beginning to disappear. Workers who led union actions in the factory and tended their machines with their heads down for a week after the coup are beginning to be arrested. In the slums, a van comes with soldiers. A few names are called and a few men taken away."

Some idea of the extent of the junta's repression in the shantytowns, or *poblaciones*, was given by Barnes's article in the October 8 *Newsweek*. "Presumably, the junta believes that since the poblaciones provided the former government's main support, they must be terrorized into accepting the fact of its demise. So the local leaders are now paying with their lives for their love of Allende. Not one población has escaped the terror.

"I spoke with three women from the Pincoya población. One of them, a mother of two, had just found out that she was a widow. She told me this tearful story: 'Soldiers raided our población last Saturday at 8 in the morning. In the section where we live, they rounded up about 50 men and held them until a police lieutenant came to take his pick. When the lieutenant saw my husband, he made him step forward and told him: "Now you will pay for all you people have done." The *carabineros* took him and a few others to the police station, and the rest were arrested by the soldiers.'"

The women in this shantytown joined the long lines of relatives and friends waiting outside the giant football stadiums that have been converted into concentration camps. When they heard that a seventeen-year-old boy from their neighborhood had turned up in the morgue, shot in the head, they went to check the lists of the dead. "There they found her husband, Gabriel, as well as every adult male from one block of their población."

The military continues to cordon off sections of the city of Santiago to conduct "searches." The October 1 *Der Spiegel* described the results: "At night when the curfew has emptied the streets, mop-up squads move in. In the morning, passers-by find huge pools of blood on the sidewalks, or corpses covered with newspapers, as for example on the business street of Huérfanos. Slum dwellers fished forty-five bodies out of the Río Mapocho not far from the Paduel airport, and in the center of Santiago itself several bodies piled up against a bridge over the Mapocho.

"A UN official who was looking for the body of a Bolivian student counted 180 fresh bodies in the morgue, including five children. The head of the registry department has even complained in the press that his clerks are so busy identifying dead bodies that they have no time for issuing marriage licenses."

In some cases, the brutalized police have already taken advantage of the terror to shake down the population. "I joined a funeral procession of weeping families following three coffins to burial," Barnes wrote. "Carabineros . . . had raided a home in the Parque Santa María población and had picked up three petty thieves aged 18, 19 and 20. A sergeant told them they would be released if they paid 7,000 escudos — only $5, but a lot of money for the población poor. Their barrio raised the money and the youths returned home. But two hours later a carabinero patrol came back to get them. That was the last their families heard, until they found their names on the morgue list. One of the boys was so riddled with bullets that they could hardly dress him for burial. But the fate of the other two was worse. Coffins in Chile have small window doors over the face of the dead, and the women opened them for me. There were no heads inside."

The junta is capable of anything, as innumerable atrocities throughout the country have shown. Barnes reported a conversation with a worker in a shantytown. "On the day the coup took place . . . he and one of his sons saw ten high-school students marched from their school, their hands over their heads, after a brief skirmish with carabineros. They were forced to lie face down on the ground, and a policeman walked the line of prone youngsters, spraying them with machine-gun fire."

The conclusion the worker drew was: "They can kill whom-
ever they want to kill. There is nothing, absolutely nothing, that
we can do about it."

Despite the demagogic promises it continues to make to the
workers, the junta has obviously opted for naked terror to
"restore discipline" among the work force. On September 25,
the CUT was outlawed. One of its leaders, former Minister
of Labor Jorge Godoy, has been so badly tortured, according to Sourander's September 30 article, that "he has tried
to kill himself." The junta also announced September 28 that
it had captured Luis Corvalán, the general secretary of the
Communist Party, and intended to try him for treason, a capital offense. At the same time, the junta continues to report
executions of left-wing figures after rapid military trials.

In the October 7 *New York Times*, Jonathan Kandell reported: "Under the first few weeks of the military Government,
a rigid labor discipline has been put into effect. Union activity has been suspended. Workers — motivated mostly by fear
of losing their jobs — have apparently cut absenteeism sharply.
And working hours have been increased by resurrecting a
half day of work on Saturdays.

"A tour of a dozen factories in recent days appeared to bear
out management claims that employes were hard at work, although their enthusiasm may have been partly explained by
the suspension of dozens of workers alleged to be leftist extremists."

In the same issue of the *Times*, Marvine Howe said that the
junta's economic policy "has not been spelled out in detail,"
but that it had "made strong appeals for foreign capital, particularly American capital," and that "initial measures indicate a squeeze on the workers and encouragement to
producers."

One measure indicating a "squeeze on the workers" was the
junta's freezing of wages and refusing to grant the cost-of-
living increase due September 30 under the Allende government's law. Since prices have gone up 320 percent over the
last year, this step means a drastic cut in the workers' buying power. At the same time, moreover, the currency was sharply devalued. "What this means," Howe wrote, "is that food
and petroleum imports . . . will go up in price by over 1,000
percent."

"The military regime is seeking its advisers in the most reactionary circles," the October 1 *Der Spiegel* reported, "above all
in the Nationalist Party. Expropriated landowners have been

called in to the Ministry of Agriculture; the chairman of the manufacturers' association, Sofofa, has been called in as an economic adviser in the Foreign Ministry."

The uniformed conspirators were convinced long before the coup, one told Jonathan Kandell, that only "military methods" could "restore order." They were even more firmly convinced after the right-wing parties failed to get a large enough vote in the March congressional elections to oust Allende: "It was supposed to be a last chance for a political solution," one officer admitted. "But frankly, many of us gave a sigh of relief when the Marxists received such a high vote because we felt that no politician could run the country and eventually the Marxists might be even stronger." (*New York Times*, September 27.)

Once the Chilean bourgeoisie decided to unleash the generals, it had to accept the consequences at least for the time being. These included handing over economic management to the most retrograde elements and accepting the unforeseeable costs of brutal, irrational, and corrupt military rule. But some voices in the same imperialist center that armed and trained the local repressive machine began very quickly to express fears that the overkill in Chile might hopelessly undermine the political bases of bourgeois control over the society.

The most farsighted organ of American imperialism, the *New York Times*, raised an alarm in an editorial September 26, entitled "Off Course in Chile." It warned the generals very pointedly not to go too far: "The junta needs all the help it can get if it is to avert civil war, pacify the country and create the conditions for political and economic recovery. It will not get that help if it persists along the sterile if familiar path of military dictatorship in what was one of the Americas' few remaining strongholds of democracy."

This warning was evidently issued in behalf of a section of the American bourgeoisie. On October 1 the U.S. Senate passed the Kennedy Amendment, calling for suspension of military and economic aid to Chile until "assurances" are given of decent treatment for political refugees. Even if the bill passes the House of Representatives, Nixon need not respect it any more than he did various resolutions calling for an end to the Vietnam war. But it is an indication that an important sector of the ruling class in the United States is worried about the political repercussions of the slaughter.

In its October 7 issue, the *New York Times* issued a new warning that Chile was "Still Off Course." "In a country as bitterly polarized as Chile had become during the Allende Government's attempts to impose drastic Socialism opposed by the majority, prompt pacification and reconciliation could not be expected. But the junta will surely render these imperative long-run goals impossible if it carries out what seems to be a plan to try every major figure of that Government within its reach before military tribunals on charges of treason." The fear of the *Times* editors was that the military, in their determination to impose "order," risked destroying all the links between the bourgeois political system and the workers—thus making it impossible for the capitalists to regain any measure of cooperation from the working class.

"The trial of Luis Corvalán, the Communist party secretary-general, is a case in point. Strange as it seems to those unfamiliar with Chilean politics, the Communists not only had played by the democratic rules but had been a force for moderation and compromise within the Allende coalition, repeatedly critical of the more revolutionary Socialists."

The experienced imperialist leaders understand that mere terror cannot long maintain production in a country like Chile, even when there is a high unemployment rate. Furthermore, pure military rule has generally proven quite unstable in countries as developed as Chile. Given unlimited opportunities for looting and extortion, the ground-level command structure quickly becomes utterly corrupt. And as the top command becomes involved in directly running the economic life of the country, the contradictions in the bourgeoisie tend to become reflected in its own ranks in an acute way. Every conflict of economic interests threatens to turn into a civil war. With the military facing the bitter hatred of the decisive masses of the country, the inevitable faltering of the regime could produce a violent explosion.

"No soldier or Carabinero can venture into certain poor areas on the outskirts of Santiago except in vast army operations," *Le Monde* reported October 4. "Many have already been killed."

By backing the coup that has produced General Pinochet's murderous regime, the bourgeois parties have been hopelessly discredited in the working class. The "communitarian socialism" of the Catholic Christian Democrats is not likely to attract many workers after the party has backed a take-over by the murder machine, financed and trained by the United States, that has already slaughtered so many of "the Lord's beloved." As for the bourgeois parties' pretense of devotion to democratic principles, that has been shattered for the foreseeable future.

"The members of parliament who talked themselves hoarse defending the Congress from Allende's assaults," Ramiro de Casbellas wrote in the October 2 issue of the liberal Buenos Aires daily *La Opinión*, "did not bat an eye at the abolition of the legislative branch."

As for the reformist parties, whose leaders and activists are now being cut down in the general slaughter of the working-class organizations, their parliamentary course has also been widely discredited. "They have not defeated our socialism but only the bourgeois reformists," a worker told Bobi Sourander.

"Allende was a coward. He should have given us weapons, us workers. We don't trust bourgeois leaders with bourgeois ideas any more. . . . They wanted to make a revolution with official cars." (*La Opinión*, September 29.)

In the absence of organized resistance by the masses, it was difficult for the ranks of the armed forces to break free from the discipline imposed by their officers. But there is evidence that the unspeakable cruelty and bloodthirstiness of the chiefs has driven a gap between them and the masses of men in uniform.

"Witnesses claim that soldiers shot their officers when they ordered them to execute prisoners," the October 1 *Der Spiegel* reported. "Another soldier paid with his life for refusing to carry out such an order. He was shot as he threw away his helmet and rifle in protest. The reason was that one of his comrades, guarding a line of people standing at a bread outlet in Santiago's Mapocho district, shot a child who was crying."

Why the MIR Did Not Win the Leadership of the Workers

The following article was translated from the October 3, 1973, issue of Avanzada Socialista, *the weekly paper of the Partido Socialista de los Trabajadores (Socialist Workers Party), an Argentine Trotskyist organization.*

The MIR warned many times that there were no "peaceful" roads" to socialism. It criticized the Allende government's vac-illations and concessions to the Christian Democrats. It sparked many mobilizations. And in the period before the coup, it was the only current that developed a campaign — although an insufficient one — directed at the army, trying to turn the soldiers against the putschists.

Nonetheless, the MIR was unable to win the leadership of the working class away from the Communist and Socialist parties in order to keep the workers from being defeated. Why? Was it because victory was only possible through a "prolonged war" and there was no time to form an "armed wing" to carry this out? We think that the MIR failed because it held on to ultraleft deviations and because along with these it committed a series of opportunist vacillations and errors typical of the guerrillaist currents.

Although the MIR warned about the reactionary nature of the "capitalist state" and its apparatus, it did not uphold the Marxist position — that is, the only consistently revolutionary position — in regard to the army. Not only did it fail to remind the masses of the army's role as the repressive arm of the exploiters and draw their attention to this, but it made centrist-type statements that broached the possibility of winning the armed forces, or large sectors of the officer corps, to supporting the revolution.

For example, a month before the coup, these compañeros said in their paper, *El Rebelde*: "Today the bosses and the reactionary officers are carrying out an elaborate maneuver to bring about a clash between the armed forces and the people. . . ." As if the armed forces and the overwhelming majority of their officers have not always been in conflict with the people!

Before this, in a press conference May 22, Miguel Enríquez, one of the top leaders of the MIR, said that "some sectors of the Unidad Popular and the government . . . rather than recognize that there are some bad officers prefer to say that there are bad peasants. . . . They do not have the moral courage to admit that bad officers and bad policemen exist and criticize them."

The Chilean experience has shown once again in a tragic way that what Miguel Enríquez should have explained to the workers was that, "bad" or "good," the immense majority of the officers defended the interests of the exploiters, heading up repressive squads.

Furthermore, the MIR's vacillations helped to confuse the

masses about what kind of government the Allende regime was.

Following the press of the MIR, we see that it constantly denounced the Allende government's concessions to the Christian Democrats and the right. Following the thread of these denunciations, you can see that the Allende government did not fundamentally alter the capitalist structure of Chile (most of the factories, the land, wholesale and retail trade, etc., remained in the hands of capitalists) and that it used all means including repression to resist the advances of the workers toward changing the property relations (e.g., the land occupations). It left intact the armed forces and the police, the jails, the courts, the laws, and the constitution, all instruments of capitalist exploitation. Likewise, Allende subordinated himself to a parliament dominated by the opposition and even made room for the military in his cabinet.

However, in the face of all these facts showing that under the UP government Chile remained capitalist, the most that the MIR was able to denounce was the existence of "reformist sectors in the UP and in the government." That is, it didn't even define the government as a whole as reformist and still less as bourgeois.

That is, the MIR never pointed out clearly to the masses that the Allende government was not their government, that while it was correct to make demands on it to carry out certain measures and to defend it from the right, they should not place any confidence in it. The MIR never clearly pointed out that the masses should rely on their own mobilizations, create their own organs of power and their own army — workers' militias — in order to go on from this to take power in fact.

For years the MIR worked among peasants, the unemployed, etc., rather than in the workers' movement. While it corrected this error, it nonetheless continued to follow incorrect guidelines that resulted from its insufficient confidence in the capacity of the working class.

Thus, instead of firmly supporting the *cordones industriales* (which developed, in spite of being boycotted by the UP and the unions, as embryonic forms of workers' power), the MIR insisted that the *cordones* should subordinate themselves to the *comandos comunales* [municipal commands], which were made up of neighborhood fighters, housewives, etc., and never became more than peripheral organizations of the MIR.

Capitulating to the CUT, the MIR opposed setting up a

coordinating committee of all the *cordones*. Nor did it try to promote the formation of workers' militias based on the *cordones*, limiting itself to forming small armed nuclei in the *comandos comunales* that it controlled.

Thus, its final slogan, "soldiers, don't follow the orders of putschist officers," which we supported, was insufficient because the MIR was not in a position—and it didn't even raise the idea clearly—to get the masses of workers to bring their full pressure to bear on the soldiers to win them over to opposing the putschists.

The reasons that we have pointed out here are the ones that we think prevented the MIR from becoming the revolutionary party of the working class that could have won the workers away from the traitorous leadership of the reformists. These reasons are what prevented them from becoming the indispensable tool that the heroic vanguard of the Chilean workers needed, and need, to prepare for and to win the fight against the national and foreign exploiters and their armed forces—the revolutionary party.

Interviews with Survivors

Intercontinental Press *obtained a number of interviews with revolutionaries who survived the coup of September 11 and escaped into exile. Two of these interviews are reprinted here.*

The first, from the October 8, 1973, issue, took place in Mexico City. The participants were Hugo Blanco, Eduardo Creus, and Julião Bordao. Blanco, the famous Peruvian Trotskyist peasant leader, had been a correspondent of Intercontinental Press while in exile in Chile. Creus, an Argentine Trotskyist, worked with Blanco in Peru and joined him in exile in Chile after both were freed from the Peruvian junta's prisons by an international protest campaign. Bordao was also in Chile as a refugee from military repression—that of Brazil, where he was a Trotskyist student leader. He was arrested during the coup, beaten, and then "released" onto the streets after curfew to face death, but managed to escape.

The second interview, from the October 22, 1973, Intercontinental Press, was obtained in Argentina. Elena Casares, a member of the Trotskyist PSR in Chile, had taken temporary refuge there after having been arrested and then released by the military during the coup. Casares was a factory worker in one of the cordones *at the time of the military take-over and gives an eyewitness account.*

Interview with Hugo Blanco, Eduardo Creus, and Juliao Bordao

Question. How extensive has the repression been in Chile?

Blanco. The military began their repression in advance of the coup, aiming to disarm and demobilize the people. They began raiding plants. For example, they raided an electronics plant in Arica in the North. In Santiago there were several raids, including one on a cemetery. All these searches were carried out under the cover of the so-called Arms Control Law, which was passed by the right-wing bloc in parliament at the culmination of the last offensive against the government in October 1972. The UP [Unidad Popular] did not actively oppose it, however. The UP deputies abstained and Allende did not veto it.

In the South, they raided the Lanera Austral factory, where they killed some workers. In the same area, the military launched a repression against peasants who demonstrated their opposition to the June 29 attempted coup. Some were dragged across the ground by helicopters or tortured in front of their families. Sailors who showed opposition to the coup were also tortured and imprisoned. All of this was part of the softening-up process that preceded the take-over. As a final test, in Santiago they raided the Cobre Cerrillos factory in the Cordón Cerrillos and the Sumar factory in the Cordón Vicuña Mackenna. Three days after these raids, they made their strike.

These escalating raids enabled the right to test the strength of the workers' movement, its capacity to resist. They also started the process of selective repression aimed at decapitating the workers' movement and the left parties. The strongholds of the left in the factory belts, shantytowns, and schools like the Universidad Técnica [Technical University] were hit, and vanguard militants were seized and imprisoned. Throughout this first phase of the repression, the military and the police had the acquiescence of Allende and the UP leadership.

When they launched their massive terror on September 11, the military were also aided by the faltering defensive line of the UP government. The UP government had called on the workers to maintain a constant guard on the factories. They did not call for seizing the factories but only for guarding them. They meant that the workers should continue working for bosses and even imperialists and that after doing back-breaking labor all day, carrying out the UP's order to produce more and win "the battle of production," they should stay on at night doing guard duty. Obviously this meant that those who did stay were mainly the vanguard. Most of the workers tired of this. So that it was essentially the vanguard that was trapped in the factories when the military launched its attack.

On the day of the coup, the military launched a massive strike against the factories and the shantytowns, seeking to massacre the vanguard. At the same time, they tried to round up all the leaders of the left parties as well as the UP ministers and deputies.

Next, the repression was directed against the intermediate cadres. The activists in the factories were fired, arrested, and murdered. The universities were closed. The University of Concepción, a well-known center of the far left, was shut down and formally abolished. The diplomas of its graduates were revoked. In the Universidad Técnica, the military carried out a massacre on the first day of the coup, slaughtering about 600 persons. There was also a massacre at the Instituto Pedagógico [Teachers' College].

There are reports that every fifteen minutes a body is cremated in Santiago. Many persons have seen bodies lying in the street. Murders have been seen in broad daylight. For example, if someone goes out for bread or something like that, he is likely to be bullied by the Carabineros [riot police], and anybody who protests is simply shot down. There was one occasion when the Carabineros started beating people in a food line and when some persons objected, the whole line was slaughtered.

The football stadiums have been turned into gigantic prisons in Santiago, Concepción, and Antofagasta. The island of Quiriquina has also been converted into a prison. Innumerable military tribunals have been set up. There are ten in Valparaíso alone, for example. There are a lot of executions going on, and the junta is threatening to punish any kind of resistance with death. Any act of sabotage in word or deed is supposed to be punishable by summary execution.

An all-embracing campaign of intimidation against the population began at 3:00 p.m. on September 11, when the junta gave the order that everyone was to remain in their homes, that no one could be on the streets. Many people could not get home. For example, I had to walk thirty-five blocks to get to my home. The next day there was a curfew around the clock. It was only lifted on Thursday [September 13] at noon. The people were kept imprisoned in their homes. It was certain death to be on the street.

While the military held the population pinned down and atomized this way, they carried out almost indiscriminate mass raids. They broke into the houses of everyone who had been denounced by some rightist or another, beat up whatever persons they found, tortured the inhabitants in front of their families, shot some on the spot, and dragged others away to prison—where, needless to say, they continued torturing them. The troops destroyed everything they could not carry away. They were given free rein to take all valuables. This is the way the putschists egged on the soldiers to carry out the repression. They offered them booty.

The brunt of the repression was directed against the *cordones* [term for both the industrial belts and the workers' organizations in them] and the shantytowns. Massacres took place in the squatters' settlements of Lo Hermida, La Legua, and Nueva Havana. Many of the nationalized factories where organization of the workers had reached its highest level were razed. This happened to the Sumar and Cristalería plants in the Cordón Vicuña Mackenna and to the Cobre Cerrillos plant in the Cordón Cerrillos, as well as many other factories.

The armed forces were turned into a murder machine. Many persons were killed immediately on being taken prisoner, or the next day, as it occurred to the military. The objective of the repression was to clear the left out of all the factories and centers, by killing them, driving them out, and arresting them. In this way the workers' movement was decapitated.

Q. What is the situation now of the political exiles who found refuge in Chile under the UP government?

Blanco. The campaign against foreigners is a very important aspect of the repression in Chile. Being pointed out as a foreigner, especially one from another Latin American country, can mean instant death. This campaign is obviously not the work of the Chilean bourgeoisie or the putschists alone. Most of the foreigners played no role in the government. This is obviously an action directed by the imperialists, by the CIA.

Chile has been turned into a trap. Or since the Chilean nation-

al anthem says that the country will be either the refuge of
the oppressed or the grave of the free, perhaps we should say
that it has been turned into a tomb.

Since Chile had opened its doors to political refugees, many
revolutionists were concentrated there. Mainly these were Brazilians. There were also Argentines, Uruguayans, Bolivians,
Dominicans, Venezuelans, and others from the Central American countries. So the coup was an excellent opportunity for the
imperialists to trap this entire vanguard. At the same time,
it could piously wash its hands of the affair. The blame was
on the junta. The imperialists and the other Latin American
bourgeoisies could look on innocently. They were not the ones
killing, jailing, and torturing this vanguard, only the Chilean
junta. But this was really an international repressive operation
by the various bourgeoisies, headed by the imperialists.

For example, the Uruguayan and Brazilian governments
backed up the junta in this campaign by claiming that the
persons from their countries who went to Chile had the objective of developing terrorist operations. Thus they gave the
junta carte blanche to murder the Uruguayan and Brazilian
compañeros.

There was an enormous pogrom, similar to the Nazi persecution of the Jews. Leaflets were dropped from airplanes and
helicopters. The radio stations called on the people to turn in
all foreigners, who had come to Chile to kill Chileans. That
gave rightists who didn't like foreigners a chance to run to the
nearest police station and sic the military and police on every
one they knew about. There was a good probability that those
arrested, especially if it was by the army or the air force, would
be killed on the spot.

Q. How were you able to get out of the country?

Blanco. As soon as the curfew was lifted, I had to get out
of my house. I took refuge in the Swedish Embassy and later
in the home of the Mexican ambassador, which I was finally
allowed to leave to come here to Mexico. But many Chileans
who had taken refuge in the embassy and in the ambassador's
house were not given exit permits, and in some cases only
some members of a family were allowed to leave. For example,
there was the case of Alejandro Chilén Rojas. They gave visas
to his wife and daughter-in-law and grandson. They are here
in Mexico City. But he was not allowed to leave. His crime

was mainly publishing books; he worked for the Quimantú. publishing house.

The Mexican Embassy deserves special credit for getting refugees out. They are doing everything they can. But don't think that it is easy to get into the embassies. They are surrounded by police. The day before I left I saw them capture three persons who were trying to make it into the ambassador's home.

Creus. I would like to add one thing to what Hugo said about the repression. There were wholesale expulsions of activists, mainly from the factories of the nationalized sector that had been seized by the workers. The junta itself has said that 15 percent of the workers in these plants have been fired.

Q. What has the Chilean experience shown about the theory of the "peaceful road" to socialism?

Creus. This theory did not have much to do with reality. The class struggle never stopped. The workers occupied factories and the peasants took land without asking the permission of the UP. On the other hand, the rightists kept up a constant attack on the government. They pressured the government to use the police to repress the workers who wanted to advance the process of socialization. For example, on many occasions when the workers occupied the factories, it was the Allende government itself that cleared them out. On other occasions, it repressed the people in the shantytowns who were pushing for direct distribution of food and other supplies. Finally the repression by the right escalated, and they began attacks on factories and the poor neighborhoods while Allende was still in office.

In this whole process, the role of the Communist and Socialist parties was to act as a brake on the popular mobilization. Part of their policy was the "dialogue" with the right and the campaign for production. They did not tell the workers to organize to push the developing situation forward, but to work harder and harder, even in the factories that were still in the hands of the imperialists.

Although the masses were on the offensive throughout most of the UP government's term in office, they were held back by their reformist leaderships. When the right went on the offensive in October, the reformists kept the masses in a strictly defensive position. The workers saw the need to arm and talked about organizing defense committees. But the Allende government said that there could be no armed forces but the Carabineros and the military.

Q. Did opposition to this reformist policy develop in the Communist and Socialist parties?

Creus. In the CP I saw only individual dissidents. In the SP there were dissident currents but in the end they capitulated to their reformist leaderships. The real effect of these left currents was to reinforce reformism. Militant workers joined the SP in the hope that they could win it over to a revolutionary line and they became trapped in a reformist structure.

Q. How extensive was the resistance to the coup?

Creus. There was no organized resistance. The workers wanted to fight. But in the absence of a genuinely revolutionary organization there could be no organized resistance. There was some resistance by snipers. There was some resistance by groups besieged in places like the Instituto Pedagógico, but they were slaughtered. They tried to put up a fight in the Universidad Técnica, but they were massacred. There was resistance in the shantytown of La Legua, but there was a massacre there like the one in Lo Hermida.

Q. To what extent were the workers armed?

Creus. The left organizations had a lot of guns. But these weapons were not in the hands of the workers. They were kept in special arsenals by the leaderships. This was another aspect of the bureaucratic organization of the left parties. Even if the leaderships had wanted to arm the workers, there was no organization suited to this task. There was the case of the governor of Talca, for example. He wanted to resist and did put up a fight with a few people but it was only a small group.

It was no good having guns if they were not in the hands of the workers. And there was no organization to enable the workers to resist in an organized way. So the resistance was minimal; the amount of weapons in the hands of the workers was minimal. But with the proper organization, the resistance could have assumed gigantic proportions.

Q. Did any splits show up in the armed forces?

Creus. There were two types of opposition to the coup. There was a sector of the officers who were against the take-over. It was led by Prats. But it was very weak. Nonetheless, this division could have been exploited by the proletariat if it had had a really revolutionary leadership. A reformist leadership could not take advantage of it. When Prats told Allende that the only way out was to fire sixteen generals, Allende said he didn't have the strength to do it. So Prats and the other anticoup officers had to resign.

The common soldiers were another matter. Among them there were revolutionary elements ready to fight alongside the working class. There was murmuring in the armed forces against the putschist plans, rather than active opposition. In the absence of a revolutionary organization, such opposition could only take an isolated, atomized form. There was a case where a Carabinero shot a lieutenant and a captain and called on the others to join him. But he was alone and so no one else followed him and he was killed. It is probable that such incidents occurred in many places but in a disorganized way.

The case of the sailors in Valparaíso shows how the reformists disorganized any opposition in the armed forces. When the sailors manifested their disapproval of the June 29 coup and the military's plans for a take-over, the officers repressed them. And the government endorsed this repression. It approved it first by its silence and later explicitly.

Q. There are some elements in the U. S. Communist Party that accuse the revolutionary left of provoking the coup by promoting the nationalizations and a socialist policy. What is your opinion of that?

Creus. Those who provoked the coup were not the left, because the only thing that could have stopped the coup was the advance of the struggles of the working class, toward more nationalization, workers' control, measures that would have strengthened workers' power, including the arming of the proletariat. These measures, as well as encouraging the soldiers to resist the coup, are the only thing that could have blocked it. But instead of advancing this development, the UP leadership held all this back and even assisted the repression. So it is not the revolutionary left that provoked the coup but the reformist leaderships — basically the Communist Party, and also, of course, the SP leadership.

Q. What about the MIR [Movimiento de Izquierda Revolu-

cionaria— *Movement of the Revolutionary Left]? What kind of alternative did it offer to the reformist leadership of the UP?*

Julião Bordao. At no time did the MIR really seek to win the masses away from the UP's reformism. This is the key for assessing the MIR. In the period before Allende took office, the MIR's political line could be characterized as ultraleft. They raided banks and did all the things that are called urban guerrilla warfare. But at no time did they try to win the masses away from reformism. Instead they threw themselves into vanguardist actions.

Then when Allende was elected, the MIR changed its line, but they really just turned the coin over. From a policy of urban guerrilla warfare, they turned to capitulating to Allende, essentially to an opportunist line. Although they retained their organizational independence from the UP, they were basically drawn in behind its policy. The line of the MIR in fact became integrated with that of the UP. They launched attacks periodically on the UP, but the central aspect was their support for it.

That is, just as they did not seek to win the masses away from the reformists in the first phase of their activity, so they did not do so in the second. They tended in fact to support the left wing of the Socialist Party, helping it to keep the most militant workers from going beyond the framework of the UP.

Creus. As the comrade says, the MIR was unable to build an alternative mass leadership. It should be noted that the MIR did nominally have a caucus in the union movement, the Frente de Trabajadores Revolucionarios [FTR— Front of Revolutionary Workers]. But this was only an appendage of the MIR and suffered from all its defects. The MIR was essentially a bureaucratic organization and the FTR also suffered from this bureaucratism. It was impossible by such methods to organize an independent workers' vanguard.

The social base of the MIR was first of all peasants and then the inhabitants of the shantytown belts around the cities. They had very little in the workers' movement. This led them in an opportunist way to underestimate the *cordones industriales*, which were the vanguard of the working class. They put their emphasis on the *comandos comunales* [community commands], which combined the shantytowns and some other sectors and in which the workers were included but in a diluted way. No real *comando comunal* existed; there were only embryos that were not even on the level of the *cordones*. We were not against the *comandos comunales,* but we thought that the fundamental thing was to strengthen the *cordones industriales*, which should have been the axis of the *comandos comunales.*

Along with their opportunism, it should be noted that there were spontanéist and adventurist attitudes in the MIR. At times they planned seizing factories and streets in sudden actions that were not prepared by previous mobilization of the masses and by discussion. This obviously led to failures. At times they tried to substitute the action of groups of their own members for that of the masses. For example, when they tried to take some factories back from the rightists who had occupied them while the workers were out, they wanted to have Mirista groups do it, instead of trying to organize the workers themselves, who were beginning to see the need to do this. This happened specifically in the AG factory.

As the comrade said, they failed to put up their own candidates in elections when they had the strength to do so. Instead they gave uncritical support to the leader of the SP left wing, Altamirano.

Q. What is the role of the fascist groups in the repression?

Creus. Everybody is calling the junta a fascist government. We don't think that what exists in Chile is fascism. I don't say this to try to prettify the junta at all, or to minimize its guilt. This does not mean that it is any less barbarous; it could hardly be any more barbarous. The fact is that if the military has not established a fascist regime, it is not because it doesn't want to. Fascism, as we define it, is a mass movement. It involves political gangs repressing the masses. But there are only the embryos of this type of fascist gangs in Chile.

At present, the repression is being carried out almost entirely by the armed forces. If the fascists have been involved in any of this, we have no news of it. On the other hand, the fascists are playing a role by informing on leftists and by offering the junta trucks and everything it needs. But the repression, the massacres, are being carried out by the armed forces.

Q. How great a defeat do you think the Chilean workers have suffered? How soon will they be able to recover?

Creus. The working class has suffered a very grave defeat.

The entire vanguard is being crushed. The leadership in the *cordones* and the left parties is being annihilated — not just the top leadership, but the intermediate leadership and now even the activists in the factories. The entire student body at the University of Concepción, for example, has fallen under the repression. It is a defeat from which it will take a long time to recover.

Blanco. This is a defeat of catastrophic proportions because it comes in the context of a series of defeats in Latin America. The coups in Uruguay, Bolivia, and Brazil, for example, have reinforced the reactionaries. Argentina is one of the few bulwarks left. In the present situation, it represents a great hope for a new rise in Latin America.

Q. What can we do outside Chile to help minimize this defeat?

Blanco. We have to develop a worldwide campaign to restrain the repression in Chile. In the first place, we have to stop the executions and killings, many of which take place every day. Secondly, we have to win more humane treatment for the prisoners and force the military to abolish its special tribunals. The demonstrations that occurred throughout the world in the wake of the coup had an immediate effect. A few days after the initial massacres, it was evident that they were trying to apply some restraint. So, I think that this campaign must be continued in order to save many lives from the slaughter that is going on every day.

The situation of the foreigners in Chile is extremely grave. The world has not seen such a hysterical pogrom since the years of Nazism. This is something that should interest not just the left organizations but all organizations that claim to uphold human rights.

The demand should be raised that the Chilean government give exit permits to all political exiles and give them safe-conduct passes out of the country. Chile has signed the Latin American treaty on asylum, and if it denies the right to leave to one single exile, it is violating this treaty. So we must demand that this treaty be respected and that the cordons around the Latin American embassies be removed.

At the same time, we have to fight to assure the exiles new places of asylum and keep them from being returned to their countries. For example, sending some Brazilians back to their country means just killing them in Brazil instead of Chile.

The organizations that defend human rights must campaign to get the exiles out and to a place where they will be in no danger. There are in fact Brazilians who have been forced to take refuge in their own embassy because in the face of the kind of terror the Chilean junta has unleashed, they preferred to die in their own country.

It should be pointed out that many of the Brazilians who were in Chile had never participated in the revolutionary movement but were studying, or working, or had some other non-political reason to be in the country. But the fact that they have to escape from Chile—because it is a capital crime there now to be a Brazilian—means that they cannot return to Brazil, because going back under these conditions means that they would unquestionably be regarded as political criminals.

It is important to expose the junta's almost unprecedented campaign of terror against the population. Despite stories of armed resistance, what has been going on has essentially been a massacre of a defenseless people.

Interview with Elena Casares

Question. What happened in your factory when the coup started?

Answer. I went to work on the day of the coup just like any other day. By about 9:00 in the morning, a comrade came around to tell us that the presidential palace had been surrounded by tanks again. This had happened before, on June 29. So we all stopped work and went to listen to the radio to see what was happening. We heard Allende speaking. He seemed to be saying good-bye, a very emotional and populist farewell. I and all the other comrades in the factory felt that he was saying good-bye to life, too, because he seemed to be saying that it was all over.

The president told the people to resist and not to falter. But we didn't know what to do. We knew the coup was coming, but the leaderships of the political parties and even the leaderships of the *cordones* didn't have a line on how to fight it.

So the leaders of the union in our factory went out to make contact with the leaders of the *cordón* and the other plants. Then the interventor came. (He was an official sent in by the government to keep the factory running. There had been a big battle between the workers and the management and so the government sent him in as kind of an arbitrator.) He told us what the situation in the city was like. He said that a fight had started and that we should keep calm and wait to see what happened. We were to stay in the factory and fight if necessary. On the other hand, he said that the workers who wanted to go home could leave — especially the women.

So only the vanguard stayed, the ones who wanted to resist, who wanted to defend the factory. We organized a defense committee, a food committee, a medical committee, and so on. I organized the communications committee. Then I went into the city. I wanted to find someone with military experience because none of the workers had any and we had no way to fight. I hoped to find somebody to teach us, to tell us what to do, because we were getting no leadership, either from the *cordones* or from any party. We were lost. The CUT [Central Unica de Trabajadores — United Federation of Workers] didn't make any announcement over the radio or anything, so we had to do something.

But when I got to the city, a battle was going on. It would have been suicide to try to go on and risk getting caught in the cross-fire between the military and the snipers.

So I went back to the factory and stayed there. None of the comrades could contact any of the leaders of the *cordones*. So we were really without any direction, without any help. The only communication was with nearby factories.

By 3:00 in the afternoon, the military decreed a curfew. I discussed the situation with some of the comrades and we decided that I should leave because there was an air force base right near the factory and there was a danger of airborne infantry coming in. We would not be able to resist because we did not have anything to resist with. I left because I was a foreigner and so it was dangerous for me to stay and dangerous for the comrades, too. There was no point in it.

So, I went to spend the night at the house of a friend who also worked in the factory. All night long we heard gunfire. We were very tense, and we got especially nervous when we heard about the death of Allende. The junta announced it over the radio. (By 9:30 in the morning the military had already taken over all the radio stations. The only news we got was from them.) They said that Allende was dead, that he committed suicide. This shocked the girls I was with. It shocked them very much. We knew Allende was a very weak man and all that. But he was still a leader; he was the great leader in Chile.

We didn't know what to do, so we just stayed in the house. In the streets, even though it was a proletarian neighborhood, many, many Chilean flags went up. This was supposed to be a sign that Chile had been "liberated," liberated for the right, of course. There were a lot of people in the neighborhood who supported the coup. I was very surprised at this and we were afraid somebody would denounce us.

What we felt was that there was chaos. We did not know what to do. We didn't hear any news. We were desperate.

The next day I went to the factory because I thought the curfew had been lifted. I found out that it hadn't when I got there and they told me.

About 280 people worked in the factory and there were about thirty on defense. It was a very weak defense; they were not armed.

Then they told me to go to a meeting in the factory across from ours. There were more people on defense there — about eighty. The work force was normally about 260, more or less the same as in ours. But here the mood was more combative.

But in this factory the defenders were not armed either. It was a bottle-making plant, a place where they make glass.

They started to make molotov cocktails with the bottles but not very many.

When we arrived at the meeting, some comrades from our party, the PSR [Partido Socialista Revolucionario — Revolutionary Socialist Party], were leading it. They explained that the Cordón Vicuña Mackenna was fighting very hard against the military and that our *cordón,* the Cordón Cerrillos, should do the same thing, but that it was totally disorganized — there was no leadership — the workers had to take it into their own hands to organize the *cordón* and factories for armed defense against the military.

At this very moment, the military burst in. They had been watching us from the air. They arrested all of us and took us to the air force base that was quite nearby. The women were separated from the men. There were about four women and eighty men. The men were taken to a runway and made to lie on the ground while they were searched.

About an hour later, all were released, except me and a few others, because the military had been given about eight different versions of the meeting, and they could not figure out what it was about — whether it was just a meeting to calm the people or what. We came to the conclusion that they were more lost than we were.

They were very worried by the armed defense at other factories that were already engaging in gun battles against the military. So we think they were much more interested in those factories that were already fighting against them than they were in us, who were just starting to organize.

I was kept there one day, since I didn't have any documents. During this time, I had a chance to see how they worked. I saw officers, soldiers, and medics. Some were very depressed by the outcome of the coup. They hoped that everything would go off very quickly and that there would be no resistance.

Also, I saw something very interesting. This was the base of the four airplanes that bombed La Moneda. The planes were English; I don't know what they are called. But the pilots were not Chilean. I would say they were Yankees. I could not hear them talking, but North Americans have a very typical look. The only other possibility is that they were English, but I don't think so because the English aren't the ones for that sort of thing; they are very bureaucratic.

When my comrade finally brought my documents, we were allowed to leave. We left in the midst of a gunfight. The workers in a factory across from the base were shooting at the military. But they surrendered a few minutes later because the armed forces had weapons that the workers didn't have.

There were about 500 men at the base. They left very often in trucks to fight against two shantytowns opposite the base. In one, called La Legua, there were very combative people. This shantytown put up a hard fight; they had some weapons that they had received from the government.

From the base I was able to see the fight in La Legua. I could see that many, many people were being killed, including soldiers themselves. The military had helicopters with fifty-caliber machine guns and they could just gun the people down from the air. But even so, the people in this shantytown fought the military for three days. I would say they fought very hard and that many soldiers were killed, too.

In La Legua, I was told, they had some way to make "Miguelitos," that is, nails made to puncture tires. So they stopped some police vans and killed about 160 cops. The people of this shantytown were mostly what is called marginal, largely unemployed. It was not a proletarian neighborhood.

When I left the base, I didn't go back to the factory because there were a lot of troops surrounding it.

Q. What information do you have about other areas?

A. The Cordón Vicuña Mackenna was the best organized before the coup. Many factories, I would say eight or ten, fought very long and very hard. This cost the lives of many, many people. At one factory, for example, the workers put up a hard fight, but when they saw the soldiers surround the plant and realized they could not hold out, they surrendered and turned over their guns. The military shot them down on the spot, in view of another factory that was about to surrender. But when the workers there saw this, they started fighting again.

In the group that were executed, there were about sixteen women, so there must have been about 160 men, because women were usually about 10 percent of the work force.

The Sumar factory had gotten some guns from the government, and it also put up a hard fight. All the people there were killed. In general, in all the factories where there was resistance, everybody was killed. They were executed right on the spot. At Sumar, a synthetic fibers plant, there was an explosion. This factory wrote a heroic page in history and a sad one, too, because all the workers are now dead.

Q. You said that the CUT [the trade-union federation] did not issue any statements or instructions after the coup. Did it issue any statements at all?

A. Not after the coup. Before, they called on the workers to resist in the factories. And I would say that they share the responsibility for the extermination of the vanguard that was concentrated in the plants. Everybody knew a coup was coming, and we didn't think it was a good idea to try to put up a fight there because we knew that if the military came in they would kill everybody. The workers would be trapped like rats because they had nowhere to run. But the CUT said to resist in the factories and so the vanguard is now dead.

Q. How did you come to work in your factory and how long did you work there?

A. I worked in the factory about two weeks. I went to work there as a result of the activity we were engaged in. This factory was occupied after the first coup on June 29, as were all the other factories. The workers there went on strike. And we started to work with them, organizing them, helping them, putting out a strike bulletin, raising funds, and making contact with other factories. I was involved in this. Finally the government intervened the factory [i.e., sent an administrator to run it]. Then the workers asked me to come and work inside the plant and so I took a job there.

Q. How were the cordones *organized and what has happened to them since the coup?*

A. The *cordones* were set up to provide a centralized leadership for groups of factories. They were to coordinate work in the factories and give special help to those that had trouble or went on strike. Another objective was to help to organize the distribution of supplies.

Generally, the *cordones* were led by the Socialist Party. They were run in a bureaucratic way and the masses of the workers were not involved. The ranks were never consulted; all the decisions were made by the leadership. It was always the same leaders who took charge of things. The ranks were never encouraged to participate.

We tried to promote participation by the rank and file. We thought it was vital for them to feel that they and not just the leaders were making the decisions. I think things could have developed differently if such participation could have been achieved. As it was, it was only the trade-union leaders who were brought together in a centralized organization. They tried to widen the organization by bringing in the people of the shantytowns, students, and peasants to participate in the meetings. But the main participants were always students from the shantytowns. They could not broaden the *cordones* enough.

Q. What is the situation of the cordones *now?*

A. I would say they don't exist any more. Not as organizations. So the people don't know what to do. The only place people are coming together is in the separate party organizations. For example, in the shantytown we are familiar with, the members of the Communist Party, the Socialist Party, and the MIR [Movimiento de Izquierda Revolucionaria — Movement of the Revolutionary Left] are still trying to carry on resistance against the military. Even in this situation where the military control everything, they are trying to do something because they are desperate. They are not defeated. They want to do something, but they don't know what to do. There are still a lot of guns around. Most of those in the hands of the people were given out by the Socialist Party.

The Communist Party had a lot of guns but they were all in the hands of the bureaucrats. They did not distribute them among the rank and file. The ranks did not have any military instruction; no defense committees were formed; they don't know how to use guns.

But they [the CP] do have guns; they have more guns than people.

There was a rumor going around when I left Chile that the people were going to fight this week. They were going to call a general strike and then start fighting. So there is some vanguard left. But I don't think this will happen because people are afraid of the military. They are afraid they will be fired or executed.

Q. How did you finally get out of Chile?

A. Since I had not had my papers changed, I was still considered a student. So I was allowed to leave without any difficulty. But before I did, my house was searched and we were treated very badly by the cops.

Q. What is your opinion about the political conditions before the coup and what were the alternatives?

A. I would say the crunch had to come. It was something nobody could avoid. The class struggle had reached such a pitch that I would say that from their point of view the military had no choice but to act as they did. The people and the workers also realized that a decisive confrontation was inevitable. In the last few mass meetings, such as the one on September 4, they asked Allende to arm them because they saw a coup coming. But the reformist parties refused to see this. They blinded themselves to it. They called everybody ultraleft who warned that a crunch was coming.

The only way the coup could have been prevented was if the proletariat had developed its own power. If it had moved toward this, it would at least have been able to fight the military on something like more equal terms. They could have taken the initiative from the military and not let them pick the time and the place for the fight. At the end, there was no middle ground. Even the military commanders who were against a coup had to withdraw. The class struggle was too sharp. There was no room for negotiating. It was the bourgeoisie or the workers. The one who struck first would be the victor.

Chile and the Global Struggle for Raw Materials

By Dick Roberts

The coup in Chile reconfirms a central tenet of Lenin's theory of imperialism: the *ever-increasing* need of the advanced capitalist countries to monopolize sources of raw materials in the underdeveloped world.

Lenin wrote in *Imperialism* (1916): "The principal feature of modern capitalism is the domination of the monopolist combines of the big capitalists. These monopolies are most firmly established when *all* the sources of raw materials are controlled by the one group. And we have seen with what zeal the international capitalist combines exert every effort to make it impossible for their rivals to compete with them; for example by buying up mineral lands, oil fields, etc. Colonial possession alone gives complete guarantee of success to the monopolies against all the risks of the struggle with competitors, including the risk that the latter will defend themselves by means of a law establishing a state monopoly. The more capitalism is developed, the more the need for raw materials is felt; the more bitter competition becomes, and the more feverishly the hunt for raw materials proceeds throughout the whole world, the more desperate becomes the struggle for acquisition of colonies."

A number of aspects of the development of imperialism in the period after World War II seemed at first glance to contradict Lenin. Most of the colonial possessions of Dutch, French, and British imperialism in Asia and Africa won formal political independence. Imperialist investment as a whole proceeded more rapidly in the advanced countries than in the underdeveloped countries. Furthermore, investment in the underdeveloped countries increasingly shifted toward manufacturing indus-

From *Intercontinental Press*, October 8, 1973

tries, rather than the agricultural and extractive industries that constitute sources of raw materials.

The net fixed assets of all U.S.-owned foreign affiliates in 1970 was $69 billion. Of this 51 percent were located in only six countries: Canada, 27 percent; United Kingdom, 11 percent; West Germany, 7 percent; France, 4 percent; and Belgium-Luxembourg, 2 percent. Mexico and Brazil occupy a special position in U.S. investment in the underdeveloped world. In 1970, Mexico had 2 percent and Brazil 3 percent of total U.S. foreign investment.

U.S. foreign investment in the rest of the world stood at $29.9 billion. In terms of industries this broke down as follows: agriculture, 1 percent; mining and smelting, 4 percent; petroleum, 42 percent; manufacturing, 34 percent; public utilities, 8 percent; trade, 4 percent; finance, 3 percent; insurance, negligible; other, 4 percent. (*Implications of Multinational Firms for World Trade and Investment and for U.S. Trade and Labor*, Committee on Finance, United States Senate, February 1973, pp. 404-5.)

Moreover, nationalization is increasingly taking place in the "neocolonies." Before Salvador Allende was elected president of Chile in 1970, Christian Democrat Eduardo Frei had formed "mixed companies," in which the Chilean government owned 51 percent, with the giant U.S. copper firms of Anaconda, Kennecott, and Cerro. Even more noteworthy is the increasing ownership of Middle East oil demanded by the Arab and Iranian governments.

Nevertheless, none of these developments contradicts Lenin's basic thesis. The overwhelming majority of raw materials in the underdeveloped world remain owned and controlled by imperialist monopolies. This is increasingly necessary from the standpoint of profits. And to the extent that one or another neocolony has succeeded in nationalizing or partly nationalizing foreign holdings, imperialism's drive to tighten its hold elsewhere has been all the more reinforced.

The increasing instability of U.S. oil holdings in the Middle East, for example, is certainly one of the factors that impelled Nixon to press for victory in Southeast Asia, with the potential reward of oil leases in the South China Sea. Moreover, it is a factor in Washington's détente with Moscow. The imperialists are hoping to gain Moscow's help in maintaining U.S. control of oil resources in the Middle East and at the same time are looking toward a long-term, possibly more stable, source of natural gas in the Soviet Union's Siberian fields.

Raw Materials Consumption

Central to imperialist strategy is the fact that the United States consumes more raw materials than can be domestically produced. The disproportion is growing. Harry Magdoff emphasizes this point in *The Age of Imperialism* (1969). "It is true," writes Magdoff, "that in recent years technical innovations have increased the utility of domestic ores. Nevertheless, the tendency to increasing reliance on foreign sources of supply persists, partly to get one's money's worth out of an investment already made, partly as a protective device to keep the lesser quality ore sources in reserve, and partly for immediate financial advantage where foreign ores are more economical. As specialists in the field see it, in the absence of a further breakthrough in technology that would make the very low grade iron ore, derived from taconite and similar rock, decidely cheaper than foreign ore, the prognosis is for increased reliance of our steel industry on foreign sources of ore. Thus, it is anticipated that about half of the iron ore to be consumed in 1980 will be met by foreign sources, and that by 2000 the import ratio will reach 75 percent."

Magdoff cites the example of the jet engine—a commodity whose usefulness to the imperialists goes far beyond commercial travel. Of the six critical materials used in the jet engine, three are entirely imported: columbium from Brazil, Canada, and Mozambique; chromium from South Africa, Turkey, Rhodesia, the Philippines, and Iran; cobalt from Zaïre, Morocco, Canada, and Zambia.

The physical dependence of the United States on foreign sources of raw materials is summarized in the following list adapted from *U. S. News & World Report*, December 4, 1972. Of the total world output of key minerals each year, the United States uses the following proportions:

	Percent
Natural gas	57
Silver	42
Lead	36
Aluminum	35
Petroleum	32
Tin	32
Nickel	30
Copper	27
Steel	19
Coal	16

Thus, according to *U.S. News,* "with 5 per cent of the world's people, [the] U.S. consumes 30 per cent of world's minerals." There is hardly a sharper expression of the fundamentally predatory character of imperialism. What is most important from the standpoint of the present discussion, however, is that the dependency is increasing. A 1971 report by the Committee on Interior and Insular Affairs of the U.S. Senate declared: "The United States consumes between 30 and 40 percent of the total world [nonfuel] minerals production. If present demand trends continue and unless future recycling and reuse augment supply, the U.S. demand for primary minerals is expected to increase an estimated 400 percent by the year 2000."

A projection of the increasing dependence on imported minerals adapted from U.S. Department of the Interior data appeared in an article by Lester R. Brown in the November 5, 1972, *New York Times.* It is summarized in the following table showing mineral imports as a percentage of mineral consumption by the United States in the given years, with projected figures for the year 2000:

	1950	1970	2000
Aluminum	64	85	98
Chromium	-	100	100
Copper	31	0	56
Iron	8	30	67
Lead	39	31	67
Manganese	88	100	100
Nickel	94	90	89
Phosphate	8	0	2
Potassium	14	42	61
Sulfur	2	0	52
Tin	77	-	100
Tungsten	-	50	97
Zinc	38	59	84

Brown, a senior fellow with the Washington Overseas Development Council, wrote, "In per capita terms, Americans consume perhaps 20 times as much metallic ore as the average person living in the poorest countries. If the consumption levels of these countries should ever begin to approach those now prevailing in the rich countries, pressures on mineral supplies, particularly of the scarcer minerals, would quickly become a matter of global concern.

"For example, in 1967 the average American consumed approximately one ton of steel, while worldwide [per capita] consumption was 0.17 tons. To raise the present global population to United States consumption levels would require a six-fold expansion of production."

Brown, of course, finds such an expansion inconceivable. And it *is* inconceivable under conditions of monopoly rule. Yet it would be a different matter under social conditions in which world production was planned and run for the benefit of the world's population instead of the privileged few.

Monopoly Control

It is not only a question of physical consumption—the *use value* of commodities—but also a question of who owns them. After all, one could argue, precisely because the U. S. need for raw materials is increasing, the neocolonies have an advantage. They could take over the companies and sell the raw materials to the United States *in a seller's market*, with demand exceeding supply, and consequently at ever higher prices! However, monopoly profit rates in the extractive industries depend on the ability of the monopolists to exploit the labor of the underdeveloped countries and to sell the product under world market conditions in which production (and consequently prices) are controlled. Only through *cartelization*—the rigging of world production and prices by a few monopolists in each industry—can the monopolists suppress self-defeating cutthroat competition and maintain monopoly profit rates. And that requires private ownership and the political power to coerce governments.

For example, the ability of the U.S.-dominated international petroleum cartel to keep Japanese oil investment in the Middle East at a minimum, and consequently to keep Japan dependent on Western oil, is primarily a political—not a monetary—question.

Paul Sweezy described a "classical" situation in his 1958 study of the profit structure of Standard Oil of New Jersey. He restated the results of his investigation in his and Paul Baran's *Monopoly Capital* (1966). In 1958, the percentage distribution by region of assets and profits of Standard Oil (now Exxon) was as follows:

	Assets	Profits
U.S. and Canada	67	34
Latin America	20	39
Eastern Hemisphere	13	27

"While two thirds of Jersey's assets were located in North America, only one third of its profits came from that region," Sweezy and Baran wrote in *Monopoly Capital*. "Or to put the point differently, Jersey's foreign investments were half as large as its domestic investments but its foreign profits were twice as large as its domestic profits. The indicated profit rate abroad is thus four times the domestic rate."

Moreover, we can be certain that if the study were repeated today, the results would be even more pronounced. That is because the percentage of Exxon's holdings located in the Middle East—where the ratio of profits to investment is highest—would be much greater than it was in 1958. Additionally it should be underlined that the *reinvestment* of the extractive industries' profits in the foreign nations where they are located is sufficient for the expansion that is undertaken in most cases. The ratio of profits to initial investment is thereby all the more increased.

Further, under the now prevailing conditions of intensified competition among monopolies of advanced capitalist countries for international markets, the monopolies' need for control of raw materials *will be intensified*. As control of markets for finished products is undermined by international competition, the monopolists have ever greater need for access to and control of sources of cheap raw materials. The search for these resources will take on a more rapacious and frenzied character. The underdeveloped world cannot escape the effects of intensified international monopoly competition. In fact, it will be forced, as always in the epoch of imperialism, to bear a disproportionate share of the burden of imperialist contradictions.

Add to this the fact that the No. 1 bastion of imperialism, the United States—which already consumes 30 percent to 40 percent of the world's raw materials—aims to increase its share at the expense of its imperialist rivals as well as of the neocolonies, and the explosive content of the struggle for raw materials is clearly revealed. "In the period of crisis the hegemony of the United States will operate more completely, more openly, and more ruthlessly than in the period of boom," Trotsky wrote in the 1928 "Draft Program of the Comintern." "The United States will seek to overcome and extricate herself from her difficulties and maladies primarily at the expense of Europe, regardless of whether this occurs in Asia, Canada, South America, Australia, or Europe itself, or whether this takes place peacefully or through war."

The interimperialist war that Trotsky foresaw in 1928 did

not solve the central contradictions of imperialism that brought it about. They are reemerging on a world scale. And since a new interimperialist war is virtually precluded because of the even greater hegemony of the United States today than in the 1920s when Trotsky was writing, it is all the more incumbent upon us to pay attention to the ways in which imperialism "resolves" its contradictions short of interimperialist world war.

U.S. Investment in Chile

U.S. investment in Latin America has been on a sharp up-swing since the early 1960s, as the graph from the September 12 issue of *Business Week* shows.

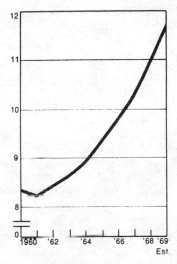

U.S. BUSINESS'S STAKE IN LATIN AMERICA

Total U.S. direct investment in billions of dollars

Before Allende was elected in 1970, Chile was taking its place alongside Mexico, Brazil, and to a lesser extent Argentina and Puerto Rico, as a rapidly expanding market for U.S. multinational investment. Second only to Brazil, Chile had received $600 million in U.S. "aid" (primarily military hardware) during the six-year period of the Frei government.

In their contribution to *The Chilean Road to Socialism* (Dale L. Johnson, ed., 1973) entitled "Multinational Corporations and Chile," James D. Cockcroft, Henry Frundt, and Dale L. Johnson wrote: "At the time Allende assumed office, more than one hundred U.S. corporations had established themselves in Chile. Among these were twenty-four of the top thirty U.S.-based multinational corporations. These included the major auto producers, four of the biggest oil companies, Dow and

DuPont chemicals, International Telephone and Telegraph (ITT), and other big industrials. In recent years the ranks of the industrials had been joined by multinational banks and corporations operating in the service sectors." The book value of these investments was nearly $1 billion, with ITT's telephone company ranking highest, at $200 million, according to *Business Week,* April 10, 1971.

Cockcroft, Frundt, and Johnson describe the operations of another conglomerate, the Rockefeller International Basic Economy Corporation: "IBEC operates in thirty-three countries and in 1970 derived 60 per cent of its profits from Latin America, although only 33 per cent of its assets were in the region. In Chile, IBEC has a ready-mix cement plant, a petroleum-products manufacturing and marketing concern, a construction firm, a mining enterprise, and four investment and management companies. Through these investment companies Rockefeller interests have penetrated many Chilean firms. IBEC now participates in thirteen of the twenty-five largest Chilean corporations and controls over 50 per cent of the stock in three of them. In short, IBEC in Chile operates as ITT does everywhere: it grows by achieving financial control of more and more independent firms."

Thus the most powerful sector of U.S. finance capital, the Rockefeller empire itself, tries to solve the problem of overproduction of capital, of "superabundant capital" as Lenin called it in *Imperialism,* by swallowing up small manufacturing firms in Latin America. Finance capital, which has already monopolized the extractive industries, spreads into manufacturing and services.

That process tends to weaken the indigenous bourgeoisies and tie them more closely to the imperialist power. Sectors of the "national bourgeoisie" are transformed into a rentier class. They relinquish their own firms for the "blue chip" securities of the American firms that have bought them out. This, by the way, becomes an added cause of the balance-of-payments deficits of the underdeveloped countries: the indigenous bourgeoisie invests more in the U.S. stock and bond markets than U.S. corporations invest in the underdeveloped countries.

In Chile, however, the economic centrality of the copper trusts still overshadowed the incursions of foreign capital into the manufacturing and service industries. When the book value of all U.S. investment in Chile stood at roughly $1 billion, with ITT at $200 million or 20 percent, the book values of the copper firms were: Cerro, $15 million; Kennecott, $80 million; and Anaconda, $186 million. Thus, even in 1970 the interests of the copper firms amounted to 28 percent of total U.S. investment.

But this understates the case because these are figures *after* Frei's 51 *percent nationalization.* The April 10, 1971, *Business Week* stated: "The total U.S. investment in copper in Chile is generally said to be around $600 million." So in book-value terms the copper interests prior to Frei's nationalization came close to 50 percent of U.S. investment. An ironic admission of the understated book values of these corporations came in Anaconda's claim in 1971 that "the new Marxist government of Chile has stolen $1.2 billion worth of mines and properties from the Anaconda Company."

The *Wall Street Journal* reported January 6, 1971, that "Anaconda stands to lose heavily by the expropriation. Its Chilean holdings have been valued at about $400 million in three major mines. The company estimates that two thirds of its total annual copper sales of $600 million come from Chile." The same article reported that a quarter of Kennecott's copper was mined in Chile. These two firms had reaped monopoly profits for decades.

In *The Chilean Road to Socialism*, the Chile Research Group at Rutgers University notes: "According to the U.S. Department of Commerce, in the period between 1953 and 1968 U.S. mining and smelting operations in Chile (about 90 per cent copper) earned $1,036 million, while new investments and reinvestment of profits together totaled only $71 million." A return of almost fifteen times investment. This is the typical monopoly profit rate in the extractive industries of the underdeveloped world (although the rates in petroleum tend to be higher).*

An indication of the long-term importance of the Chilean copper companies in the world investment patterns of U.S.

---

* It may be asked why, if the profit rates are so high in the extractive industries, the imperialists do not invest more in these industries. The answer is that monopoly profit rates depend on *restricted production.* An increase in investment does not produce a proportional increase in profits. Thus, the raw materials monopolies tend to become closed off. They cannot provide extensive outlets for "overproduced capital," which consequently tends increasingly to flow into manufacturing investments in the underdeveloped countries.

imperialism is the close ties of these companies to the central financial sectors of the American ruling class. Cockcroft, Frundt, and Johnson observe: "The Stillman-Rockefellers of First National City share control of Anaconda Copper with the Morgan interest group. Ten of the twenty-four top multinationals in Chile share directors with First National City Bank.

"The Morgan interest group has a strong presence in Chile through its ties to Kennecott Copper and other corporations present in the country. The Morgans [partners in the Morgan banking group] also have an interest in Anaconda copper (as well as another major copper producer not in Chile, American Smelting and Refining)." The third of the major copper firms in Chile, Cerro, was founded by the J.P. Morgan Company in 1902.

In the period just prior to Allende's coming to power, the copper trusts had begun a large expansion program. Chilean copper accounts for 21 percent of the world's proven copper reserves. Given the long-term expectation of increased demand for copper, especially in the United States itself, the copper trusts were preparing to reap the profits. This is why, in the last period of the Christian Democratic government, an estimated $500 million had been poured into the three copper firms, aimed at expanding production from 685,000 metric tons in 1970 to a future capacity of "well over a million tons," according to the April 11, 1971, *New York Times*.

Behind-the-Scenes Strangulation

Marxists are not "economic determinists" pure and simple. In fact, the level of class consciousness of the Chilean workers — and of oppressed peoples internationally — was more determinative of the specific history of Chile in the Allende period than the place Chile occupied in the sphere of U.S. imperialist investment.

From the outset Washington believed that it was too risky to directly intervene with U.S. military forces in Chile, given the world unpopularity of the U.S. aggression in Southeast Asia and the political sophistication of the Chilean masses themselves. The *New York Times* spelled out this opinion from the start. "There is no point in trying to minimize the importance of what has happened in Chile," the *Times* editors lamented on September 6, 1970, as they announced Salvador Allende's election victory. "This result, unprecedented in the Americas and virtually without parallel anywhere, is a heavy blow at liberal democracy. It may mark the demise of the ailing

Alliance for Progress, which was undertaken 'to improve and strengthen democratic institutions.'"

The words, of course, are the hypocritical jargon of liberalism, but the meaning is plain enough. In the same editorial the *Times* emphasized: "All the United States can do in this situation is to keep hands off, behave correctly and hope for the best. Dr. Allende is a Chilean, preferred by a plurality—though not a majority—of Chilean voters. . . . Whatever troubles Chile may face would only be compounded by even the appearance of American interference."

That analysis signified that world imperialism would resort to behind-the-scenes strangulation. The Chilean market was boycotted and its credit was cut short. But overt and covert "aid" to the Chilean military—where the imperialists' best hopes remained —was continued.

Lenin's central political message in *Imperialism* was that the world imperialists, having "divided" international markets among themselves, do not bring humankind closer to peace. They prepare the ground for further war.

There cannot be a long-term perspective of "peacefully co-existing" with the oppressive system of imperialism. Whether one is talking about the relations between postcapitalist states and imperialism, or between the neocolonies and the big powers—or between the workers of the advanced countries and their own ruling classes—the watchword must be "prepare for the final struggle." The Unidad Popular's failure to grasp this central principle of Leninism was its fatal error.